W9-CWC-793

LONG-TERM CARE FOR THE ELDERLY

Long-Term Care for the Elderly

A Comparative View of Layers of Care

Betty H. Landsberger

HV
1451
.L36
1985

WITHDRAWN

INDIANA
PURDUE
LIBRARY
FORT WAYNE

ST. MARTIN'S PRESS
New York

© 1985 Betty H. Landsberger
All rights reserved. For information, write:
St. Martin's Press, Inc., 175 Fifth Avenue, New York, NY 10010
Printed in Great Britain
First published in the United States of America in 1985

Library of Congress Cataloging in Publication Data
    Long-term care for the elderly.

    Includes index.
    1. Aged — Services for — Cross-cultural studies.
2. Long-term care of the sick — Cross-cultural studies.
3. Aged — Institutional care — Cross-cultural studies.
I. Title.
HV1451.L36   1985   362.6   85-10793
ISBN 0-312-49668-0

rst
10 - 16 - 86
INDIANA
PURDUE
LIBRARY
FORT WAYNE

CONTENTS

to the memory of
Hugh B. Hatch and Margaret Macdonell Hatch
and
Ernst Landsberger and Annie Winter Landsberger
who gave long-term care to hope and human values
throughout their long lives

FOREWORD

The development of services for old people in one country can derive great benefit by drawing upon similar experiences in others, as long as cultural, economic and structural differences are properly understood and taken into account.

In the field of ageing, we have had relatively slender resources on which to base inter-country comparisons and the literature in this field is still very scant. An International Congress of Gerontology with a limited social science element every third year, the quarterly Bulletin of the International Federation on Ageing, material from the World Health Organization and a few research agencies together with the United Nations World Assembly on Ageing have provided the principal mechanisms for exchanges between policy-makers and practitioners, apart from Conferences on special issues. However, the high cost of international travel and the need to spend time in a visited country limits participation at even these useful events.

This means that, at a personal level, books continue to provide the principal resource for the majority of people; but reliable texts which combine information and analysis in different national settings are still few and far between. If they are written by a single author they may lack sensitivity to national differences; if written by a team from different countries and disciplines, they may lack comparability. For this reason, I welcome the publication of Betty Landsberger's valuable contribution to the literature on long-term care for old people. She describes the settings, the people involved and the strategies being developed in the United States, Great Britain and Germany with additional references to Scandinavian countries in a thoughtful and incisive way. This helps our understanding of the policies and their implication for practice during a period of rapid change in which long-held beliefs about the place of institutional care within the scheme of things are being challenged on both economic and ideological grounds.

Long-Term Care for the Elderly is a useful book in its own right, as well as being a model for a comparative study dealing with practical realities within a conceptual framework. It draws out some of the current arguments about the relative merits of differing

vii

systems of delivery, the sectors through which it is organised and about the critical role of co-ordination and liaison when a range of agencies and disciplines may be involved in the networks of care supporting old people on a long-term basis.

Betty Landsberger's study should certainly be of value to those working in the countries she has studied; but its lessons have much wider implications. It also appears at an opportune moment in relation to far-reaching discussions in many countries about the nature and scope of the welfare society itself. 'Is it to be extended or dismantled?' and 'What are the key elements, as far as older people are concerned?' are serious questions for all of us with their best interests at heart.

David Hobman CBE
President, International Federation on Ageing
Director, Age Concern England

PREFACE

This book arose from the author's share of the intense and widespread concerns about how to improve the life of the many very elderly people who need help in handling long periods of disability and infirmity.

Knowing these concerns at first hand in the United States, the author took advantage of an opportunity to visit Britain and West Germany in 1984 to become acquainted with the thoughts and actions of those and other European countries. The 1982 World Assembly on Aging, convened by the United Nations, had stimulated many nations and international study groups to produce descriptions and updates regarding the condition of and provisions for older people. These always included attention to long-term care. The reports were not only useful to her, but the author feels that they constitute a literature which should be more widely known than is usual amongst gerontologists, health professionals and the public at large. Consequently, some of these documents are quoted frequently and sometimes extensively herein. Studies and writings from within individual countries were also helpful sources of information about particular topics.

The literature led to making first hand visits to several kinds of sites and programs which both Britain and West Germany have developed for their infirm elderly citizens. These visits ranged from training programs for *altenpflegen* (old people's nurses) in the Ruhr to geriatric day hospitals in London, and from the headquarters of the German Gray Panthers in Wuppertal to an aftercare program attached to a hospital in the upper reaches of England's Lake District. The author is greatly indebted to all of the many people who made reading materials and visits possible and has included references to this help under Acknowledgements.

It is clear that no matter how rich the literature and how helpful the hosts, any foreign visitor on a single visit must emerge with a very inadequate view of each part of the picture. In spite of this inevitable limitation, a responsible effort to look at the same social phenomenon in various countries does produce valuable insights and new ideas about approaches and techniques, and because of this the project was undertaken. However, the author wishes to offer an apology for any inadequacies and inaccuracies still present in her account, though the reviews of the original text made by many knowledgeable people will have picked up most of the errors originally there.

It is hoped that this study in a modest way demonstrates the values of comparative study for gerontology. The larger hope is that learning of other nations' experiences and approaches regarding long-term care for the elderly will be of some help as each nation attempts to develop better forms of care.

ACKNOWLEDGEMENTS

Special kinds of help are needed for a study which must be carried out away from home. These include support from home in the form of arrangements for taking over tasks during one's absence as well as financial support. Away from home, beyond the comfort of their hospitality, one requires of the hosts a great deal of time and effort to collaborate with the project in order to make suggestions and offer introductions and explanations.

This American's study of long-term care for elderly people in several European countries was made possible and enriched by generous assistance at home and abroad. The School of Nursing and the University of North Carolina at Chapel Hill made possible a six-month stay in Great Britain to learn about the care of elderly people there and in different parts of Europe.

People as individuals and people in various organizations offered essential orientation and suggestions about the British scene. Dr Robin Huws Jones, CBE, from the world of social work, Miss Marjorie Simpson, OBE, from the world of nursing and Professor Brian Abel-Smith of the London School of Economics, who has a special acquaintance with social policy in the European Economic Community, were among the persons who made suggestions and opened doors at the outset. Persons at the King Edward's Hospital Fund for London provided a warm and helpful home in London, and Professor Pinker and the London School of Economics gave a very supportive academic home to my husband and I. Dr Sheila Peace and her associates at the North London Polytechnic, Mrs Sally Greengross at Age Concern, Ms Alison Norman at the Centre for Policy on Ageing, and Mrs Linda Thomas at the Royal College of Nursing were sources of good ideas about where to go and what and whom to see. The libraries of the Centre for Policy on Ageing, the King's Fund and the Royal College of Nursing were great resources. Elderly patients themselves, nurses, social workers, health visitors and physicians — all of them on the front line of long-term care — were most generous in introducing me to people and sites at first hand.

In West Germany, many persons made the special effort to explain to me in English the nature of work and care for the elderly in that country. Among them were Dr Margret Dieck at the German Center for Gerontology in West Berlin; Dr Willie Rückert at the German Foundation for Care of the Elderly in Cologne; Herr Hen Tröost of the German Workers' Welfare Organization and Herr Brandt of the Bundesarbeitsgemeinschaft der Frein Wohlfahrtpflege, located in Bonn. Frau Christa Romberg and Schwester Anagret Taake, both of whom work in Duisburg with the Christophorus Werk of the Diakonisches Werk der Evangelischen Kirche in Deutschland, provided information about training people for work with the elderly. Several officers of the Senioren Schutz Bund at their headquarters in Wuppertal gave a stimulating introduction to their organization, also known as the German Gray Panthers.

Persons from Denmark, Sweden and Norway communicated by letter and sent books and booklets by mail. The same is true for the WHO Office for Europe at Copenhagen, the International Federation on Ageing, EURAG, the United Nations Office for Aging in Vienna, and the Centre de Liason d'Etude, d'Information et de Recherche sur les Problèmes des Personnes Agées at the Commission of the European Communities in Brussels.

Indebtedness is expressed to many authors and teams of persons whose writings have been quoted in the book, often at some length. Many of these materials — the Country Reports prepared for the World Assembly on Aging are an example — are not copyrighted, while copyrights are held by authors, publishers or both on other works cited extensively here. Appreciation is expressed to all whose work has seemed so appropriate that excerpts have been included. Copyright holders who have generously given permission to use materials include the following: Alison Norman, author, and the National Corporation for the Care of Old People (now, the Centre for Policy on Ageing), publisher of the book *Rights and Risk*; the Writers and Readers Publishing Co-operative, publishers of *The Alienated*, by the late Gladys Elder; Ellen Newton, author of *This Bed My Centre*; Dr Philip Selby, holder of the copyright for the following work: Selby, P. and Schechter, M., 1982. *Aging 2000 — A challenge for society*. Lancaster, England: MTP (published for the Sandoz Institute for health and socio-economic studies), a book quoted throughout this volume. Others are the authors, Dr E.M. Goldberg and Ms N. Connelly, and the Policy Studies Institute, holders of the copyright for *Effectiveness of Social Care of the Elderly*, published by Heinemann; the Centre for Policy on Ageing, publishers of *New Literature on Old Age 44* (March-April 1984) and *Organising Aftercare*, from which excerpts are reprinted here; Age Concern England, publishers of the *Age Concern England Handbook*, from which a section has been reprinted; Dr Malcolm Johnson, author of 'Involvement of Patients and Relatives in Discharge and Aftercare'.

The Beth Johnson Foundation, the Department of Adult Education at the University of Keele and Age Concern England hold the copyright for *Care in the Community: Recent Research and Current Projects*, edited by Frank Glendenning. The author is grateful to those three organizations for permission to quote excerpts from the article by Olive Stevenson, 'Social Trends in Care for the Elderly' and from 'Caring for the Carers' by Sally Greengross.

The article by Dr Johnson mentioned above appeared in a publication not itself copyrighted, entitled *Home from Hospital — to What?* It was issued by the Continuing Care Project under the direction of Mrs G.M. Amos. Her articles and that of P. Thursfield in that volume are gratefully acknowledged. Other individuals and organizations whose non-copyrighted material has been used extensively are Pensioners Link/Task Force, London, publishers, and R. Pearson, author of *An Independent Old Age: Provisions for Pensioners in Scandinavia*; the Equal Opportunities Commission, the producers of *Who Cares for the Carers?*; Age Concern Greater London, who provided material from the 1984 Health Forum; and Jean Fisher, Maura Hunt, Felicity Watson and Linda Gardner, all of whom generously shared descriptions of their projects for liaison between hospital and home.

The 1981 Final Report of the White House Conference on Aging held in Washington, DC has been cited extensively. Other material regarding the United States was provided by Ambassador John MacDonald of the Department of State. The statement of principles prepared for the Selby and Schechter book, *Aging 2000 — A Challenge for Society* by Dr Leo Kaprio of the World Health Organization's Office for Europe is reprinted here. The author wishes to acknowledge this excellent contribution to the literature on services for the elderly.

In expressing appreciation for the help from so many persons, the author is of course not attempting to place responsibility for the contents of this book on anyone other than herself. That responsibility rests entirely with the author. The very able assistance of three persons with typing which had to be done very rapidly and well is gratefully acknowledged. They are Norma Dawlings, Sheila Picken and Jean Pilgram, from London and Cambridgeshire.

I owe a special debt to my husband, Dr Henry Landsberger, who took time from his own demanding research tasks to give his expert help with the German language. The German dimension was added to this study because he acted as able interpreter in conversations, as translator of printed material and as locator of organizations and maker of appointments.

I am confident that all who gave their help to make this study possible will join the author in this statement: that our work will have been worthwhile if people in towns and cities, in states and nations, wherever they are, address the needs of their infirm elderly people with some new information, new insights and new determination to provide care they regard with pleasure and with pride.

1 LONG-TERM CARE IN CONTEMPORARY WESTERN SOCIETY

Introduction

The presence of very old people in large numbers is something altogether new. Persons over 75 and even those over 85, are a growing proportion of the populations of all industrialized countries of the Western world, and this may soon be a phenomenon almost world wide. The topic of the very old was frequently on the agenda when representatives from 124 member states met in Vienna at the United Nations World Assembly on Aging during August of 1982. It has caught us all unprepared, the sudden arrival on the national doorstep of this host of unexpected and unannounced guests.

People everywhere feel that what we have hastily found to provide for the elderly in general, but the very old in particular, is not serving anyone very well. Governments feel the arrangements are too costly, and elderly people say they vary from tolerable to terrible. 'We haven't yet got it right,' is the British way of making this admission. A high priority of our time is to orient ourselves to the reality of the life of very old people in contemporary societies, in order to put it right.

Very large numbers of people in the upper registers of age are as fit as ever they were. Nevertheless, it is recognized and documented that very old people are vulnerable on a number of scores: they are illness-prone, accident-prone, poverty-prone and isolation-prone. Above all, and because of their vulnerabilities, they are disability-prone and thereby many are made dependent on help from others to keep up the essential activities of living, sometimes just as surely as infants and young children are dependent upon others for their survival. But the dependency of older people is made infinitely complex because it represents a demotion from independence. This inevitably leads to psychological and social, as well as physical problems, between the elder person and those who give the needed help. There is cogent meaning behind the assertion, 'I don't want to be a burden.' It is no wonder that the question of how to provide the needed care for long-lasting disability of their very old populations has baffled societies everywhere.

One reason for the failure to find good solutions has been the very unfortunate timing: the awareness of the numbers of very elderly people in need of care has come just when economies everywhere have been experiencing high rates of inflation, high numbers of unemployed and low rates of economic growth. How to provide the needed long-term care of disabled older people in the present economic conditions remains an unanswered question.

Perhaps one reason it is unanswered is that other questions must be answered first. Just how should we perceive the economics of an aging population? That topic was addressed in a searching article by Robert Butler (1978), the first director of the National Institute on Aging in the United States. He argued for an end to 'narrow gauged' discussions of the costs to society of maintaining its elderly people. Longer life expectancy, he reminded his readers, is a triumph, not a tragedy. This triumph brings with it the need for new forms of social policy making. According to Butler, we must have much more knowledge about aging, of course on the bio-medical front, but also in the economics of aging and the social policy issues arising from the connections between health and wealth.

Butler pointed to the lack of prudence when there is little research-based information about services for which a society is making large expenditures. This is very much the case with long-term care services. He noted that the expenditure for research on this kind of enterprise amounts to less than 2 per cent of the billions expended on nursing homes alone. Thus, there is little established fact to enlighten the constant discussions about all of these observations: nursing homes cost too much; there are not enough home care agencies to meet the need; and, even though everyone is now enthusiastic about family members supplying the care (with the possible exception of some family members, and sometimes the patient), many elderly people do not have such an asset: with the high probability of widowhood among them, many live alone and have no relative to serve in the capacity of carer.

'A Comparative View' in the title of this book is intended to signal that various countries have so far responded differently to the needs for long-term care within their elderly populations. There is meant to be an implication that it is worthwhile to look at what other nations are doing. The view of these differences in care put forward here is that there is more to any nation's provisions for long-term care than appears on the surface: we need to look at them in some depth, both at home and abroad.

These considerations lead to the chief point of the book: finding satisfactory solutions to meet the needs for long-term care is such a large and serious problem that each nation must give it very careful thought. We need to take care not to get stuck with the makeshift solutions which resulted when we threw together something to 'get through today and get by till tomorrow'. None of these is to be accepted uncritically as a starting point, and it is of primary importance that we find the right starting point. Gerontologists from 16 countries who prepared a report entitled *Aging 2000 — A Challenge for Society* to be used for the 1982 World Assembly on Aging made this statement about the current situation, worldwide:

> The report suggests that most countries have not found adequate solutions to the problems caused by the aging of their populations, indeed many do not even have the beginning of adequate social policies for preventing or coping with such problems. There appears to be an urgent need for more information about the elderly and aging societies, as a basis for sound policies and programs. (The Sandoz Institute Study, p. 13)

The fundamental needs and rights, along with the prospects for comfort and recovery of the elderly individual who is disabled and needing the care must be appreciated: that individual is ultimately what it is all about. The interests of his or her family — especially if one or more are to be the care-givers — must be given equally careful consideration. What kinds of care, skills and supports are needed to help the patient regain the ability to function independently must be identified. These are the first questions to address; not, 'How can we cut the costs of nursing home care?' nor, 'What kinds of community services do we have available?' nor, 'What kinds of care are reimbursed by public and private insurance?'. Matters of service delivery and financing must not lead; they must follow after consideration of human rights, national values and ethical standards have shown us the directions we wish to take. We cannot decide upon the qualities needed by the service-delivery personnel nor whether the price is right until we know what it is we want.

It is certain that many persons upon reading the foregoing paragraph will have thrown up their hands at visions of the expensive, impossible things which that would lead us into. However, for our own sakes as individuals as well as for the public good, it is advisable not to make money the prime consideration at the outset of this inquiry. The experience of disabled elderly persons in modern society is a reality quite likely to confront every one of us as individuals, not once but several times. First it will be through great-grandparents and grandparents; then, with parents and parents-in-law, uncles, aunts and older friends — finally, our own generation, including ourselves; and we may live to see our own children grow old. Some nations are beginning to see two generations beyond retirement. No one needs to have a very broad social conscience to feel some real concern over the issues of aging policy, though in fact many people develop quite a social conscience in the process of facing these issues.

To look at what other nations are doing in the matter of long-term care is a step toward taking the kind of careful approach and broad perspective needed by any one country as it hunts for and decides upon the solutions it wants to live with.

Theoretical Framework for the Investigation

Taking a close and careful look at the responses which nations are making to the long-term care needs of their very elderly people means that we must look at more than the surface features of institutions and programs. I suggest that it is worthwhile to think of layers beneath, consisting of attitudes, beliefs and values on the social as well as the personal level, brought into play, evoked, by the responses a society makes when people are in need of care. The contents of these layers vary from nation to nation, and any one country needs to look at others to have standards of comparison for evaluating what is found on home ground. At least three of these layers can be distinguished. The description of what the layers are purported to contain makes it clear that they are as much a part of the effect of any program upon elderly lives as money and services.

First, let us be clear that on the surface of our metaphorical sphere are the services, goods, treatments, institutions, information, human interaction and all that make up the visible caring acts and events. Chapters 2 through 6 contain descriptions of the various forms of care. There are not only differences, but many similarities from country to country: some form of home-help service exists in virtually every country in Europe and North America, and there are always nursing homes, whether or not they have just that name.

The layer which lies just beneath this surface is the nature of common beliefs about the proper role of government — both central and local — in relation to the population's needs and the national resources. When we look further into this layer in Chapter 7 we shall note that the country-to-country differences in these beliefs seem to vary like the departments of a bank: the concept in some resembles a beneficent trust officer and in others, a tough loan officer.

Another important layer lies just under this one, and it also reflects attitudes. It consists of the principle of inviolability of the individual against being shaken up, pushed around or over-powered by his or her society. Such rights as respect for privacy and freedom of speech and conscience are backed up by guarantees in constitutions, statutory provisions and legal decisions. In the ways they come to play in matters concerning older people, these vary quite substantially from country to country as we shall see in the material presented in Chapter 8.

Those two layers together constitute the beliefs about how the responsibility for resources to meet particular human needs is divided between the state and the individual; and, beliefs about the necessity for individual freedom to be protected, and to be limited. In matters of elderly care, the two layers become joined because those acting for the state with power over resources may not guard against extending this to power over the individual rights of those persons receiving resources.

Finally, when the outer surface and these layers are peeled away, we are at the center, the heart of the matter: the reactions of this generation of elderly individuals whose needs are to be met by the care. Chapter 9 contains some statements from the center. Ultimately the reason for it all, it seems very strange indeed that it is here that we know very little. A case exists for insisting that evidence must come from older people themselves, that others simply cannot speak for them with authority, and yet there is very little evidence about the experiences of today's older people in their own words. The bureaucracies have warehouses full of paper about regulations for elderly programs and statistics about their operation: think only of Social Security. The philosophers and social scientists have filled libraries on the matter of the proper role of government and, in recent years, about the welfare state. Lawyers and judges have filled other libraries with material about human rights and civil liberties. But much less has been put down for us by older people themselves about their own condition. We have heard enough to know that there are problems of respect, dignity and self esteem, but the evidence as yet is slim. All the more important that efforts be made to get down to this core of whatever program of care we might examine.

Data for the Study

The sources of information used for this study have consisted primarily of reports available in the English language and produced by groups who met together in international meetings and committees to examine the present and future condition of the elderly and recommend the programs needed for older people. The following are prominent examples: reports prepared by the separate countries for the World Assembly on Aging, and the report of the *Plan of Action* accepted at the Assembly itself in August, 1982. References to that Plan are made as 'WAA'. Reports have been published since then by the International Federation on Aging and the United Nations. *Aging 2000 — A Challenge for Society* (Selby and Schechter, 1979), is a compilation of survey responses from a small working group of experts from 16 countries about problems of the elderly, carried out by the Sandoz Institute for Health and Socio-economic Studies and the United Nations Centre for Social Development and Human Affairs. This report is referred to throughout as 'The Sandoz Institute Study'. Various reports from the European Economic Community on both aging and poverty in European countries have been helpful, one of them cited extensively as CLEIRPPA (Collot *et al.*, 1982). Reports on aging have also come from the Office for Europe of the World Health Organization. Materials from Britain and West Germany (referred to as UK and FRG, respectively) predominate, but frequent reference is made to Scandinavia and to other countries referred to in the international reports. The Final Report of the White House Conference on Aging held in 1981 has been drawn upon frequently for information about the United States.

Some materials from a particular country have been cited frequently because of their relevance to one or another of the layers which have been identified in the previous section. One such source helpful in understanding the 'role of government' layer in the Federal Republic of Germany in Flamm's book, *Social Welfare Services and Social Work in the Federal Republic of Germany*. Alison Norman's book on *Rights and Risk* has been used extensively for material addressing the situation in the United Kingdom regarding the layer representing human rights' protection as has the Goldberg and Connelly book (1982) for thorough descriptions of programs important for long-term care.

A book comparing elderly care in the United States with Scotland also included a careful and perceptive look at the role of government with respect to nursing home care in the two societies. This book, by anthropologist J.S. Kayser-Jones (1981) is entitled *Old, Alone and Neglected: Care of the Aged in Scotland and the United States.*

We have indicated earlier that the elderly must themselves inform us about the core of the matter, the experience of today's disabled older person who receives care, and that these sources (at least, published in the English language) are very few and far between. It is true that there are some organizations which truly seem to consist of old people and are run by old people as well as for old people; prominent here are the Gray Panthers of West Germany as well as the US, and in the latter country, the Older Women's League. Their newspapers and meetings appear to contain authentic statements of older people's claims and points of view, but they are not apt to contain as much about long-term care as about Social Security.

As for statements in their own words from individuals, a principal source is a tiny paperback from Britain: the words on the cover say: '*The Alienated : Growing Old Today*, by Gladys Elder OAP'. (People outside Britain may need to be told that OAP means 'Old Age Pensioner'.) Another is from a resident of nursing homes in Australia and is entitled, 'This Bed My Centre' (Newton, 1979).

The few available materials of this kind consulted, though not quoted directly are mentioned herewith for the sake of the interested reader. Age Concern England has published Seabrook's compilation of individuals' statements entitled *The Way We Are,* and there is journalist-emeritus Mary Stott's book entitled *Ageing for Beginners*. There are some American statements of this kind, with Maggie Kuhn (Hessel, ed., 1977) as always, out in front leading the pack. Carobeth Laird wrote *Limbo* (1979) as her memoir about the year she spent in a nursing home in the south-west United States. 'Not a tale of horror or of filth and overt cruelty', it is an account of her own day to day experiences and those of the others there with her in what she described as a 'dehumanizing atmosphere' (p. 1). Another book which should be included among these is by Eva Salber, herself retired and a doctor, well-acquainted through her research with many poor elderly persons in a rural area in the southern United States. Dr Salber performed the Herculean tasks of making several visits to each of more than a score of rural residents, taking along her tape recorder to have a verbatim record of the interviews, and then she edited the transcriptions to preserve the original words and thoughts of the speakers.

Printed materials have been supplemented by opportunities to converse with many experts in gerontology and people working in services for elderly people in Great Britain and West Germany, and by correspondence with officials in the Scandinavian countries and international organizations.

It is evident that this study includes very little systematically gathered quantitative data and little presentation of such data from sources who have collected and reported them. There has not been an attempt to include all of the established texts in the references. The reader therefore needs and deserves an explanation of the approach taken by this book to the literature on the subject of long-term care. It is an approach which seems to the author to be suitable given the confusions and dismay in almost all countries over the very unadvanced state of the art. Each nation must at this stage direct some of its attention away from the care-giving activities and the financial problems connected with the present system for long-term care and look toward establishing the goals it wishes to select and attempt to achieve in the years ahead.

The theoretical framework and the descriptive material presented in the pages to follow are designed 'to serve as a guide to further reading rather than as an encyclopedic reference'. That quotation comes from a book edited by Mishler *et al.* (1981) entitled *Social Contexts of Health, Illness and Patient Care*. In their statement which follows, the authors express exactly the present writer's view of what the reader will find, and not find, in this book:

It is selective rather than comprehensive in coverage ... This selective approach reflects, as well, our view that the book should serve as a guide to further reading rather than as an encyclopedic reference. We neither intend nor assume that this is the 'last' book that professionals and students in the health care field may read on these topics. Rather, we hope it will serve as a beginning for the development of their own thought, as a stimulus to further reading and exploration, and as a basis for reflection on their own practice. (p. ix)

References

Butler, Robert, (1978) 'The Economics of Aging: We are Asking the Wrong Questions'. In *The Economics of Aging*, a National Journal Issues Book. The Government Research Corporation, Washington, DC

Collot, C., Jani-LeBris, H. and Ridoux, A., for CLEIRPPA, (1982) *Towards an Improvement in Self Reliance of the Elderly: Innovations and New Guidelines for the Future*. The Commission of the European Communities, Brussels

Country Reports for the World Assembly on Aging (1982)
— *Aging in Norway: Humanitarian and Developmental Issues*. Royal Norwegian Ministry of Health and Social Affairs, Oslo
— *Aging in the United Kingdom*, Department of Health and Social Security, London
— *Just Another Age: A Swedish Report to the World Assembly on Aging*. The National Commission on Aging, Stockholm
— *Report on the Situation of the Elderly in the Federal Republic of Germany*. The German Center of Gerontology, Berlin
— *US National Report on Aging to the United Nations and the World Assembly on Aging*. Department of State, Washington, DC

Elder, Gladys, (1977) *The Alienated: Growing Old Today*. Writers and Readers Publishing Co-operative, London

Flamm, Franz, (1974) *Social Welfare Services and Social Work in the Federal Republic of Germany*. Deutschen Vereins für Offentliche und Private Fürsorge, Frankfurt

Goldberg, M. and Connelly, N. (1982) *The Effectiveness of Social Care for the Elderly*. Heinemann, London

Hessel, Dieter, (Ed.), (1977) *Maggie Kuhn on Aging*. Westminster Press, Philadelphia

Kayser-Jones, J.S., (1981) *Old, Alone and Neglected: Care of the Aged in Scotland and the United States*. University of California Press, Berkeley

Laird, Carobeth, (1979) *Limbo*. Chandler and Sharp Publishers, Novato, California

Mishler, E.G., Amara Singham, L.R., Hauser, S.T., Liem, R., Osherson, S.D., and Waxler, N.E., (1981). *Social Contexts of Health, Illness and Patient Care*. Cambridge University Press, Cambridge, England

Newton, Ellen, (1979) *This Bed My Centre.* McPhee-Gribble Publishers, Melbourne, Australia

Norman, Alison, (1980) *Rights and Risk.* National Corporation for the Care of Old People (now known as the Centre for Policy on Ageing), London

Salber, Eva, (1983) *Don't Send My Flowers When I'm Dead.* Duke University Press, Durham, NC

Seabrook, Jeremy, (1980) *The Way We are.* Age Concern England, Mitcham, Surrey

Selby, P. and Schechter, M., (1982) *Aging 2000 — A challenge for society.* Published for the Sandoz Institute for health and socio-economic studies, referred to herein as 'the Sandoz Institute study', Lancaster, England MTP

Stott, Mary, (1981) *Ageing for Beginners.* Basil Blackwell, Oxford

White House Conference Staff, (1982) *Final Report: The White House Conference on Aging, 1981.* The WHCoA Staff, Washington, DC

World Assembly on Aging, (1982) *Plan of Action.* From the meeting of the United Nations World Assembly on Aging in Vienna, Austria, August, 1982. (Referred to herein as WAA)

PART ONE

THE SURFACE LEVEL: PLACES, PEOPLE AND
PROGRAMS FOR LONG-TERM CARE OF DISABLED
ELDERLY PERSONS

2 CARE IN INSTITUTIONAL SETTINGS

Where do people go for the long, slow process of regaining strength and recovery after they have been brought through the initial trauma of a serious illness or accident? Who provides the 'tending and treatment' they need during that period while their disability prevents their caring for themselves in normal fashion? In the following chapters we shall see a wide variety of answers to that pair of questions as one looks from one country to another. While disability is not limited to very elderly people, they form the vast majority of people in that position, and it is their plight under consideration here.

The Limited Role of Hospitals

It is usually the hospital where people are taken and treated at the onset, the acute stage of severe illness and injury. When the critical stage is past, hospitals often do begin the process of rehabilitation toward decreasing the disability. However, care for the long-term to recovery is seldom regarded by hospitals as their function, and they resist the role of long-term care provider.

In virtually all countries there are limits, often set by reimbursement practices, on how long patients can remain in hospitals. In France, for instance, this is six months (Collot *et al.* for CLEIRPPA, 1982, p. 220). In the US this depends, for patients coming under Medicare, on the patient's diagnosis, but stays are short. The average older person's stay on a single hospital visit in 1978 was 8 days (Federal Council for the Aging, 1981, p. 49). Stays amounting to several months do occur infrequently in West Germany (the FRG). Only in Britain are there geriatric wards in some hospitals where patients remain until they die, sometimes being there for as long as three or four years, but such long stays are no longer frequent. Nowhere are hospitals without the problem of 'bed blocking' which the increasing numbers of severely disabling chronic illnesses bring about.

Part of the reason for the general lack of involvement of hospitals with the particular needs for long-term care of the elderly is the very slow development of interest in geriatrics as a medical specialty in virtually all countries. The achievements of Great Britain in this respect are, therefore, worthy of note. Not only is there sophisticated training for doctors as part of the general practitioner preparation and for the specialty of geriatric medicine; some centers have developed clinical work and training in psycho-geriatrics as well. A 1977 publication from the US National Institute of Health (Kane and Kane) reported that geriatrics had tripled as a specialty-choice in Britain in the ten years between 1963 and 1973, and that young physicians were being attracted to this specialty.

Carboni (1982) has investigated reasons for the development of the specialty of geriatric medicine in Great Britain while this has not occurred in the medical profession in the US.

Accompanying the development of geriatrics in medicine is the requirement for a six-month course in geriatric care as a part of the preparation of all State Registered Nurses. In most hospitals with a (consultant) geriatrician, the geriatrician and nurses form the core of a multidisciplinary team for geriatric care, along with physiotherapists, occupational therapists and social workers.

Among other advantages of this attention to the development of professional expertise, is the aura of rehabilitation and recovery of independence which it brings to the care of elderly patients. This has reached lately into the possibility in most instances for bringing effective management and even recovery from incontinence, a problem long considered hopeless.

The combination of involvement of physicians with special interest and funding from the National Health Service also has helped make possible the development in Britain of Day Hospitals. These are set up to care for patients who are collected from their homes and brought in for the day, one to five days per week, for therapy and for monitoring. A recent innovation in an Inner London borough has involved making use of such premises at night for a Night Shelter for older people with mental problems. It currently gives the older people respite care with a nurse in charge for one night or a few nights in a row, to give the home carers a rest from their responsibilities, or to tide them over in an emergency. Although Britain is the leader and innovator in these special-purpose uses of hospitals, day hospitals are becoming popular in the Scandinavian countries and in the Netherlands as well, and are viewed there as parts of the system.

Nursing and Residential Homes

When elderly patients are still in need of nursing care when they leave hospital, the destination very likely to be chosen is a nursing home, especially for any patient who is very disabled at the point of discharge. It is probably the easiest choice, the path of least resistance, for the hospital personnel to take — whether or not it is the best for the patient. There is great variation in nursing homes, and while some offer very fine nursing care, it is never easy to get a place in exactly those good homes where there are rehabilitation services, more personnel and less dehumanizing treatment of patients. Those good homes are likely to have no vacancy. But, be that as it may, most elderly people needing nursing care for some period of time outside of their own homes are to be found in nursing homes.

Up until two or three decades ago, when the numbers of very old people were much smaller, nursing homes existed, but were needed much less than now. On a very large scale in the US and to a lesser extent in most European countries, the numbers of these institutions have increased rapidly. While regarded as necessary, this increase has generally been viewed with some alarm. Gerontologists and the general public in most countries would agree with the opinion of the Sandoz Institute Study group (Selby and Schechner, 1982). They told the Americans not to look upon community-based services for the disabled elderly simply as 'alternatives to institutions'. The US should build up a variety of services and think of 'the *institutions* as alternatives'. (p. 69)

In Britain and Holland as well as in the Scandinavian countries there has been a trend in that direction. An explicit shift in policy away from institutions and toward community-based care has occurred during the preceding decade.

Whether or not there is the long-term trend away from institutional care everywhere, which the Sandoz Institute Study group hoped to see, there will continue to be a need for those institutions in the short-run — at least for the next 15 to 20 years. The Sandoz Institute Study group noted that as yet, 'few countries offer formal programs of community-based home services' (p. 72). In a later chapter we shall see that progress has been made. Several European countries have made substantial starts toward building community services for infirm elderly people. But to do so requires a fairly long period of time, during which care under present institutional arrangements would continue to be necessary.

It is important, therefore, to see what form these institutions currently take, and to become aware of the suggestions from various sources for ways to improve them.

Apart from the Scandinavian countries and the Netherlands, these are run as private ventures nearly everywhere, operated on either a for-profit or not-for-profit basis. Seldom are the costs of care covered by insurance as is care in hospital, not even in the FRG where health care costs of most kinds are very likely to be covered for most people. A great deal of the cost is paid for by patients or their relatives out-of-pocket, or, better said, out of savings. Ultimately much of the cost of nursing home care *is* paid for by the state, but payment comes through means-tested financial support schemes in Britain and the FRG, as is the case with Medicaid in the United States. The matter of financing nursing home care is to be considered at greater length in Chapter 7.

In order to discuss nursing homes as institutions, it is difficult in the mid-1980s to decide just which ones of the places where infirm elderly people are cared for should be included as 'nursing homes'. The practice followed here has been to include in this chapter information about residents' lives, personnel employed, etc, from the British 'residential care homes' (run by local authorities) and the German 'altenheimen' (elders' homes, also run with public financial support) in the discussion of nursing homes. It must be made clear that in Britain and the FRG, as in France, there are in fact many 'nursing homes' which are different from the homes receiving direct public support for operating to care for elderly who need a home rather than care. As is the case with nursing homes in the US, the independence of these entities (whether for-profit or not-for-profit) makes it difficult to enforce standards of the care they provide. However, having said that, the distinction between these and the publicly-operated homes is becoming blurred:

(1) A sizeable portion of the nursing homes is almost entirely supported ultimately by public money because patients' bills are paid by the above-mentioned means-tested programs. On the basis of this, efforts to enforce standards are being made by the agencies through which payment is made.

(2) In addition, the populations of people served are quite similar, because the residential homes do in fact care for many dis-

abled people along with a few who are completely fit. Goldberg and Connelly (1982) cite a study of residential care homes which found that the recently admitted residents 'had a much greater degree of physical and mental frailty than people admitted ten or more years before' (p. 217). The institutional character of life in the homes as well as the needs of the residents seem to call for a broad rather than a narrow definition of 'nursing home' for our purpose here.

The Nature of the Homes and Their Providers

The activities of voluntary organizations in providing homes of both residential and nursing types are well known in many countries, especially in Britain, the US and Norway. Sometimes run by religious organizations, sometimes connected with military service or lodges or professional associations, the voluntary sector has played a substantial role in caring for older people from retirement to the end of their lives, including their care when very ill and infirm. In the US approximately 20 per cent of nursing homes are run by voluntary, non-profit groups. This pattern continues, but the voluntary sector can in no way expand sufficiently to accommodate the large numbers needing nursing home care today and tomorrow.

A special case is the role played by voluntary organizations in Germany. The FRG Country Report for the World Assembly on Aging (WAA) stated that 'In organized care for the elderly, the non-governmental welfare organizations (operated by six large roof organizations) operate around 55 per cent of the institutions for the aged' (p. 76). Not only this, but they operate 34 per cent of the FRG hospitals. These six large roof organizations of the major churches and other religious societies, together with voluntary welfare organizations, are in fact depended upon in the FRG, not only to provide services to the elderly along with other age groups, but to train personnel for nursing occupations, social work and administration. As examples of the magnitude of these activities: The Catholic Caritas Association runs 1280 hospitals, nursing homes, homes for the handicapped and convalescent homes with a total of 186,000 beds; 1630 old age homes; and 710 training and continuing education establishments for social, sociopedagogical, social welfare and nursing occupations with 26,780 places (Flamm,

p. 44). The German Non-denominational Welfare Association runs 800 homes, hospitals, etc, providing 75,000 beds and operates 60 training centers. (Flamm, p. 45). The other roof organizations run similar enterprises. Flamm explains that the Basic Law of the FRG guarantees their freedom to carry out such activities, and churches have the right and do levy taxes to support these activities. Most services provided, however, must be paid for by those who receive them.

To look again at the general picture, the nature of the population served by nursing homes, like many residential homes (the latter operated in Britain by Social Services departments of the local authorities) has changed quite dramatically in recent years, partly as a result of the deinstitutionalization policy with respect to mental hospitals. Another factor has been the development of domiciliary care services which have enabled care at home to continue until people have reached a very disabled state. In any case, the residents are very elderly — the average age in one country was 83, in another 82; they are frequently very infirm indeed, and many appear to be suffering from dementia. Their care is often much more likely to be viewed as custodial than restorative.

While sometimes numbers are much larger, the situation frequently found is that the 30 or so residents sit around the walls of a large lounge for most of the day, with the TV constantly going, though few, if any, appear to be listening or watching. In some homes meal-time is a social event, with residents sitting at tables for four or six, but in other settings the meal means a tray brought to the chair, TV still going. In those homes which do have single rooms, the residents who are not bedfast tend not to remain there nor return there during the day, but stay in the 'public' areas of the home, (Peace, Kellaher and Willcocks). In any case, it is quite common to have four or more beds in one room rather than singles When the staff contains some dedicated and capable carers, there are attempts to communicate with patients, but physical care and other duties have been found to take up most of the staff time, leaving little opportunity for purely social contact (Rückert, 1980). The language of the staff describing the day itself indicates what the work consists of: 'We get them up at 7, they have breakfast at 8, we bath them between 9 and 11, etc'. How different from: 'The patients get up at 7, eat breakfast at 8, take their baths after that, etc'.

Not always, but very often, standards of cleanliness and nutritive meals are maintained. Care of physical needs is provided, but on the whole, environments in homes for long-term care are lacking in opportunities for independent pursuits, stimulation or activities, no matter how much superhuman effort the staff makes.

A combination of surveys and estimates (in many places the exact numbers of people and places are not known) indicates that at present well over two million people in industrialized countries live in these institutions for elderly people. There are approximately 1,400,000 in the US alone. In Sweden in 1972 the number of nursing home beds was a little over one-third of the number of beds in their hospitals, according to Kane and Kane (p. 80). While it is recognized that they are often used as a scapegoat for frustration over society's generally poor treatment of the infirm elderly, there is genuine dismay over what life in these homes apparently does to peole who live there for a long time. (It is important to note that a large number are short-term patients.) Tobin wrote of the long-termers in a research review in 1978 that 'The literature is replete with descriptions of the institutionalized elderly as disoriented and disorganized, withdrawn and apathetic, depressed and hopeless. These characteristics are frequently ascribed to the singular effects of institutional life' (Tobin, p. 219).

It is reassuring, therefore, that many large-scale studies of nursing homes and residential homes and their residents and staff have been made in recent years. Only some of this work from the US, the FRG and Britain is noted here, but similar research has also been done in other countries, principally at centers for gerontology; this has been the case in Norway, Sweden, France and the Netherlands.

In 1977 the National Center for Health Statistics in the United States carried out a nationwide study of people then being cared for in nursing homes. That survey was but one of a great many studies of nursing homes in the US which have been reported upon, often in the *Gerontologist*, one important source, and frequently also in publications from the Committees on Aging of the US, Senate and the House of Representatives. One of these is *Special Problems in Long-Term Care* (1980).

In the FRG, there are at least two major sources of studies and reports with information about health and health care of the elderly. The German Center of Gerontology (Deutsches Zentrum für Altersfragen) in West Berlin concerns itself with all aspects of the life and needs of older people. This center was responsible for the publication in English of a comprehensive report on provisions for older people (Dieck, 1981) and for the FRG Country Report for the WAA which is cited frequently in this present study. The German Foundation for the Care of the Aged (Kuratorium Deutsche Altershilfe) located in Cologne, concentrates upon systematic dissemination of information about aging and the elderly population to the general public, and about developments in the care of elderly people to the six major voluntary agencies who are, as has been noted above, the essential trainers and employers of care providers. The latter function consists of staff management and training as well as architectural and design problems in institutions where old people are cared for. The Kuratorium has made very detailed observational studies in nursing homes leading to an analysis of the time required for the many caring tasks performed by personnel (Rückert and Zimmerman, 1978).

Recent large studies of the health care of elderly people in Great Britain have been commissioned by the Department of Health and Social Security. Three of these of special relevance are the study of different kinds of care provision by Wade, Sawyer and Bell (1983); the study of residential life in local authority operated old people's homes by Peace, Kellaher and Willcocks (1982); and the survey of studies of the effectiveness of social care programs for the elderly by Goldberg and Connelly (1982).

The US survey made very clear the great problems of disability throughout the population of patients in nursing homes. 45 per cent of them were found to need round-the-clock nursing care. Other findings from that study are to be looked at in greater detail in the next section of this chapter.

From the German studies it is clear that the proportion of the elderly in institutional care there, 4.5 per cent of those over 65, is very much like the 5 per cent figure found for the US. In all countries the proportion in institutional care rises to a much higher figure for those over 75, and especially for those over 85, than the percentage for elderly people between 65 and 75.

A problem of quality of care identified in the German WAA Country Report was the difficulty produced by the conflict between the needs for flexibility in what may be needed by infirm elderly persons, and the distinctions by status of different jobs within a nursing home staff. Consistent with the noting of rigid demarkations of tasks by jobs in the German homes was the description of the staff as a hierarchy, with the matron in charge often setting the tone and determining whether care was patient-centered, clock-centered or cleanliness-centered. Several different sources of information about the FRG homes spoke of the influence exerted by the matron of the institution.

The study in Great Britain by Wade, Sawyer and Bell also found that 'leadership style' of the person in charge played a crucial part in the type of care given to the elderly, though they did not specifically point to problems of hierarchy and status. They described the care provided by staff as varying from task-centered to person-centered.

Peace, Kellaher and Willcocks made a study of 100 homes, 1000 residents and 400 staff members. They found that the care of older people in the institutions studied seemed to be directed, by buildings and behaviour of staff alike, toward a public, social model. 'Residential life is currently constructed socially, on an assumption that residents will be prepared to live out their lives in a public setting,' they say (p. 48). The authors felt, in fact, that the experiences of the older people in the homes was out of balance in the public, social direction, and that it is important to bring about a better balanced life for residents by increasing the private and personal areas. The content of their interviews with the 1000 patients led them to conclude that this change would bring an improvement in the acceptability of institutional life for elderly people. They propose that the problems with institutional living lie in the combination of losses of one's own territory, of privacy, and of control over one's own daily activities and living space — together with being a part of a situation where the expectations of those in control continually push in the direction of social, public experiences. It is that change from the personal, private type of living which they have known, to a social, public existence which has made institutional care objectionable to so many elderly people. This finding has special importance for the sizeable proportion of the elderly who are very likely to require care in an institutional setting because they are on their own, have no family member or other person to give needed help, and may reach a point where they cannot manage in their own homes.

Needs Prompting Plans to Increase the Numbers of Nursing Homes

In spite of the fact that almost nowhere do people like the existing institutions for disabled elderly, whether they are called nursing homes, residential homes, altenheimen or lôgements — there already are many of them in most of the industrialized countries, and the forecast, from the Sandoz Institute experts (Selby and Schechter, 1982) like the general public, is that more will have to be built.

The Sandoz Institute Study report has noted that the need for more nursing homes was brought out by West Germany, France, Sweden, Japan and Australia (p. 76). The UK has set a goal of having available 25 residential home places for every 1000 people over 65 and 10 places per 1000 in nursing homes (p. 74). Responsible for this perceived need is the rapidly increasing number of very old people. Sweden, for instance, expects a 37 per cent increase in people over 80 between 1980 and 2000; by 1990, almost 30 per cent of Norway's elderly population will be over 80. And already in 1979, the CLEIRPPA report stated that within the member states of the European Community, 'over a third of the elderly population is made up by people aged 75 and over, ranging from 35 per cent in Italy to 41 per cent in France' (p. 11).

It is among the very elderly that there are the large numbers of severe problems of disability which prevent people from managing on their own, even when they do receive some services from the community, and which call for more assistance than family members (often very old themselves) can give.

The *World Health Statistics Quarterly* (Kovar, Vol. 35, Nos. 3 and 4 1982) presented figures from the 1977 US survey of nursing home residents to make explicit these disabilities. They pointed out that 40 per cent of the patients were 85 and older, and that approximately 20 per cent of people aged 85 and over were living in long-term care institutions. Then they went on to give the details of disability:

The 1977 survey of long-term residential institutions revealed that almost all of the residents needed continuous care. The elderly residents had multiple chronic conditions or impairments, and over 90% needed help in one or more basic activities such as bathing, dressing or moving about. Over half (53%)

had been in another health facility, usually a short-stay hospital (34%), before they were admitted. Arteriosclerosis was the most common primary diagnosis (23%), representing 45% of residents: 38% had heart trouble, and 27% arthritis. Hypertension, stroke, chronic brain syndrome, diabetes, and permanent stiffness or deformity each afflicted more than 10%. About a third had impaired sight and an equal proportion impaired hearing. About 3% of those aged 65 and older were blind and 1% were deaf. ...

Among the 450,000 residents aged 85 and older, the prevalence of chronic disease and impaired functioning was even higher: 63% had arteriosclerosis, 44% heart trouble, and 42% were senile. Only 4% could bathe independently, dress, move about, eat, remain continent and use the toilet and 45% required help in at least five of these six activities. They needed continuing round-the-clock care and 48% were receiving intensive nursing care. (p. 249)

The particular problem of mental disability needs special note. Goldberg and Connelly (1982) note from their study in Britain that it is not unusual when over half of those in a residential home are 'confused'. Research by Maule and Williamson in a British city produced figures about the presence of mental disorder in those over 75 as compared with those between 62 and 75 which have been pictured in the graph presented in Figure 2.1.

Figure 2.1: The Effect of Age on the Prevalence of the Common Mental Disorders

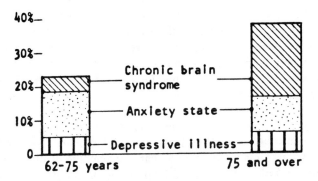

Source: Edinburgh Study: M.M. Maule and J. Williamson, 482 subjects over 62

The value of preventive care for old people, often stressed in the FRG Country Report, has relevance with respect to keeping minor disabilities of all types from becoming serious disabilities by virtue of accidents and rapidly worsening physical conditions. Abrams (1980) in *Beyond Three-Score Years and Ten* reported results of the survey of people over 75 living in the community, conducted by Age Concern in Britain in 1978 (Abrams, 1980, p. 9). The average person over 75 'was afflicted by approximately six ailments ranging from rheumatism and difficulty in walking to incontinence and difficulty in passing water. Apart from those actually bedfast or chairfast, at least one-third have some physical difficulty in carrying out ordinary household tasks such as taking a bath, getting into bed, putting on shoes, etc. Only a bare minimum of those with such difficulties received any help with them' (p. 9). The *Chartbook on Aging* (White House Conference on Aging, 1981) reported that one-third of those over 85 in the US 'needed help' with either bathing, dressing, eating or use of the toilet. For the 75-84 group that figure was only 12 per cent. It would seem important and prudent from many points of view to make this a target group for the improved primary health care for the elderly which the WAA gave high priority in its *Plan of Action.*

The Need for Professional Interest to Improve Nursing Home Care

There is cause for alarm in the combination of developments noted in the preceding section:

1. The undoubted need for a great deal of nursing care in the rapidly increasing population of very old people,
2. The universal dissatisfaction with nursing homes in the institutional form they have taken in most countries,
3. The expressed intentions of so many countries to build more nursing homes.

It is an urgent matter to attempt to identify the aspects of the system which are responsible for the continuation of the unsatisfactory nature of many nursing homes. The Sandoz Institute Study report has pointed to their isolation from the rest of the health care enterprise and especially its leading professional people:

In more developed nations, with high concentrations of professional manpower in institutions like the hospital, resources
tend to be allocated more to health services than to social services, and more to acute care than to chronic care. One result is
a tendency to ignore or minimize chronic care needs. Indeed, a
vivid example is furnished by the medical dramas of US television, which are overwhelmingly dramas of acute illness;
chronic care receives a relatively small share of public attention.
... Unfortunately, in many areas, the principal chronic care
institution, the nursing home, is poorly developed as a site of
professional care. It is isolated from centers of research and
academic training. Physicians may visit irregularly. Poor working conditions may contribute to high rates of staff turnover,
(and, finally) hospitals around the world are keyed, typically, to
acute care, for which technologically elaborate procedures are
necessary. The chronic care needs of the elderly tend to be
poorly funded, and the institutions that serve them have severe
staffing shortages. Rehabilitation is rarely offered. According to
UK, US and Swedish experts, doctors and nurses usually are
unfamiliar with geriatrics, and tend to turn away from the
elderly in frustration and even with hostility. Institutions for the
elderly tend to become 'storage' facilities. (pp. 70-1)

That situation raises again the matter of the underdevelopment
of doctors' interest in geriatric medicine almost everywhere, with
the single exception of Britain. The relationship of this to the
specific failures in meeting the health needs of the elderly was also
commented on by the Sandoz Institute experts (Selby and
Schechter, 1982):

Geriatric medicine appears to be universally underdeveloped.
West German experts report that many doctors lack knowledge
of the diseases common in old age. Superficial examinations
lead to erroneous or partial diagnoses: for example, 'senile
dementia' is given as a diagnosis without any effort to rule out
infection, drug reaction, or other acute and reversible illness.
This is a complaint voiced by experts in the US and other countries. Japanese experts report a shortage of trained personnel
and an over-emphasis on acute care to the neglect of chronic
care.

'Enormous price tags have been placed on medical care', according to US experts. Yet, insurance coverage is malde-signed for the elderly — not covering preventive or chronic care at times, and often not paying for needed items such as dentures. Iatrogenic or practitioner-caused illness is considered by the experts to be far too common in the US, and drugs in general are not well managed. The typical elderly American is on multiple medications — up to about 13 at any one time. (pp. 54-5)

When geriatricians are on the scene and playing a significant part in health care, the contributions they do make are notable. The British geriatricians' achievements prove the Sandoz Institute group's observation of the important role of geriatrically trained doctors. The proposals of one British geriatrician, Dr J. Malone Lee (1983) regarding what nursing homes and health care should be like, provide a sample of the leadership so badly needed in all countries.

Dr Malone Lee has called for the development of nursing homes where the different kind of medical care appropriate to the health care needs of the very elderly is practised by teams of health professionals, and where social care is recognized as an integral part of the therapeutic picture.

The acute care, disease-curing model appropriately provided by hospitals for the population up to about age 70 is really inappro-priate for most of the illnesses of people over 70 and 75. Trying to 'cure' the older person's heart problem with medical treatment designed for the younger patient may, and often actually does, make the older patient worse. Malone Lee distinguishes between what he would *not* do — 'cure' the physical disorders (of which most very old people have several, due to normal degenerative processes) — and what he *would* do — 'restore' the ability of the very old person to carry out the activities of his or her daily living: very different activities, calling for different physical strength and physiological functioning from the younger person's.

The medical care for the rehabilitation and restorative regimens possible in the nursing homes and their day centers which he visualizes must be as much purpose-built as the structure itself. The development of the different approach called for is a tre-mendous challenge to the medical profession and, he adds, a challenge which must be met, given the very fast-growing numbers of health problems due to the fast-growing population of very elderly people. More beds in today's hospitals, says Dr Malone Lee, would be the worst response to this challenge. What is needed are often not beds at all, but restorative home environments (at home or in a nursing home) where medical, nursing, physiotherapy, occupational therapy, psychological and social work expertise join in the combination necessary to make the person recover ability to maintain an active, independent, interesting life of his or her own design.

With Dr Malone Lee's specialty in clinical and research work centered on urinary functioning and incontinence problems, special note may be taken of his citing the following episode as an example of the need to combine social and medical care. In a ward where virtually all 12 or so very elderly patients were 'incontinents', an enterprising assistant of his set about redecorating, using objects and photographs of the years between the two world wars, a period holding many memories for all of the patients. Appropriate music was found and played and films were shown. It was not long before the incontinence problems were gone: 'There wasn't a single soul weeing,' Dr Malone Lee reported.

On that note of insistence, if not conviction, that good nursing homes are a possible achievement, we move on to a matter closely related to just that: namely, personnel and their training.

Personnel and Training

All countries alike regard personnel as crucial in determining the care received by residents of nursing and residential homes. Countries also agree that the large costs of institutional care are personnel costs. Thus, it is personnel which costs the most and means the most in nursing homes. But, is it really thought about most? Looking from country to country, one sees a great deal of variety in the occupational categories put together to make up the personnel who operate these homes. Each country has much food for thought in the various staffing options in existence. Each country would do well to give very careful consideration to the staffing pattern it outlines and finances, and the training methods it designs and finances, since the outcome and the expense of the entire enterprise depend so heavily upon personnel. Not only is that the case, but without intending to overlook grave obstacles, it is possible to bring about institutional change by making changes in personnel practices.

This is, however, a choice point calling for a very broad perspective on the purposes and goals of institutional care. It is a choice point involving the self-interest of each of those professionals and paraprofessionals who know the situation best. It may well be the choice point where the consumers need to have at least as much to say as any other group involved.

There are two points regarding personnel and training which received frequent mention, not only in the WAA Plan of Action, but also from the Sandoz Institute Study experts. One of these is the need for more people to be trained for work with the elderly — indeed, that training for work with old people should be a part of the training of all who are working or preparing to work in all of the human care professions. The other point is that all personnel must collaborate in their caring with each other and with the elderly persons and their families. The word 'interdisciplinary' was often linked with geriatric care. Recommendations 6 and 7 and paragraph 55 from the Health and Nutrition Section of the WAA *Plan of Action* follow:

Recommendation 6

The trend towards increased costs of social services and health care systems should be offset through closer co-ordination between social welfare and health care services both at the national and community levels. For example, measures need to be taken to increase collaboration between personnel working in the two sectors and to provide them with interdisciplinary training. These systems should, however, be developed, taking into account the role of the family and community — which should remain the interrelated key elements in a well balanced system of care. All this must be done without detriment to the standard of medical and social care of the elderly.

55. Those who give most direct care to the elderly, are often the least trained, or have insufficient training for their purpose. To maintain the well-being and independence of the elderly through self-care, health promotion, prevention of disease and disability requires new orientation and skills, which should be made available to the elderly themselves, as well as to their

families, and health and social welfare workers in the local communities.

Recommendation 7

(a) The population at large should be informed in regard to dealing with elderly who require care. The elderly themselves should be educated in self-care.

(b) Those who work with the elderly at home, or in institutions, should receive basic training for their tasks, including the importance of participation of the elderly and their families, and collaboration between workers in health and welfare fields at various levels.

(c) Practitioners and students in the human care professions (e.g. medicine, nursing, social welfare, etc.) should be trained in principles and skills in the relevant areas of gerontology, geriatrics, psychogeriatrics and geriatric nursing.

The Sandoz Institute Study report had this to say about the manpower and education needs for improving provision of services:

'In both less developed and more developed countries, a general priority is for training more geriatrically-orientated professional, paraprofessional and volunteer workers. Emphasis is placed on training them to work as inter-disciplinary teams, and to be familiar with preventive geriatrics and the possibilities of services in a wide variety of settings, including the home, day hospital, sheltered housing, day-care center, hospital and nursing home.' (p. 79)

The Sandoz Institute Study group also made these points:

'The training of geriatric nurse practitioner and other non-physician care givers is a US recommendation, partly as a means of economy. Recommendations for the training of nurses and paramedical personnel are also made by experts in Sweden, Italy and Egypt. Polish experts want visiting nurses to be trained as the main coordinators of comprehensive home care' (p. 80)

'The need for geriatric practitioners is often noted by the

experts', was a comment directed to the medical professionals in the Sandoz Institute Study report. The broad-based type of preparation for geriatric care referred to many times was described in this recommendation from the French representatives: 'Train all professional care givers in geriatrics, especially the inter-relationships of somatic, psychological, social and economic conditions and philosophical outlooks' (p. 66). Clearly, the Sandoz Institute Study called for persons in medicine and nursing, as well as those in the allied health professions, who were by no means 'specialists' in the usual sense of the term as workers apart from others of their profession. Rather, all were to be trained to approach their older patients as 'whole persons', with the doctor able to appreciate the importance of a problem with a pension, and a social worker sensitive to behavior which might indicate a hearing problem.

Above all, each must be ready to exchange information with the others. The necessity for working in interdisciplinary teams which they emphasized is consistent with this approach, since the social worker can only report his or her suspicions to the doctor who must make the diagnosis and supply treatment, while the doctor can only say to the social worker that bringing down Mrs T's anxiety depends upon solving her pension problem, and would the social worker see what can be done about it?

In its Country Report for the World Assembly on Aging, Norway related the nature of the health problems of older people to the kinds of professional services required for their care. They too, saw the special need for team work.

> As in most other industrial countries, the most common diseases among old people are cardio-vascular diseases, cancer, kidney diseases, and diseases of the nervous and motor systems. Mental illnesses are another large group, and other very usual complaints are connected with reduced vision or hearing. It has been registered furthermore that old people often suffer from side-effects of medicines, social isolation and loneliness.
>
> A characteristic of the general spectrum of disease among old people is that a number of complaints often occur simultaneously, and the sum of these complaints results in reduced mobility, unsteadiness and a tendency to fall, incontinence in respect of urine and defecation, as well as isolation and mental suffering.

These four groups of symptoms again have four features in common — they often have many causes, they lead to loss of independence, there is no simple form of treatment, and help from other people becomes a necessity.

These conditions have often been considered an unavoidable consequence of advanced age, but this evaluation is incorrect. Diagnosis and treatment must — more than in the case of acute illnesses at other times of life — include an understanding of physical, mental and social conditions, and their inter-relations. The treatment must not only be centred on what is diseased or functionally impaired, but must also focus on the strong aspects of the patient, on the qualities and abilities which can be exploited and developed so that the patient will be able to function for as long as possible in his/her own normal environment. The treatment does not consist of ordinary medical treatment alone, but also includes ergotherapy, physiotherapy, improvements to housing etc. The treatment must be carried out by different professional groups (doctors, nurses, ergotherapists and physiotherapists, experts in home-adjustment and furnishing etc). These must work as a team, with a clear and realistic objective, and must have respect and understanding both for the patient and for others in his/her environment.

In this last area there is today far less progress than is desirable as regards interest in, knowledge of and cooperation concerning old people's problems. (pp. 18-19)

Such interdisciplinary teamwork functions apparently very well in the British setting where there are geriatric physicians to take the lead. It is possible that this is an essential feature, given the facts of professional status in the health professions. If so, as Dr Malone Lee has said, it constitutes a great challenge to the physicians to bring about what the Sandoz Institute Study experts and the WAA, along with Norway have called for.

A British program of training for geriatrics functions according to the Sandoz Institute Study specifications. It is conducted at the Middlesex and the University College Hospitals in London. A nurse is the co-ordinator of the four-week module for geriatric training for the medical students together with some students each from nursing, physiotherapy, occupational therapy and social work. There is a wide variety of lecturers, and the students each work up a case study for presentation to the whole group. The course involves field experience in out-of-hospital settings as well as in hospital.

To return to the topic of personnel: The amount of staff time needed for care of persons with disabilities is itself a subject needing careful scrutiny. The most painstaking research into staff time needed for various disability levels of patients has been carried out by Rückert and his associates at the Kuratorium in Cologne. That research has documented in minutes and hours the staff time needed for each of the tasks performed for patients in a typical day in the usual nursing home situation. The research findings of the British teams reported by Wade and by Peace raise the question, however, of how desirable is the practice in the usual nursing home situation combining most of the 'doing' on the staff part, and the counterpart patient role consisting of passivity and dependency? 'For how many patients is this kind of caring actually necessary?' is a question which must be addressed, and its answer depends upon a number of factors in addition to levels of disability.

Descriptions from Denmark and Sweden of the housing complexes for older people containing 'assisted flats' and custom built adaptations, sophisticated alarm systems and nursing staff always available on the premises, presented in a report by Pearson (1981) suggest that there are ways for getting away from the usual nursing home and nursing care situation and fostering more independent self care on the part of patients with much disability. While there are bound to be a proportion who do require care for feeding, bathing, toileting and turning in bed, there are many who need much less care from others, given the right aids and adaptations along with skillful physiotherapy, occupational therapy, and a nursing staff who have time and will to encourage independent care. Undoubtedly, Britain, Denmark and Sweden can teach other countries much in these respects. Solutions to the problem of long-term care which require less staff time in the long run and build patient independence are worthy of study.

Another major question about which countries may learn valuable lessons from each other is the matter of what personnel and job categories are involved in caring for elderly patients. The presence of nurses is clearly indicated in every country, but there is wide variation in the proportion of nurses on the staff, and in the duties they perform and do not perform. This is related to physician presence on the one hand and to other personnel who supplement the nursing staff. Dependence on nurses is increased where there is little physician involvement, and this is the case almost everywhere. In the US, it is common for the contact with physicians to be via a telephone conversation with the nurse; physician visits to patients are few and far apart in most nursing home situations. The same is likely to be true in the FRG and in British nursing homes and residential homes. According to Kane and Kane's report, Sweden should be quite different, since there are requirements for physicians to be on the staff of nursing homes, the number required dependent upon the size of the home. However, it was suggested to the Kanes that these regulations were not always complied with there.

In West Germany there exists a category of personnel which serves in a major way to supplement the nursing staff for nursing homes and old people's homes, called 'altenpflege'. This term is translated as 'old people's nurse', and the important features are that besides much instruction for nursing care in their training, they receive much more instruction than do regular nurses about the various needs of old people, state services and benefits for the elderly, etc. The training has been a two-year course, and it is being upgraded now to three years in length. There is a state examination and a registration system as for nursing. Altenpflegen form the chief part of those caring for patients in nursing homes, for residents in old people's homes and in some places they offer home care along with community nurses. Begun in the mid-sixties as a job which could be taken up by middle-aged women needing employment, the number of jobs has expanded greatly. It is now regarded by young people as a good career, and they form a large part of the people employed in this job at present.

Because this vocational category provides persons who fill such a need in the FRG and are depended upon so greatly for the long-term care in that country, other countries may want to consider making such an addition to their long-term-care workforces. German authorities have observed that it is the combination of gerontological content along with the content for nursing which results in the special qualities that these carers bring to their work.

Still another type of carer, and training therefore, is being developed in Duisburg by a Deaconess who is a nurse from the religious order based at Kaiserswerte, where Florence Nightingale received her training for nursing. In this case, the job being developed is to assist in providing care for old people in their homes, under the direction of the Sister in charge of a Social Services

Station in that city located in the Ruhr region (Taake, 1984.) It is designed to be part-time work, especially suitable for housewives who want to engage in this as useful, paid employment compatible with their own responsibilities at home. The hours worked may be, say, from 6 to 8 in the evening, though a more conventional 9 to 12 each morning might be the case for some. There is a 'fit' worked out between the worker's available time and the client's needs with the aim of having continuity, i.e. one person provides the care needed by one client, though some are able to serve the needs of more than one. The training course consists of lessons much like the content for the altenpflege training, a combination of instruction for nursing skills with instruction about aging and gerontology. The ability to recognize social and economic needs and physical needs and to work flexibly are emphasized. Altogether, the training consists of 320 lessons, all offered in evening sessions, and extending over a period of two years. Enrollees begin to work in the course of the initial three-months' introductory training when they meet for two nights per week. At the center where this model is currently in operation, there are 80 of the caring-assistants on the staff along with 14 nurses.

The very notable thing about these developments in Germany is that they are innovations in personnel for long-term care capable of making a great difference in the available pool of people trained very specially for the work which needs to be done. Training for both kinds of jobs from the beginning has been fashioned to prepare for the care of older people. It is therefore tailor-made and should provide a better fit than jobs which have been altered from their original shapes. Clearly, those responsible for personnel — the element in long-term care which costs the most and means the most — should consider such developments as those very carefully indeed.

The Home Help vocation is described at some length in the chapter on Community Services. Home helps have become a prominent part of domiciliary services in virtually every European country. Unlike the German altenpflegen and the care assistants just described, the home helps at the outset had no nursing duties nor nursing training whatever. In fact, in most countries they still have no preparation for their jobs. But, like the 'Home help — home health aide,' a kind of worker funded to a very small extent under the Older Americans' Act in the US, their duties are in fact beginning to include care of a nursing type for their infirm elderly clients. As this trend is certain to continue, those institutions training for nursing care might well consider development of training programs like Duisburg's. Those people employed as home helps who wanted to qualify for a step up in a community services career could then do so by completing such training.

In Britain, the training department of Age Concern England regularly offers such short courses on a variety of topics. The same course may be scheduled for different locations throughout the country on separate dates. Another voluntary organization doing the same is the British Association for Services to the Elderly, which has organized such courses on almost a monthly basis.

Networks are needed so that professional people, volunteers and interested members of the public know that these offerings are available. The Centre for Policy on Ageing in London provides a valuable service in disseminating announcements of such courses on all aging-related topics well ahead of the events themselves. Several pages of their bi-monthly publication *New Literature on Old Age* contain current events and announcements of courses coming during the months ahead. The following listing from that publication for June of the past year represents a sample of this type of training activity:

June 1
The prospects for prevention in geriatric medicine
A one-day symposium of the Royal College of Physicians and Surgeons of Glasgow.
Details: Honorary Secretary, Royal College of Physicians and Surgeons of Glasgow, 234 St Vincent Street, Glasgow G2 5RJ.

June 8
Home from home: issues in adult family placement
Study day planned by British Association of Social Workers (BASW) which will be concerned with the use of adult family placements for various groups of clients.
Details: Conference Organiser, BASW, 16 Kent Street, Birmingham B5 6RD.

June 8, 15, 22 and 29
Working with the elderly mentally infirm
The aim of this course is to provide an overview of the many different problems which result in confused behaviour in elderly residents or patients; to then study practical approaches to the prevention, alleviation and management of these problems. The course is aimed at staff in social services, homes for the elderly and the NHS.
Details: London Boroughs Training Committee, 9 Tavistock Place London WC1.

June 11
Positive approaching to continence
An Age Concern training course.
Venue: Training Resource Centre, Birmingham.
Details: Training Dept, Age Concern England, 60 Pitcairn Road, Mitcham, Surrey CR4 3LL.

June 12
Management of the elderly confused person
Day course organised by the National Demonstration Centre in Medical Rehabilitation of the Elderly.
Details: National Demonstration Centre, Day Hospital, Kingston General Hospital, Beverley Road, Hull HU3 1UR.

June 18
'We'll take good care of you ...' — public sector residential living
Seminar organised by BASE (British Assoc. for Service to the Elderly) — London group. Speakers from the Centre for Environmental and Social Studies in Aging.
Venue: King's Fund Centre, London NW1.
Details: BASE, 2 Twyford Avenue, Acton, London W3 9QA.

June 19-20
Normalisation and services for elderly mentally ill people
Two-day course organised by the King's Fund Centre.
Details: King's Fund Centre, 126 Albert Street, London NW1 7NF.

June 19-20
Resources on confusion
The course will seek to show what resources are available to help people to understand the nature of confusion, as well as explore ways of helping people and their carers.
Fees: £45 (£35 to Age Concern groups)
Venue: Birmingham
Details: Age Concern England, Bernard Sunley House, 60 Pitcairn Road, Mitcham, Surrey CR4 3LL.

June 19-21
Living with dying
The Lisa Sainsbury Educational Foundation conference. A conference for nurses concerned with symptom control, terminal care and family support at all ages.
Details: Deputy Director of Studies (External), St Christopher's Hospice, 51-53 Lawrie Park Road, Sydenham, London SE26.

June 26-27
The contributions of volunteers to primary health and social care
The purpose of this workshop is to examine the importance of developing a partnership between providers of care in local government and the health services and volunteers.
Fees: £100 per person inclusive of accommodation and meals.
Details: School of Applied Social Studies, University of Bristol.

June 27-29
Services for mentally frail elderly people
A course to look at some of the rehabilitative and supportive services offered to elderly mentally frail people with special attention to services using volunteers.
Fees: £45 (£35 to Age Concern groups)
Details: Age Concern England, Bernard Sunley House, 60 Pitcairn Road, Mitcham, Surrey CR4 3LL.

June 28
Vitamin deficiency in the elderly
One-day symposium organised by the Health Services Research Centre, Medical School, University of Birmingham.
Details: Health Services Research Centre, Department of Social Medicine, Medical School, University of Birmingham, Birmingham B15 2TJ.

July 4
The challenge of geriatric long-term care
One-day conference organised by the Univ. Hospital of South Manchester. Subjects will include art and the environment; space for quiet and study; the activities organiser; the use of music and reminiscence and the viewpoint of the patient, nurse and doctor.
Fees: £12 incl. lunch and refreshments.
Details: Dept of Geriatric Medicine, Teaching Unit 4, University Hospital of South Manchester, Nell Lane, Manchester M20 8LR.

References

Abrams, Mark (1980) *Beyond Three-Score Years and Ten.* Age Concern, England, Mitcham, Surrey
Centre for Policy on Aging, (1984). *New Literature on Old Age 8* (44) March-April, 1984. Centre for Policy on Aging, London
Country Reports for the United Nations' World Assembly on Aging (1982)
— *Aging in Norway: Humanitarian and Developmental Issues.* Royal Norwegian Ministry of Health and Social Affairs, Oslo
— *Report on the Situation of the Elderly in the Federal Republic of Germany.* The German Center of Gerontology, Berlin
Carboni, D., (1982) *Geriatric Medicine in the United States and Great Britain.* The Greenwood Press, Westport, Connecticut
Collot, C., Jani LeBris, H. and Ridoux, A., for CLEIRPPA, (1982) Towards an Improvement in Self Reliance of the Elderly: Innovations and New Guidelines for the Future. The Commission of the European Communities, Brussels
Dieck, Margret, (1981) *Social and Medical Aspects of the Situation of Older People in the Federal Republic of Germany.* The German Center of Gerontology, Berlin
Federal Council on the Aging, (1981) *The Need for Long Term Care* (DHSS Publ. No. OHDS 81-20704) Washington D.C.
Flamm, Franz, (1974). *Social Welfare Services and Social Work in the Federal Republic of Germany.* Deutscher Vereins für Offentliche und Private Fürsorge, Frankfurt
Goldberg, M. and Connelly, N., (1982) *The Effectiveness of Social Care for the Elderly.* Heinemann, London
Kane, R. and Kane, R., (1976). *Long Term Care in Six Countries: Implications for*

the US DHEW Publ. No. (NIH)76-1207. The John E. Fogarty Center, National Institutes of Health, Washington, DC

Kovar, M.G., (1982) The public health impact of an increasing elderly population in the USA. *World Health Statistics Quarterly 35* (3 and 4) 1982

Malone Lee, James, (1983). Contradictions in care: A twentieth century dilemma? Inaugural address to the British Association of Service to the Elderly, London Group. Kings College, London, December 3rd, 1983

Maule, M.M. and Williamson, J., The Edinburgh Study (1975). Quoted in Amos, G. (ed.) *Going Home? The Care of Elderly Patients after Discharge from Hospital.* The Continuing Care Project, 1975, Birmingham, England

Peace, Sheila, Kellaher, L. and Willcocks, D., (1982) *A Balanced Life? A Consumer Study of Residential Life in One Hundred Local Authority Old People's Homes.* School of Applied Social Studies and Sociology, The Polytechnic of North London, London

Pearson, Rosalind, (1981) *An Independent Old Age: Provisions for Pensioners in Scandinavia.* Task Force and Pensioners' Link, London

Rückert, W., (1980) *Organizing Nursing Services in Nursing Homes* (available only in German). Schriftenreihe der Bundesministerium für Jugend, Familie und Gesundheit, Bonn

Rückert, W. and Zimmerman, R.E., (1978) Measuring nursing needs of older people related to actual nursing times in institutions for the aged. *Akt Gerontologie 8,* 373-7

Selby, P. and Schechter, M., (1982) *Aging 2000 — A challenge for society.* Published for the Sandoz Institute for health and socio-economic studies, referred to herein as 'the Sandoz Institute Study', MTP, Lancaster, England

Taake, Annegret, (1984) *Curriculum for Training Older People's Care Assistants.* Social Service Center of North Duisburg, Duisburg, West Germany (mimeo)

Tobin, S., (1978) Old People. In Maas, H.S. (ed.), *Social Service Research: Review of Studies.* National Association of Social Workers, Washington, DC

United States Congress, (1980) Special problems in Long-Term Care. Committee Publ. No. 96-208, a report of the Select Committee on Aging of the House of Representatives, United States Congress. The US Government Printing Office, Washington, DC

Wade, B., Sawyer, L. and Bell, J., (1983) *Dependency with Dignity.* The Bedford Press, London

White House Conference on Aging, (1981) *Chartbook on Aging.* The White House Conference on Aging Staff, Washington, DC

World Assembly on Aging (1982) *Plan of Action.* From meeting of the World Assembly on Aging in Vienna, Austria, in August, 1982. (Referred to herein as 'WAA')

3 CARE IN THE FAMILY

Patients in the United States who require skilled nursing care for some months are likely be sent to a nursing home for most of that period of time. In many countries — the UK, the FRG, Sweden, Denmark and France — they would have been kept in hospital for those months. When finally the time comes to leave hospital or skilled care in a nursing home, however, the most likely destination is to go home where the patient will be cared for by a member of the family. The figure for this destination at the point of hospital discharge was reported to be between 50 and 60 per cent in *Home from Hospital* (Todd, *et al.* 1979). For those disabled elderly who are being cared for at any one time, the percentage at home is a higher one. Walker (1983) has quoted the British Sociologist Peter Townsend's observation that 'nearly three times as many bedfast and severely disabled people live in their own homes as in all institutions put together' (p. 106).

Recommendation 5 under 'Health' in the WAA *Plan of Action* had this to say: 'A proper balance between the role of the institutions and that of the family in providing health care of the elderly — based on recognition of the family and the immediate community as the key elements in a well-balanced system of care — is important'. Much concern has been voiced in Britain that things have recently been pushed out of balance. Finch and Groves (1983) noted that public expenditures for institutional care were being reduced by governments at the same time that they were expressing 'renewed enthusiasm for so-called 'community' provision of various sorts, and a reliance on the recently designated 'informal sector' of welfare provision that is, families, friends and neighbours who provide care for the dependant' (p. 5).

The change in Britain from less to more dependence on families and friends was examined in the context of recent history in a report from the Equal Opportunities Commission (EOC) (1982):

The initial intention of policies of community care in the 1950's and early 1960's was to remove elderly and physically or mentally handicapped people from the large, impersonal, geographically isolated institutions, and to place them in smaller residential homes and hostels in a local setting. The aim was to improve the quality of care given to the patients and to enable them to retain contact with family and friends. Primary responsibility for care, however was to remain with public authorities. During the 1960's and 1970's the concept of community care changed from a policy of 'care *in* the community' to one of 'Care *by* the Community'. The idea that care of those who are unable to care for themselves should be provided by those closest to them has been clearly expressed in the recent White Paper on the elderly *Growing Older.* '... families are, as they have always been, the principal source of support and care.' (p. 2)

(The White Paper goes on:)

'... the primary sources of support and care for elderly people are informal and voluntary. These spring from the personal ties of kinship, friendship and neighbourhood. They are irreplaceable. It is the role of public authorities to sustain, and where necessarily, develop — but never to displace — such support and care. Care *in* the community must increasingly mean care *by* the Community.' (p. 2)

The report notes that:

This policy however presupposes both that a family are able and willing to accept the enormous responsibility and commitment which caring entails and that the disabled or elderly are themselves willing to be cared for by their families. Neither of these assumptions are necessarily true in all cases. (p. 2)

The growing numbers of very elderly persons likely to be needing this care must be taken into account together with other societal developments:

Ironically other societal changes have reduced the numbers who are in a position to provide care. Many frail elderly for example have no children; Mark Abrams survey of people aged over 75 revealed that:
'30% had never had any children and another 45% had had only one or two. Among the many women living alone almost 40% had never had any children. Some of those who had had

children have outlived them so that at the time of the survey 35% of all respondents had no living offspring.' (pp. 2-3)

and

The 'traditional' pattern of family life has also been substantially altered by the increased participation of married women in the work-force; in spite of rapidly rising unemployment in recent years over 70% of married women aged between 35-54 are economically active. (p. 3)

The EOC opinion is that more and more care will be given by families, but at a cost to the women of the family:

For those who succeed in combining work and caring the opportunity costs are considerable. Caring inevitably restricts the type of employment that can be undertaken to work that is near-at-hand, possibly part-time, but certainly with working hours that fit into the carer's routine. Such employment is unlikely to be well paid or to offer good prospects for advancement. (p. 6)

Despite this imbalance between those needing care and those able to provide it the concept of care by the family may gain more credence among policy makers simply because the increase in the numbers requiring care has coincided with an economic recession and the presumed availability of large numbers of unemployed people may be seen as a way of reconciling the need for more care with less money. Married women who wish to re-enter the labour market after bringing up their children may be especially vulnerable in this particular political equation.

The shortfall of provision for those requiring care must mean that most of those unable to fend for themselves will have to rely upon their own and neighbourhood resources for their daily needs. Hence it is likely that families will find themselves faced with a cruel conflict of demands which force them to assume a caring role; the pressure will undoubtedly be greatest upon those family members with the least influence and opportunity in the labour market; usually these are the women of the family. (p. 3)

The Sandoz Institute Study (Selby and Schechter, 1982) brought into this picture the support which the carers at home must have if the 'informal sector' is going to be expected to do its part:

> Without informal services, many elders would not be assisted at all. ... Experts in a wide range of countries propose ways of helping families to help their elders. One major approach is to provide those professional and voluntary services that bring problems within manageable proportions for the informal care givers. This category would include services at home during the day in health and social facilities such as hospitals and senior centers. The home services would be provided by professionals, especially nurses and physiotherapists, as well as lesser-skilled personnel, such as home-health aides and home-maker.
>
> Another major approach is to subsidize the true or surrogate family in maintaining the elder, with 'family incentives', (or other terms for financial payments). The Italians suggest that the state remunerate private individuals and organizations willing to help the dependent elderly. (p. 82)

Attention from an officially organized group of international experts to the reality of the family caregiving situation was good news to those in Britain and in West Germany who had begun to examine the situation of care for elderly people in their homes.

Who the family carers are and what their needs are, has been a subject addressed in the studies conducted by the Continuing Care Project in Britain for a dozen years (See especially the chapters on 'Who Are the Carers?' in their 1978 report.) They have found that the family carer is usually a spouse, as old as or older than the elderly patient. When that is true, there are likely to be serious physical disabilities on the part of the carer. A great deal of the time, the carer is a daughter or daughter-in-law. She is quite likely to go out to work and may especially need to do so because of the increased expenditures associated with the patient's illness. The Equal Opportunities Commission report focused upon the problems of that situation:

> The effects of caring upon employment opportunities for women are more drastic than they are for men, and not only because a disproportionate number of carers are women.

Studies have shown that the caring occurs at a much earlier stage in a woman's life than it does in a man's; most male carers are approaching or past retirement age, they have already secured their pension entitlement, and they have achieved whatever success in employment was theirs to achieve.[2] For women caring can represent yet another disruption to their pattern of employment to follow that caused by the break for child-rearing, thus further diminishing their chances of future advancement, and reducing their pension entitlement.

Despite the social and economic restrictions experienced by carers, there is no doubt that for many people the emotional rewards of caring far outweigh the disadvantages. However, the existence of intangible advantages does not justify the continuation of policies which ignore the basic rights of women who want to play a full and active part in society. The rewards of caring are more likely to be forthcoming when the caring role is freely chosen by the carer, and she is welcomed by her charge. (p. 7)

The Country Report of West Germany for the WAA noted the career difficulties daughters experienced there when they gave up their employment to care for parents with long-term disability. One political party in the FRG has drafted a law to introduce into Parliament in 1984 to provide insurance for nursing care which will make family carers (and neighbors and friends) eligible to receive payment for the time and work they spend on giving care. This bill has gone so far as to provide for family care-givers the security that when they themselves receive pensions, they shall not have been disadvantaged due to having had to renounce income from outside employment to dedicate themselves to the care of the infirm. Though the chances for the bill to be passed at this time are slim, it is important that the bill includes the concept of realistic provision for social security status as well as financial payment of family carers for their services. (*The Frankfurter Allegemine*, 12 May, 1984)

Awareness is growing in every country that this can be a situation of exploitation. Home carers need a share of services like respite care and home helps. The various domiciliary services which are provided for elderly patients in those countries which do provide them, are allotted first to those persons who have no family member at home. With the large number of very old people living alone, completely on their own, few if any of these services are left for serving the patients with a family care-giver. The family member, therefore, is in the position of contributing her, sometimes his, services without payment and, by being there with the patient, keeps out the community workers with their various kinds of care. Thus with respect to help from outside, family care-givers and their patients are the real have-nots.

It is not always recognized that caring for elderly relatives is a task requiring formidable knowledge and skills with which most of us are unfamiliar. Though there are those difficulties in obtaining services, certain benefits are available in many countries in the form of financial help. In Sweden, the family member is eligible for payment, and in Britain there is both the Attendance Allowance and the Invalid Care Allowance, but a great deal of knowledge is required to meet the requirements for these benefits and receive the first cheque. In fact, several questions arise in family caring where clear legal information is necessary. In every one of the industrialized nations there are organizations and government departments offering services for which elderly people are eligible; most people do not know what or where they are. A special asset to learn about in Britain is the service providing the aids and adaptations for a variety of disabilities; these help the disabled person to carry out many activities independently and can lessen the physical demands on the carer. There are many skills of home nursing which it is essential that the carer learn to perform. Correct information about physical and mental health problems which occur in many older people is frequently needed for daily care as well as essential in a crisis.

Consequently, a great service to the British carer is a book entitled *Take Care of Your Elderly Relative* (Gray and McKenzie, 1980). It contains detailed and accurate information, brought together in one 'manual', as it were, on that wide variety of topics. Its special value comes from the credibility of the authors who have assembled this information: Dr Muir Gray is a physician who has concerned himself with health of elderly patients, and Miss Heather McKenzie is a barrister who has served for a decade as director of the National Council for Carers and Their Elderly Dependants. The tone of their book is as important as any single part of the contents: that the home carer is faced with a very complex task requiring knowledge and skills as well as physical and emotional support. Preparing oneself to cope and obtaining the help (financial, informational, etc.) which is available will some-times change the nature of family caring dramatically. A book of this type designed for the special conditions obtaining in other countries is a support needed by family carers.

In the United States, the White House Conference recommen-dations included attention to the needs for support of family carers. Their Recommendation 209 stated this case:

Whereas families provide 60 to 80 per cent of all care given to dependent older persons, but receive inadequate assistance from the federal and state governments, therefore be it resolved that
— families providing personal care for disabled older depen-dents be eligible for reimbursement for such care, and
— federal income tax credit be extended to family care-givers, and
— states be encouraged to provide tax credits for, or cash pay-ments to family care-givers, and
— respite care be readily available through federal and state programs. (p. 118 of Final Report WHCOA, 1982)

Another committee apparently worked on the same problem and formulated Recommendation 217. A summary of the con-ference delegates' reactions to this recommendation is given in the following excerpts:

Recommendation No. 217 Committee 7 Synopsis

... the support system for older persons remains anchored in the family and extended family and therefore national policy should be redirected to provide greater resources, particularly home health care, in-home supportive services and a variety of reimbursement systems ... to families who are caring for their older members.

Scores. Total number of responses: 468   Net score: 386

Favorable	404
Neutral	5
Unfavorable	18
Unclassified	41

Staff Summary. (72 Responses analyzed) In responding to

this recommendation a large number of delegates reiterated their belief in home health care and the vital role of the family in this regard. Tax credits or alternative forms of reimbursement to the family were given thorough consideration. Delegates also placed strong emphasis on the importance of providing safeguards to prevent abuses of the elderly or of the reimbursement system.

Excerpts from Responses.   Pro — 'This is basic.' 'This recommendation should start a national trend.' 'Tax credits are highly recommended.' 'This is another basic theme of the 1981 WHCoA.' 'Important support to both individuals in need and their families.' 'It is only through some form of support that people may be able to keep family at home.' 'This is extremely deserving of consideration.' 'Emphasize family; we should provide *all* possible opportunities for older individuals to remain at home.' 'Good idea — the safeguards are imperative.' 'The growing number of elderly and the rising LTC costs make this desirable.'
  Miscellaneous — This is an important and complex issue — how monitor against abuses?' 'Family may not be the basis for support, suggest TRIAGE concept.'
  Con — 'No, monetary gain should come last.' 'Stop paying families for doing what they should normally and lovingly be doing.'

Still another, Recommendation 213, emphasized the special importance of assistance in the case of particular cultural and ethnic groups.
  Major research into the family care situation has been conducted by Elaine Brody. In a report in 1979, she wrote:

The family has a legitimate right to systems of support; the community has a responsibility to create them and to prevent the problems raised by parent care from reverberating down through the generations. (p. 16)

Brody, who has characterized the carer as 'The woman in the middle', has dealt in her research and writings with the complexities involved in the family care of disabled elderly people in the context of American society.

Psychological and social aspects of caring with special impact on women in Britain have been addressed in chapters of two recently published books. In the first of these, *Care in the Community* (1982), both Stevenson and Greengross wrote of the emotional aspects and family dynamics of middle-aged persons caring for elderly relatives. Stevenson noted the relative paucity of attention to the dynamics of family life in the later years and suggested that:

> Part of the denigration of old age is affected by ignoring the intensity and significance of emotional dynamics. A form of depersonalisation sets in by which many professionals, sadly including social workers, do not consider family problems in the same terms as they would consider those where there are children. This is manifestly absurd. The relationships of a lifetime carry through to the end. (p. 15)

Greengross also recognized ways in which the lot may be a tougher one for one who cares for an older family member as compared with the responsibilities of child care. This was presented in the case of a single woman:

> One caring daughter who had looked after her demented mother for several years could only express immense gratitude to a hard pressed community psychiatric nurse who took her mother out for a short ride in her car occasionally, as part of a relatives' support scheme. This was the daughter's only break from a relative whose needs transcended the boundaries of day and night in a situation in which time was meaningless and they were both marooned in an isolated world of their own. Her gratitude and low expectations were typical of many such care givers.
> One study of young mothers at home found that almost half of them suffered from depression for which they had sought medical treatment. Yet they could all look forward to a time when their children would be independent. The isolated caring daughter, however, knows that only her mother's death can bring her respite. Her guilt at entertaining such thoughts and her feelings of failure, together with increasing isolation and withdrawal from social contacts, make it impossble for her to leave her dependant relative, even for a short time. The single mother demands nursery care. The caring daughter is grateful for a few hours respite. (pp. 18-19)

Again over family relationships, Stevenson's thoughts are affirmed by Greengross:

> ... fragile family relationships may be broken by the demands of this caring task. We tend to ignore the psychological implications of caring and the role reversal that this inevitably brings ... Research focused on the intergenerational dynamics of family care is urgently needed. (p. 19)

Noting that there is 'increasingly heavy cost' to those who become the carers, Greengross points to the several parts of the carer's life which are touched by this cost. One important fact is the length of time often involved: 'about half of the carers interviewed in a survey had cared continually for over five years'. She goes on to note that another survey found:

> ... one working woman in eight was responsible for the care of a dependant relative and that men carers tended to be older and near or past retirement age. Nissell (1980) has examined the task of caring, the heavy physical work often involved, how time has to be allocated and carefully planned so that life loses all spontaneity. Restricted opportunties and difficulties in maintaining a job make it impossible for many caring relatives to continue to work and their reduced incomes then have to cover many additional costs such as laundry, special transport and heating. (p. 20)

The survey by Crossroads (Bristow, 1981) added further details of the sometimes painful conditions of carers:

> Carers are often unaware of their needs and the take up of various benefits is low. They are prevented from allowing others to know of their problems through guilt or shame ... 68% of them suffered from some degree of ill health. Over half those at home were caring for a husband or wife and were therefore elderly themselves and anxious about who would look after their partner when they died. ... Many are exhausted, irritable and under constant strain through lack of sleep. (p. 22)

Both Stevenson and Greengross make the connection between the emotional strain, the complexity of the family relationships involved and the fact that there have been reports of family violence: verbal as well as physical abuse of the elderly by the carer and also abuse of the carer by the older person.

One particular aspect of 'the economic cost of caring' alluded to by both authors is a fact noted in earlier references in the chapter: that the pension rights of the carer are given a severe blow when it is necessary to give up one's job. Observations in the quotation from Amman's (1981) study of aging in Western Europe indicate the ominous picture into which this fits:

> In all pension systems, retirement leads to a *lower income* for almost all population groups; this means that groups that already had a low income during their working lives will be *even more socio-economically deprived* after retirement and will be driven towards the poverty line. This is a form of *structurally transmitted social deprivation* that can scarcely be made good by individual efforts. The groups primarily affected are unskilled workers, semi-skilled workers, women (most of whom worked in subordinate positions) and the disabled. (p. 13)

Greengross put forward several suggestions for what must be done for the family caring situation. She noted the fact that in Sweden some payment is made to the carers (a measure as noted above, also recommended in the Sandoz Institute Study report). However, Greengross combined the need for interventions with cautions about the manner of intervening in this delicate human situation:

> Many are in need of practical help on a scale which could be given without too much difficulty. Any intervention, however, must be in a form acceptable to people who are reluctant to voice their needs. Insensitivity may easily destroy the existing caring relationships and cause great distress to the old person. Preventive work, spanning health and social care, income maintenance, housing and adaptations to the home, is essential and we have to reach out to carers while they are still supportive and loving and not beaten down by the strains of their task. (p. 22)

A need she stressed was for paths which carers can take to find persons responsive to their problems:

> It is essential to harness community effort and motivate self-

help, to change attitudes and discuss dementia, incontinence, problems of sleeplessness and isolation, anger and grief, openly and to help care givers and their elderly relatives to know what the future holds for them. Services tailored to changing needs and a recognition of different and sometimes conflicting interests within the caring family unit can enable its members to care for much longer and more effectively, while preserving the dignity of the old person concerned. (p. 23)

'Changing needs' includes perhaps the most difficult point encountered in a family caring situation, and that is how to bring it to an end when the need to do so is brought about because the care-giver can no longer cope, or when, for whatever reason, the need to do so is felt by the older person, the caring person or perhaps both of them. This situation calls for sensitive counselors very well acquainted with the existing alternatives for a place to live in the form of sheltered housing, nursing homes, etc, and with the financial benefits which might be found to maximize the options available.

An agency does exist in London which plays exactly this role. It is called 'Counsel and Care for the Elderly' (CCE) and is a completely independent charitable organization with its own funds for operating to achieve its purposes, described by CCE itself as 'offering a free comprehensive advisory and counseling service used by thousands of elderly people, their relatives and professionals. It helps to find nursing home places for hundreds of elderly people who can no longer cope on their own'. Its founding and history have been described in a booklet by Graham (1982).

A feature of importance is the very careful and lengthy on-the-job training given to persons coming onto the staff in order to keep the level of their service to clients very high. The information the agency collects and keeps deals with (1) government programs and charities which can be tapped into to help pay for care or, in the case of some charities, for providing care; and (2) with the characteristics of privately operated nursing and residential homes and other types of housing which may be appropriate.

Once contacted by a client, the staff member establishes the sources of help appropriate and then acquaints the client and family with all of the steps to take vis à-vis the bureaucracy or private organization involved. On the basis of their acquaintance with the client's characteristics and expressed wishes, together with their detailed knowledge of acceptable homes, the agency makes suggestions which the client then follows up. Such a responsibly run agency, independent of ties with any of the interested parties, can play a unique role in helping with decision-making in a situation usually very emotionally charged and full of needs for complete and accurate information.

Thoroughgoing and perceptive consideration of family carers and care itself are also contained in the chapters of the book edited by Finch and Groves (1983). They introduced the book, entitled *Labour of Love: Women, Work and Caring*, by describing its focus as this:

The tension between women's economic independence (actual, potential or desired), and their traditional role as unpaid 'carers'. (It explores) the dilemmas which caring poses for women, the tension between paid work and unpaid caring (which can be hard work) and the social policy issues raised by the particular topics under discussion. (p. 2)

The chapter by Graham encompasses the subject from the intimacy of caring — its basis in emotions and the very self-identity of both women and men — to its significance for major social policy decisions and for the organization of the world of work. For the kinds of paid work open to women involve giving care, and those jobs are used by women as their way into the world of work. Just as home care is not paid for at all, these jobs are underpaid. This constellation provides additional reinforcement of the tie between women and caring and low (or no) pay.

Graham distinguishes between the two elements of caring, both of which are involved for the giver and the receiver of family care: the *feeling* part of caring, and the *active work* of caring. These become so inextricably combined that there is inevitably a resistance to 'care' institutionalized into 'services'.

Whether provided through the institutions of the state or through the intervention of 'good neighbors' in the community, both carers and their dependants recognize that the substitute services are not 'care', since they lack the very qualities of commitment and affection which transform caring-work into a life work. (p. 29)

Alan Walker is the author of another chapter penetrating

deeply into the matter of family carers in today's society. His analysis suggests that it is to the state's advantage that community services do not go to the elderly person being cared for by a family member because the state's 'main concern is to ensure the continuance of the prime responsibility of the family for the support and care of its own members.' (p. 191)

Walker points out various means by which the state explicitly and implicitly supports and reinforces the sexual division of caring. Nor, he says, does the state lose any opportunity to make the point that caring for husbands, children and elderly family members is to be done by women as a duty 'beyond price'. (For example, wives are not paid the invalid care allowance when it is their husbands they care for.) Walker found, incidentally, those in the higher social classes are more likely than the poor to provide themselves with assistance (from home-helps, for instance) when incapacitated.

Walker's chapter, along with some others in the volume, described the various costs to family carers in the form of physical and psychological illness as well as disturbances in family relationships.

A great deal of attention then, is being given in Britain, as well as in Germany, to the special needs of women who are family carers. The Equal Opportunities Commission listed numbers of support services and recommendations for benefits for carers in a 1982 report. Age Concern has given priority to this cause. If, however, the giving of care by female relatives is as thoroughly ingrained as the *Labour of Love* authors have found it to be, and if the state continues to pursue the path which will save money, the improvement of matters for family carers will require a great deal of pressure from a multitude of sources.

However strong the carers' case for redress, it can not be overlooked that in the current picture, it sometimes happens that the last thing to receive consideration is the well being of the patient. The expediency for the state, the interests of others in the home — all may be put ahead of the care needed by the patient in order to recover. The interests of carer and cared-for must be kept in careful balance, and assistance from well-designed community services will help maintain that balance. The next chapter describes these services and their development.

References

Amman, A. (1981) 'The Status and Prospects of the Aging in Western Europe'. Euro-social Occasional Papers 8. European Centre for Social Welfare, Vienna

Bristow, A. (1981) *Crossroads Care Attendant Scheme: A Study of their Organization and Working Practices and the Families Whom They Support*

Brody, E. (1979) Woman's changing roles, and care of the aging family. In *Aging: Agenda for the Eighties*, A National Issues Journal Book. The Government Research Corporation, Washington, DC

Equal Opportunities Commission, (1982) *Who Cares for the Carers?* Equal Opportunities Commission, Manchester, England

Finch, J. and Groves, D. (eds.) (1983) *Labour of Love: Women, Work and Caring.* Routledge and Kegan Paul, London

Graham, Hilary, (1983) 'Caring: a labour of love'. In Finch, J. and Groves, D. (eds.) *A Labour of Love: Women, Work and Caring.* Routledge and Kegan Paul, London

Graham, Robert, (1982) *Compassionate Strangers.* Counsel and Care for the Elderly, London

Gray, J.A. Muir and McKenzie, Heather, (1980) *Take Care of Your Elderly Relative.* George Allen and Unwin, London

Greengross, Sally (1982) 'Caring for the Carers', in Glendenning, F. (ed), *Care in the Community: Recent Research and Current Projects.* The Beth Johnson Foundation in association with the Department of Adult Education, University of Keele and Age Concern England, Stoke-on-Trent

Frankfurter Allgemine (1984) 'Hessen's Draft Law for Nursing Care Insurance' May 12, 1984, Nr. III/Seite 3

McDermott, M. and Bromley-Wiggins, (1978) Who are the Carers? In Harnoen, John. *Getting Better? Report 2, The Care of the Elderly Returning Home from Hospital.* The Continuing Care Project, Birmingham, England

Nissell, M. and Bonnerjea, L. (1980) *Family Care of the Handicapped Elderly. Who Pays?* Policy Studies Institute, London

Selby, P. and Schechter, M. (1982) *Aging 2000 — A Challenge for Society.* MTP Press (Published for the Sandoz Institute for Health and Socioeconomic studies) (Referred to herein as 'the Sandoz Institute Study'), Lancaster

Stevenson, Olive, (1982) 'Social trends in care for the elderly'. In Glendenning, F. (ed.) *Care in the Community: Recent Research and Current Projects.* The Beth Johnson Foundation in association with the Department of Adult Education, University of Keele and Age Concern England, Stoke-on-Trent, England

Thurstans, J. Ed. (1979) *Home from Hospital: Questions and Answers.* The Continuing Care Project, Birmingham, England

Walker, Alan, (1983) 'Care for elderly people: a conflict between women and the state'. In Finch, J. and Groves, D. (eds.) *A Labour of Love: Women, Work and Caring.* Routledge and Kegan Paul, London

White House Conference Staff, (1982) *Final Report on the 1981 White House Conference on Aging.* WHCoA Staff, Washington, DC

4 COMMUNITY SERVICES

The benefits of services which can be provided to disabled persons in their homes to enable them to maintain and regain strength and independent functioning has been the great contribution of European countries to long-term care needs. During the past 25 years Great Britain, West Germany, France, the Scandinavian countries and the Netherlands have provided leadership in developing a dazzling array of these services. A report from CLEIRPPA, (Collot *et al.* 1982) a research center for the Commission of the European Communities, summarized how far these had been developed by 1978:

> Although domiciliary services are not available to all elderly Europeans, the numbers of those who are able to rely on them are nevertheless considerable. Their availability varies widely from country to country, and from one type of area to another; it would appear that Greece, Ireland and Italy are the countries where there is least provision of such services, while rural areas in all the countries fare less well than the towns. (p. 37)

The health services, social services and many voluntary organizations have had a hand in these creative efforts in Europe. The opportunities to exchange ideas and engage in multicountry projects through the World Health Organization Office for Europe and the European Council and Economic Community have helped stimulate these efforts.

The Sandoz Institute Study report (Selby and Schechter, 1982) mentions these community services: home visits from the general practitioner, community nurses and health visitors, physiotherapists, occupational therapists and social workers; home helps to aid with shopping, cleaning, meal preparation, and the like; home delivery of meals; bathing aids; provision of aids which the disabled person can use (eg, a wheel chair, a telephone) and installing adaptations like handrails and commodes to improve problemmatic home environments; laundry services (particularly helpful with unmanaged problems of incontinence); alarm systems, some of them not requiring the person to push a button; and, neighborhood 'wardens' who check-in at a number of homes periodically to make sure things are alright. In addition there is provision of transport for persons to go to and from day hospitals, day centers, etc. Chiropody, hairdressing and a mobile library are other options mentioned in the CLEIRPPA report.

It is evident that such an elaborate array of services would require a great deal of careful co-ordination, especially because they come from more than one service-providing agency, and it is generally recognized that there are many problems still to work out. But, as matters stand, not only have all of these services been shown to be feasible; they are popular, and the effectiveness of many of them has been demonstrated. 'A ten-year policy in favor of community care in the UK has helped to keep many people out of institutions', it is stated in the Sandoz Institute report (p. 76). A recent book in Britain has reviewed the many evaluation studies so far performed on these community services (Goldberg and Connelly, 1982), and is a valuable source of information about the nature and purposes of the various schemes, as well as their results.

The Home Help Vocation

One of the community services which figures prominently in every country for meeting needs of the elderly who are frail or disabled is the Home Help. The homemaker-home health aide service under the US Older Americans Act is a similar service but much less commonly provided than are home helps in much of Europe. The Scandinavian countries provide them at the rate of over 30 per 1000 people over 65, and in Britain there are more than 10 per 1000.

A short article in *Ageing International* (1982) furnished comparative figures for the year 1976, on the number of home helpers in selected countries, giving the ratio per 100,000 total population. All of the Scandinavian countries are high, with Sweden the top at 923 per 100,000. 'The Netherlands, with its 599, is the only non-Scandinavian country that comes as close in its ratio of home help provision per 100,000 population. Great Britain, Finland and Belgium are next in line. The remainder of the industrialized countries provide less than 50 home helpers per 100,000 population despite similar demographic profiles.' (p. 11)

Flamm (1974) described this vocation as it was in the FRG ten years ago:

> She looks after the personal and social affairs of the aged, nurses old, ailing and helpless persons, cooperates in the health care of old people and in the implementation of medical instructions ... The voluntary welfare organisations are particularly concerned with the training of homehelpers for aged persons. (p. 153)

The role of home help is a very flexible one, as flexible as a housewife's, according to Goldberg and Connelly. Reporting a study of home helps in a London borough they gave this quotation: 'They looked upon their jobs as similar to that of a housewife and considered that all that was required of them was to do in their clients' homes the same things that they did in their own homes' (p. 64). This description was given of the usual activities of home helps:

> Their tasks often include personal care and basic nursing as well as cleaning (which the studies show takes the largest share of time), laundry work, shopping and food preparation. (p. 61)

However, in studies of home-helps as well as from anecdotes, the things they actually do for the older people, often in their own time, consist also of picking up prescriptions, coming back at the end of the day to help them into bed, and contacting relatives by telephone call to report on how a client is feeling. The number of scheduled visits per client varies in number, from once a week to more frequent calls, but visits with any one client are put on a regular basis, and continuity is maintained between a particular home-help who goes to a particular client.

This is an evolving role in the constellation of those vocations which have come into being to meet the needs of elderly people. The role is taking somewhat different directions in different countries, depending partly on the nature of the other workers available. Set up almost as a cleaner originally, that still is the most frequent task, as we have noted in the case of Britain, and this is true of the FRG. According to the Pearson report on Scandinavia (1981) sometimes heavy household cleaning is excluded from the work of home helps in those countries. The training required or made available for this vocation varies from Denmark's requirements of a training course of 120 hours, to no regular training for the job even on a voluntary basis which is true in some parts of Britain.

The Home Help led the list describing the various community services and particular benefits provided for elderly people in Norway. Their WAA Country Report presented this account:

4.3.2 Home Help

The aim of the Home Help Scheme is first and foremost to offer assistance to elderly and handicapped who, without such help, cannot continue to live in their homes. The home helper carries out ordinary housework, such as cleaning, preparation of meals, shopping and small laundry jobs. The home help scheme has now been introduced in all municipalities. The Social Welfare Board is responsible for administrating operation of the scheme, and the Board lays down the rules deciding who is eligible for home help. In the municipalities it is usually the leader of the Home Nursing Scheme who is also responsible for the home help scheme. — The Government (The State) refunds 50 per cent of the operational costs, but a roof has recently been set for municipalities where this service is expanded to an unusual degree. The refund system may also cover measures of a less traditional nature, such as a municipal caretaker arrangement.

4.3.3 Other welfare activities

Meals on Wheels.   The organization of this assistance scheme may vary. The food is either prepared in institutions for the elderly or in industrially run kitchens. The meals are distributed either by the municipal services, or by voluntary helpers. Quite often the food is distributed through service centres where there is also cafeteria-service for those who wish — and are able — to have their meals together with others.

Visiting Service.   Several of the voluntary agencies have organized visiting services both for elderly living in their homes and for elderly in institutions. The visitor's job is to try to break isolation through human contact, but he/she should also, indirectly, help the elderly to obtain any necessary services. The agencies organize courses which are intended to train the visitors for this service.

Groups for physical exercise are organized by municipalities as well as by voluntary associations. The Norwegian Association for Sport in Industrial Undertakings is also engaged in this field.

Adult education courses at a reasonable price are organized by the Oslo Extra-Mural Education Board, by The Workers' Educational Association and by political or non-political organizations. Courses and study circles are very often organized by voluntary societies, and cover all subjects and activities, from politics and religious topics to painting, dancing and tourist travel. The most comprehensive scheme for activating retired persons in associations, is run by the National Organization of Pensioners, (Norsk Pensjonistforbund). The organization has 600 local branches all over the country. Adult education courses are subsidized by the State.

Free legal assistance.   In certain cases it may be possible for pensioners to obtain legal assistance free of charge. This may either be a question of free legal advice outside court, or free legal assistance in court. Such assistance is given subject to a means test.

Personal counselling.   At the Social Welfare Offices in the larger municipalities there are social workers whose job is to organize guidance and services for pensioners. At the same time the social workers can give assistance in more personal matters. Several health and welfare centres also have a social counsellor, either as an organizer, or affiliated to the centre in some other way.

Travel tickets at reduced price.   Everybody who has reached the age of 67, may obtain a 50 per cent reduction in fares. The reduction covers travel by railway, bus, boat or plane, when the travel company is subsidized by the State. The reduction also applies for the spouse of the pensioner, irrespective of age, when the two travel together.

Holidays.   Both voluntary agencies and municipal bodies try now and then to assist the elderly to satisfy their need for holiday and leisure. Long-term patients in health institutions can benefit from reduced payment obligations while absent from the institution.

Radio and television. Impecunious pensioners with reduced mobility owing to age or permanent disability, may borrow wireless sets free of charge, through the Radio Gift Fund. The disabled can apply for a free licence.

Telephone grants. The Norwegian Telecommunications Administration operates an arrangement under which old age pensioners (and disabled) may be exempted from paying the usual subscription loan of 2000 NOK. The condition is that the pensioner does not earn more than 10,000 NOK over and above the minimum pension. A greater burden on Governmental budgets is a subsidy arrangement by which the elderly and disabled may be given a grant to cover expenses connected with the first instalment and/or running subscription. The financial means, which are appropriated through the National Insurance Scheme, are distributed to the Social Welfare Offices in the various municipalities, and then passed on to pensioners according to rules laid down by the Ministry of Health and Social Affairs. In 1978, National Insurance paid for subsidies to 31,384 old age pensioners. (pp. 29-32)

The role of *home-help organizer* has recently come into existence in Britain. This is a job within the social services department. The home-help organizer not only makes deployment of workers according to the clients needing them, but acts as a resource for planning in terms of each client's needs for what the home-help will be expected to do in each case, as well as for supervision. The roles of both home-help and organizer in some local authorities are beginning to take on new forms. Goldberg and Connelly referred to one such instance:

As a fully integrated member of the district social work team the organiser gradually undertook certain tasks previously performed by other members of the team. Latto (1982) has summed up these developments thus: 'while the growth of the organiser's role was mainly in the interface with the social work team, extensions in the home help role tended to be in the boundary area shared with the council nursing service. (p. 63)

The service is known to be very popular among elderly clients, their children and others who are aware of their needs. This role needs to be considered along with others like it — the German altenpflege, for instance, and the assistants being trained in the Duisburg project described earlier — and in relation to the professionally trained jobs of nurses and social workers. Vocations which are growing in importance must be taken into account for a cost-effective personnel policy in each country. The particular nature of each type of job, and how it fits into the total picture, should be carefully considered. Also important is the possibility for career ladders for people who make caring for elderly people their life work.

The Care System and Its Parts

People who are in contact with the infirm elderly person in order to give some kind of aid are all carers together. The points about care and carers discussed in the previous chapter regarding family care are very relevant to vocations like home-helps. The attitudes and goals of all elderly carers have effects on their clients irrespective of the relative status of their jobs. The older person will respond to 'care' in its emotional meaning to him or her, and thus the relationship with a home help may develop into a stronger one than the relationship with, for instance, the district nurse. When this is the case, the home-help is sometimes in a good position to encourage the needed exercises, diet, etc. Home-helpers can be very useful supplements for people with special training when their work is co-ordinated with professionally trained physiotherapists, nurses and social workers. Better care will result when professional persons, along with the client, recognize that this is the case. Higher paid personnel should be careful to see that job status differences do not blind them to possibilities for bringing the contributions of lower-status people into the picture, and for collaboration which respects what other persons are doing for the client.

The idea expressed by Daatland (1983) as the care system needed for long-term care of elderly persons is one which helps in the understanding of what is happening and what might happen in the development of the various vocations in caring for the elderly.

The theory put forward by Daatland, a Norwegian sociologist at the Institute of Gerontology in Oslo, has been described by Landsberger (1984) in this way:

Daatland has proposed the term *care system* for the provision of those activities necessary 'to help people manage their functions of daily living which they cannot manage by themselves'. First, let us look carefully at what he has to say about the term 'care'. Though the regular and daily burdens of care are divided between only two parties, paid personnel and the immediate family, 'care is actually a collective action depending upon direct and indirect contributions from a number of actors, including the cared-for himself'. In determining which activities and actors are instrumental to what he terms a 'care event', Daatland contends that it is the output that matters, not particular inputs. This puts to empirical test the question of what are the necessary activities and actors. Finally, he proposes that care consists of the combination of two elements: the physical acts — feeding, to provide nutrition, for example — and the social relationships of those involved in the production of the event.

Daatland adds to 'care' the word 'system' for several reasons: (1) because many different persons, and sometimes objects, inevitably are involved in bringing about the care event; (2) because of the importance of social relationships to the care of the elderly patient and to the care-givers themselves, as well as relationships to the wider society with its pressures and resources; (3) because quite different inputs to the care event come from the distinct activities and actors; and, (4) because of the interrelationships among all of these parts and particles in the care event. (pp. 2-3)

Such a view as Daatland's underlies the development of expanded roles for workers like home-helps and care assistants. The West German project for development of care assistants described in a previous chapter represents one recognition from a nurse-administrator of the possibility for creating a new and needed role. Various projects in Britain, one of them described in the next chapter, have formulated jobs representing expanded home-help roles. The variety of possibilities within the role in one such project is evident in this paragraph from Goldberg and Connelly:

Home helps were encouraged and especially recruited to undertake more varied tasks than usual, to work more unsocial hours and to respond readily to emergencies. They were encouraged and trained to deal with individual problems of clients, ranging from contact with the DHSS (Department of Health and Social Security) to negotiating with hire purchase companies over debts and with other local authority departments about housing and environmental health difficulties. In any emergencies, and particularly after hospital discharge, the home-help team was able to provide very intensive care, usually for short periods. Home-helps at times assisted in the rehabilitation of stroke victims or those who had fractured a limb. A number of specialist home-helps were recruited: a male domiciliary help who provided personal care to a number of male clients and who also acted as a handyman; a mobile emergency home-help whose service was provided free of charge for a period of up to four weeks; and finally a hairdressing service which was available to housebound clients. (p. 63)

The Country Report for the WAA from Sweden explained the vocation which they have by now begun to refer to as 'social home helps':

Social home help service was initially introduced by private initiative just over 60 years ago, but is now a local government concern. It was originally intended for families with children but, especially during the sixties and seventies, has been changed to comprise help primarily to elderly persons (90 per cent). Social home help service has today grown into an organization for both individually directed and collective measures. In 1980 some 307,000 persons aged 65 years or above received home help amounting to 44.4 million working hours.

Social home help service is in a development phase. Its object is not merely to satisfy material needs but also to help the individual to retain his intellectual, emotional and physical capacity. The pensioner can then live an active life and to the greatest possible extent look after himself. Home help service has increasingly become an overall concept for different forms of service and support given to individuals living in their ordinary homes. The object of these various services is to improve the means for living a normal life in the home even for those who have fairly considerable needs of social and medical care. Social home help service consists both of the social home help given by local government employees in the individual's home and of other local government services in the district which can be utilized collectively or individually. Examples are food service, chiropody, hairdressing, gymnastics, baths, residential service, emergency duty, security alarm and telephone service, contact and activity-creating measures, and a certain limited service for families with children. They may include escort and home instructor services. The county councils are responsible for medical care, but to some extent the home help staff perform duties of a medical character. In 1980 home help personnel performed 9.7 million hours of home medical care.

From having been earlier a job for persons employed by the hour or part-time there has been a development towards a profession requiring training and a more permanent form of employment. Altogether today there are about 70,000 home-helps, 10,500 of whom are relatives employed in this capacity. The staff are usually organized in groups responsible for service of the residents in a limited area, generally coinciding with the divisions of the medical services. The work is often planned in consultation with staff from the county council.

For the social home-help service the local authorities receive a state grant amounting to 35 per cent of the gross cost of the service. In 1980 the local authorities' gross costs amounted to Skr 3500 million. (pp. 31-2)

In the United States, the White House Conference delegates gave strong endorsement to their Recommendation 214, 'Older persons must be given the opportunity to choose alternatives to nursing homes'. The recommendation which went on to carry this out, recommendation 214A, and the statements which supplemented it, showed what is wanted in the US by way of community services:

Recommendation Number 214A:

The institutional and medical care biases in the Medicare and Medicaid programs should be modified to allow reimbursement for personal care and social long-term care services in community and home-based settings. In Medicare, the homebound and skilled requirements for home health care should be eliminated and coverage of home maker/chore services should be provided; in Medicaid, the states should utilize the new Community Care waiver.

Supplemental Statements.

1. These support services should at least include home-maker and chore services, respite care, adult day care, medical transportation, mini-day care, home delivered meals, health maintenance services, home care, group rates, foster care, adult congregate living facilities.

2. Private health insurance carriers be encouraged or mandated to provide long term care benefits as follows:

   (A) Those firms engaged in intra-state insurance trade be mandated to provide long term care benefits.
   (B) Those firms engaged in inter-state insurance trade be encouraged to provide long term care benefits.
   (C) Long term care benefits should include coverage for home-based long term care and institutional long term care services.
   (D) Insurance firms providing such insurance should be provided five years to phase in such coverages.

3. To provide adequate care and assistance in the activities of daily living, assuring continuing independence for the functionally disabled, we recommend:

   That there be multiple entry points, outreach and information and referral services, provision of in-home and group services, essential psychosocial and health assessments; and emergency resources to fill gaps.

   Implementation: Provide that all health and social professionals be used to the maximum of their preparation, e.g., nurse practitioners and psychiatric social workers.

4. The WHCoA encourage the medical profession to adopt a policy of home visitation by the physician, physician's assistants and nurse practitioners in order to make medical care available in the homes of the frail elderly. (p. 119)

Co-ordination of Complexities

The needs for care of a disabled elderly person can go unmet in situations where many services are actually available. Daatland's attention to the system of care needed for the individual is made necessary in part because of the complex array of community services and agencies present in most countries today.

Most of those services were put into place for purposes other than the needs of elderly people for long-term care. Hospitals and social services departments everywhere and particular institutions like the social service stations in the FRG were fashioned for a multitude of purposes other than elderly care. Parts of these systems have been latched onto to provide care of one kind or another for elderly people, and as this population has grown, these needs have in some places come to be a major part of the agency's load. The extent to which this has happened is not always recognized nor indeed welcomed, especially by veteran workers with a history of serving young children and families, to mention one example. One virtue of the Older Americans Act and its services is that it represents a whole new agency especially devoted to older people, present at every level of government. On the other hand, since the Older Americans Act does not cover such important matters as income maintenance, medical care, housing nor facilities for long-term care, in some respects the Act has made the system even more large and complex and impossible for needful clients to comprehend, much less manipulate to provide for their particular needs.

Thus arises, paradoxically, the need for still another service, the co-ordinator. And in fact the two workers most frequently nominated for that role themselves came into existence for other purposes — to care for cnildren and their families, for the most part — and have had to adapt themselves to services for elderly people. These two are the social workers and that valuable professional to be found most often in the United Kingdom, the Health Visitor.

The role of the social worker with respect to elderly clients has been quite peripheral on the British scene, and the same has been said about the US. Goldberg and Connelly (1982) concluded, after their survey of those studies which have looked at the question, that social workers may be involved more directly in the future. 'Their roles as mobilisers of resources, co-ordinators of services and resource persons to a variety of other carers or caring schemes may have to expand considerably' (p. 114).

It is possible that the social workers may come to serve elderly clients with the needs more general to the population — how to make the system work when the problem is one of income maintenance or housing accommodation or where to get legal aid. The health visitor, on the other hand, is in a position to help the frail and disabled elderly. The very old and ill may well have general problems, but in addition they have urgent problems of making the health care services operate to provide the help they need. As a nurse with additional training for work in the community, the health visitor has the advantage of inside acquaintance with the health problems, health professionals and the departments and agencies likely to be involved.

A case recently handled by a health visitor in London was observed by the author. It illustrates vividly how much co-ordinating help can be needed for a single patient:

An aged Sicilian couple live in a two-bedroom flat in a 6-storey building of council flats in London — not sheltered nor assisted at all, just flats. The health visitor knew that the patient, Mrs C. had been home from hospital three weeks after having had treatment for her severe arthritic condition. She had received word that the caring person, Mr C., had requested a wheel chair to be able to take his wife outside for a change of scene and some fresh air. The HV called to find out how things were going.

As it turned out, the only thing 'going' was that Mrs C was truly going from bad to worse, and so was Mr C. Not only was there no wheel chair, but there had not been any visit from the doctor during the three weeks since Mrs C had been back home from hospital. She had been refusing to eat, and refusing to get up and try to move about. She was not only bedfast, but she lay almost immobile, apparently avoiding all types of movement because of pain. She was very thin, having lost weight steadily because of refusal to eat.

Mr C suspected that her medicine might need changing to help her condition, but knew he could not take her by taxi to the GP's office as had been done always previous to Mrs C's hospitalization. When the HV urged him to ring to ask the doctor to come, Mr C seemed very reluctant; he said that he knew the doctor was too busy, that he always had too much to do to make a call to their home.

The telephone rang during the course of the HV's visit, and, most fortuitously, it was the new occupational therapist who was ringing to find out more about the request for a wheel chair. Mr C had seemed able to communicate fairly well in face-to-face conversation, but was unable by telephone to make the OT understand the situation. The HV volunteered to talk to the OT and this gave her a chance to explain the urgency, not only for the wheel chair, but for the OT to visit to see what other possibilities might exist for helping the patient begin to move about. The HV obtained a firm promise as to the time and date the OT would come to their flat, and Mr C wrote it down.

Because she was very concerned over the patient's poor condition, the HV asked Mr C for permission to contact the GP on their behalf to talk with him about the need for Mrs C to be seen by a doctor. Mr C assented, with great relief, and the HV said she would talk with the doctor that afternoon.

The patient in question was worsening rapidly, and her husband was under very great stress. At one point he sounded rather desperate, saying, 'I can't get her to eat a thing. I can't get her to move at all!' Because she had come to the home, the HV was in the middle of the spot where there needed to be a 'care system' and could see how much was lacking. She had the information and the status to set in motion immediately the services needed most urgently, whereas the husband (actually an able-bodied and intelligent man) was at a standstill. In his desperation he was contemplating how he could get his wife in a taxi to go to the doctor's office, while knowing full well that he could not get her to leave her bed.

The health visitor is the one person whose job description may call for her to go regularly to the homes of the moderately ill and frail elderly of a district. Though not yet in effect everywhere, there are some areas where annual visits are made to all residents over 75 years of age. To the extent that there are sufficient health visitors to cover that population, a means exists for keeping an eye on such a crisis as was encountered at the home of the C's. The health visitor who visits with some regularity can also notice a deteriorating situation or some out-of-the-ordinary client need. And she has the know-how to help the client make the health care system do what it is there to accomplish. The trend toward having a health visitor attached to general practitioners' offices is a promising one for elderly cases.

Some initiatives devoted specifically to co-ordination are themselves important. The idea of the neighborhood social service stations in the FRG provide an excellent example. These are described briefly in the FRG's Country Report for the WAA.

> The governments of the different states (Lander) set up the first *social service centers* around 1970. Their number has grown to almost 1400 by the end of 1981. These social service centers are new organizational forms, offering various community services, and in some cases, professional counselling. A social service center is supposed to cover the demand in its field in a given region, including the arrangement of services offered by other agencies. (p. 74)
> Note: The word 'region' in an urban setting refers to a large section of a single city.

The presence in European countries of the array of community services has come about through a productive partnership between statutory and voluntary agencies. Those in the public sector have been responsible for the development of some of the very important services for the elderly: district nursing and social work are important examples, along with the health visitor work just described. Public financing has been essential in making possible the development of innovative programs by groups in the private sector. The contributions made by the imagination, energy and determination of voluntary agencies and the commitment of volunteers are described in the next section.

Voluntary Organizations and Volunteers

Voluntary organizations have frequently been the creators of community services for older people. Their role in the development of a variety of services in Norway was described in that country's Country Report for the WAA:

> *1.3 Non-Governmental Organizations (NGO)*
> Private humanitarian or religious groups and associations have had a special role as pioneers and innovators in this field.
> *Home nursing* was initially provided by the parish and by various private organizations. In the 1950s and 1960s, this service was extended, and today it is administered and financed as a general home nursing programme of the municipalities and the State.

Home help started as an experiment initiated by private organizations. The activity soon spread and was given municipal support. Today, home help for the elderly is integrated in the system of State-supported domestic services.

A number of services, often referred to as *health and welfare measures* for elderly persons, were started in the 1950s and the 1960s by the voluntary organizations. These included meals-on-wheels, recreational facilities, social arrangements through clubs, chiropody, medical check-ups and the organization of holidays and recreation in general. These activities have become extended considerably over the last few years, and are still run by the voluntary humanitarian agencies with some financial support from the municipalities. In order to co-ordinate and increase the effectiveness of the various services of this nature, the said organizations have started, especially in the larger cities, to concentrate their services and activities in service centres.

During the last few years the elderly themselves, through pensioner's clubs, have become increasingly involved in the organization of the welfare and wellbeing of their own group. The National Organization of Pensioners (Norsk Pensjonistforbund) coordinates activities in its regional and local branches, and acts also as an interest organization of its members.

Issues relating to the aging are also dealt with by other NGOs outside the social and humanitarian field proper. The most influential of these is the Norwegian Central Federation of Local Authorities (Norskekommuners sentralforbund). (pp. 8-9)

The case of West Germany illustrates the distinction between voluntary organizations and volunteers. The latter are not as frequent in Germany as in other countries, but the opposite is true for the role of voluntary organizations in providing services by professional and other workers. The very large role played in West Germany by its voluntary organizations has been referred to in Chapter 2 where their work in nursing and old age homes and worker-training was described. They are also the developers of all forms of relevant community services: home nursing, home help, meals on wheels and transport. The voluntary organizations in Germany are, in fact, such large entities that they themselves feel that they can no longer fill the need for innovation and development. Troost (1984) of the German Workers' Welfare Organization proposed that these large associations should devote some of their resources to encourage small, community-based groups by supporting initiatives they would like to undertake. (A recent proposal he referred to as an example was made by a small organization of young people to remodel some community buildings not in use, to create small flatlets of the type needed in that community by older people.) The participation of the churches and other welfare groups is and has been probably the most important single characteristic of community services in Germany.

The EGV organization in Denmark (EGV Danecare, 1982) has played and does play a similar role in that country in developing community services along with institutional care for older people. An outstanding feature of that group is that it has created a structure for ensuring substantial participation in decision making by older people themselves. This is very seldom true in other countries including the leading organizations in the US and Great Britain, the Councils on Aging and Age Concern, respectively.

Like the Councils on Aging in the United States, Age Concern in Great Britain plays a leading role in service development both in its local groups and as a national organization. Active volunteers are important in both of these organizations, though there are paid staff members at local and national levels. The US Councils on Aging are supported and held in place by the various titles of the Older Americans' Act. In British terms, the National Council on Aging and the local councils are Quango's (quasi-autonomous non-governmental organizations).

By comparison, and though it has some support from the Department of Health and Social Security, Age Concern is much more autonomous than quasi-autonomous with respect to government. Many community services are provided by local Age Concern groups with much time given by volunteers, and the local groups raise money to help provide the services. These include the more usual services like meals on wheels and chiropody, but they do not stop there. The excerpt from *Age Concern at Work* (Dickson, 1980) includes more specialized activities like hospital aftercare and helping deaf people.

Community support

In line with its policy on accommodation, Age Concern believes that in most instances it is preferable for an old person to remain in his own home during an illness, if this is at all possible. Age Concern would like to see a wider range of support facilities within the community, such as hospital-at-home schemes, domiciliary dental care and special help for caring relatives.

The movement itself is engaged in this type of work in many different ways. Age Concern Avon runs a family support scheme to enable caring relatives to have a holiday, knowing that their elderly charge is being well looked after. Volunteer 'hostesses' have been recruited who are willing to give board and lodging to infirm elderly people for a couple of weeks, and although the scheme is at an early stage of development, Age Concern Avon has already started training volunteers.

Stroke clubs are another important part of community support. Southwark's club caters for 22 elderly people who are transported by a Red Cross ambulance hired by Age Concern Southwark. The club is run by five volunteers who spend much of their time helping the stroke victims overcome the emotional and physical problems brought about by their disability. Age Concern Stafford and District also has a stroke club, and the staff provide support for relatives and mentally frail elderly people.

Other Age Concern groups have developed clubs and day centres to bring better health care to elderly people on a day-to-day basis. A day care centre at Newquay in Cornwall was purpose-built following the designs of a local physician. It has a hydraulically operated bath-seat-shower facility for the elderly disabled, and there is also a therapy room to cater for the needs of elderly stroke cases. The centre was established with the help of a grant from Age Concern England's Operation Enterprise Fund.

Often when elderly people are recovering from illness or have simply become more frail, they require the help of some form of aid or adaptation. Most Age Concern groups are able to assist in this area; for example, Age Concern Northumberland and Age Concern York stock wheelchairs which they lend to elderly people who require them.

Much valuable work is also carried out in the field of health education. Age Concern Oldham recently played a major part in organising an exhibition on the subject in conjunction with its local health authority. Entitled '*Adding Life to Years*', the exhibition featured continuous forum sessions addressed by eminent speakers and it attracted a great deal of local interest.

Age Concern groups are active in alleviating some of the stresses of particular disabilities and ailments that affect elderly people. Age Concern England has published a book called *Management for Continence* which, as its title implies, takes a very positive attitude towards this problem. Locally, Age Concern Greater London has examined the services available for the incontinent in its area and has produced an authoritative report; in Essex the county Age Concern group has published a booklet giving practical advice to wardens on how to help residents who suffer from incontinence.

Deafness is another disability common to a large number of old people. Age Concern Kent has now been running its *Hard of Hearing Project* for over two years, which has proved immensely successful in highlighting the problems faced by deaf people and in helping them. The project has initiated a number of new services in the county including hearing advice bureaux where services offered include simple checks on hearing aids for obvious faults, advice on the variety of aids available and the correct procedures for obtaining medical audiology assistance. Volunteer visitors have been trained and now visit a sizeable number of old people's homes, clubs and day centres.

Hospital aftercare

The period following discharge from hospital can be a traumatic one for people of any age but for the elderly it can be particularly difficult, especially if they live alone or with a frail relative. Away from the highly supportive environment of hospital, they can find themselves alone without help of any kind. The statutory services are often unaware of individual problems and in many cases are unable to provide the services required.

Age Concern has played a prominent role in pioneering hospital aftercare services and the national body has recently published an Action Guide designed to encourage the development of more schemes throughout the country. Already some Age Concern groups have well-established services. Age Concern Leicestershire set up its Hospital Discharge and Extra Care Scheme in 1978. It includes a group of 'spearhead' volunteers who have a commitment to give support for older people returning home from hospital. The scheme received 302 requests for help during its first twenty months of operation.

However its activities cannot be measured simply by quoting requests for help, as each may well require the input of a number of services. These include preparing the home for the elderly person's return from hospital, welcoming them home on discharge day, the preparation of meals, putting them to bed and getting them up in the morning and so on.

Another scheme is operated by Age Concern Metropolitan Gateshead. The pilot service began in 1978 in Birtley where the scheme is now fully operational and it has since expanded to central Gateshead.

Mental health

The strain on the relatives of confused elderly people can be enormous and some local Age Concern groups are now developing services to help them cope, while at the same time trying to improve the quality of life of the mentally infirm themselves. A joint MIND/Age Concern Greater London project has established a day centre for the confused elderly in Greenwich. It is run by two full-time and two part-time staff; and in addition there are three volunteers, though the organisers hope to recruit more in time. The centre caters for ten confused elderly people. Anyone who refers an elderly person is asked to come and see the centre at work, and one of the full-time paid workers then visits the confused old and their relatives to assess whether or not the centre will be of any benefit. Lunch is provided by the meals on wheels service though, on occasion, staff help the elderly confused people to cook their own meals. Regular armchair exercises take place after the morning cup of tea, and there is a rule that everyone who is at the centre joins in whether they are visitors, volunteers or paid workers. The organisers believe this prevents embarrassment and is less patronising for the elderly people.

In Surrey, Age Concern is working in conjunction with the Surrey Council for Mental Health to research ways in which community support for the elderly mentally frail can be strengthened and increased.

Another initiative which may well be copied elsewhere in the country is that of the day-care centre run by Age Concern Bracknell. Housed in a local authority flat, the centre caters exclusively for the mentally confused, providing extensive care and support with one volunteer for each elderly person. Around thirty-five people benefit from the service each week, all of whom are severely confused and have been categorised as being incapable of rehabilitation. It is these people, even more than those less handicapped, who do not at present receive community support. The centre has received voluntary funding from a number of trusts as well as a grant from the Age Concern England Operation Enterprise Fund.

Short-stay homes

For some elderly people who have undergone hospital treatment a period of care and rest can do much to boost their morale and provide them with the strength and confidence they will need before returning home.

Ethel Tipple Court, the short stay home run by Norfolk Old People's Welfare Association (Age Concern) has already briefly been mentioned in connection with its work for those old people who live alone and require a respite from looking after themselves. However the home also contains residents who are convalescing after a period in hospital and it provides them with the opportunity to readjust themselves and gain the courage and fortitude to return to their own homes — often with the knowledge that they can return to Ethel Tipple Court for another short-stay in a few months time. Since it opened in 1978, Ethel Tipple Court has provided short-stay accommodation for over 1300 elderly people and it now also operates a seven-day-a-week day care service for a small number of frail elderly people.

Age Concern Portsmouth also has a short-stay residential home Alberta House, which was both established and is being run by the Age Concern group. Patients are helped to regain mobility and social skills after illness and are able to return home, physically and mentally more capable of looking after themselves.

Initial referrals by general practitioners or social workers are followed up by visits from a member of Age Concern's staff to each elderly person to make the necessary admission arrangements. While staying at Alberta, residents continue under their own doctors; and arrangements can be made for them to attend out-patient departments, hospital clinics and day centres.

Age Concern Avon is planning a day care centre at Pill near Bristol. At first it will open for two days a week though the organisers hope to extend this if sufficient funds are available.

Chiropody

For an elderly person the provision of adequate footcare can mean the difference between being housebound and immobile and being able to lead a normal life; and 96 per cent of those receiving priority treatment are elderly.

In its report on the chiropody service called *Step on it!*, Age Concern England published an estimate that 78 per cent of elderly people were in need of treatment while only one in six was actually receiving it. The chiropody service is clearly under-manned and Age Concern believes there is an urgent need for greater investment to establish more training schools.

As painful feet can render old people immobile, many Age Concern groups employ chiropodists at their day centres, while others run nail-cutting services using volunteers under the supervision of trained staff. In the Boston and South Holland districts of Lincolnshire, Age Concern clubs have responded to the long waiting list for treatment by paying for transport to clinics or by arranging for treatment at their own premises.

Age Concern Tameside faces a similar problem with elderly people having to wait for months before receiving attention. The group provides transport for those unable to reach the clinic on their own with voluntary drivers and a community bus.

Many other groups provide comparable services such as North Tyneside, Peterborough, Essex, Brighton and Maidstone. (pp. 8-10)

The nature of services for the future surely is dependent upon the activities of voluntary organizations. The lesson of the history of such services is that the voluntary groups are the crucial change agent in elderly services and particularly in those providing long-term care. Especially as they themselves become very large bureaucracies, it is important, as Troost has said, that they provide support for smaller groups with more flexibility to continue innovations which make services responsive to pressing needs of older people in their own neighbourhoods and localities.

Volunteers

The fact that volunteer activity is not by any means synonymous with voluntary organizations has been mentioned. In fact, the extent to which organizations' community services are carried out by volunteers is a matter where there apparently are some national differences. Germany's very large voluntary organizational role in services involves little volunteer service delivery, while in Britain volunteers are referred to as 'the key resource within the Age Concern movements' (*Age Concern England Handbook*, 1982, p. 48) and this includes the services provided by that organization.

Age Concern is only one of hundreds of British organizations through which people give their time to provide services for older people. Some of these have developed models for sheltered housing on a very large-scale basis — Abbeyfield is a leader in this. Others, like Task Force/Pensioners Link have sought to work in partnership with the pensioners to support a wide variety of activities by which pensioners 'can live a full, healthy and active life and maintain independence in old age for as long as possible'. (*Task Force Annual Report*, 1982-3). Volunteers for Abbeyfield may carry out a task regularly for the elderly living in an Abbeyfield House; Pensioners Link may help a pensioners' action group organize a demonstration for a local council meeting to provide more help for fuel costs in the winter months. Volunteers in both may be old or young people.

Mary Stott (1981) advised people entering retirement to engage in a regular job whether voluntary or paid. Her reason for encouraging people to volunteer in activities to benefit others may explain why older people do give so much time and effort in service to the elderly. 'Taking on a voluntary job means securing approval from one's fellows and achieving some status within the community. It means the certainty of company which we may greatly need ... and it means involvement, which is perhaps the most important factor of all in combatting ageism and the fear of growing old' (p. 108).

In the US, many older people are involved as volunteers through the Retired Senior Volunteer Program (RSVP), no doubt often for the reasons Stott suggested.

There exists in Britain a Volunteer Centre to help organizations in the recruitment, selection, training and support of volunteers. Some of the training opportunities offered for volunteers along with paid workers have been described in the final section of Chapter 2. Age Concern's booklet on training helpers (1983) was developed by a distinguished working party made up of professionals from many disciplines. All in all, there exists in Britain a great deal of serious attention to help for volunteers as well as from volunteers, in order to achieve a high quality of service for older people.

An experimental study of volunteers in services to infirm very elderly people was carried out by Power and others in Britain over a two year period. They developed a model for recruitment, training and continued support of volunteers in a small urban area in south-west England and have reported the results. The statistically significant positive result shown up in their preliminary analyses was that the group of very elderly people who had volunteer visits showed a slower decline in mobility, and they experienced a decline in feelings of loneliness while the control group showed an increase in loneliness. (Power, 1984).

Goldberg and Connelly (1982) feel that volunteerism may be entering into a new phase with respect to services for the elderly in Britain. Not only are the days of Lady Bountiful long past, but so are the days when the professionals regarded volunteers as second-class citizens. In an era when government is seeking to cut costs, the warning is heard everywhere that public agencies and professionals must not throw their responsibilities over to unpaid persons. This not only would exploit the volunteers but it would short-change those receiving services. There is a need for volunteers over and above the need for professional workers.

Bearing in mind what has recently been said on the subject of care in works described in the previous chapter, it may be that the volunteer combines some of the emotional aspect of caring with the 'tending' aspect of care. Thus, the pattern of service delivery provided by a volunteer may have its own special value to an infirm elderly person. The very good relationships often built between the volunteer and elderly person in Power's study testify to this.

A paragraph from *Organizing Aftercare* (Slack and Gibbons, 1979) describes necessary conditions for volunteer work in hospital aftercare and goes on to recognize the special contribution of volunteers:

> There is great potential for volunteers to work with elderly patients being discharged from hospital. Encouragement and financial assistance for this can come from a wide variety of sources — from voluntary groups already having an interest in the field, and all groups within hospitals, as well as Social Services departments. Adaptability to a particular situation is

imperative, but in general the organisation needs to be under-taken by a specially recruited co-ordinator. There is a role for a group of trained and committed volunteers, but this should not preclude liaison with a wide variety of voluntary organisations who might on occasions be able to help individual patients e.g. neighbourhood groups, national self-help groups. There is a variety of models for co-ordination of volunteers, but a deep level of involvement in the hospital and good communication with the professional staff is imperative. A co-ordinator/organiser must have sufficient authority to support the volunteers, convince the staff of the value and purposes of volunteer help, and work out the most effective way of organising referrals and making assessments. Above all, it must be borne in mind that the contribution of a volunteer, whether specially trained for the job, or a neighbour from down the street, is something quite different from that of any professional, and volunteers should not be seen as filling gaps in statutory service. (p. 31)

It is vital that volunteers will continue to contribute, as do the voluntary organizations, to the services provided in the community for those elderly people who need long-term care.

References

Age Concern England, (1982) *The Age Concern England Handbook.* Age
    Concern, Mitcham, Surrey
Age Concern England, (1983) *Training Helpers in Caring for the Elderly.* Age
    Concern, Mitcham, Surrey
Butler, A., Oldman, C. and Greve, J., (1983) *Sheltered Housing for the Elderly:
    Policy, Practice and the Consumer.* George Allen and Unwin, London
Collot, C., Jain Le Bris, H. and Ridoux, A., for CLEIRPPA, (1982) *Towards an
    Improvement in Self Reliance of the Elderly: Innovations and New Guidelines
    for the Future.* The Commission of the European Communities, Brussels
Country Reports for the World Assembly on Aging (1982)
— *Aging in Norway: Humanitarian and Developmental Issues.* Royal Norwegian
    Ministry of Health and Social Affairs, Oslo
— *Just Another Age: A Swedish Report to the WAA.* The National Commission
    on Aging, Stockholm
— *Report on the Situation of the Elderly in the Federal Republic of Germany.*
    The German Center of Gerontology, Berlin
Daatland, Stein, (1983). 'Care Systems'. *Ageing and Society 3* (1), 1-21
Department of Health and Social Security, (1983) *Elderly People in the
    Community: Their Service Needs.* Her Majesty's Stationery Office, London
Dickson, Niall, (1980) *Age Concern at Work.* Age Concern, Mitcham, Surrey
EGV Dane Care, (1982) The Ensomme Gamles Vaern, Hellerup, Denmark

Flamm, Franz, (1974) *Social Welfare Services and Social Work in the Federal Republic of Germany.* Deutscher Vereins für Öffentliche und Private Fürsorge, Frankfurt

Goldberg, E.M. and Connelly, N., (1982) *The Effectiveness of Social Care for the Elderly.* Heinemann, London

Landsberger, B., (1984) Defining the nursing of elderly people through an appropriate theory of care. University of North Carolina School of Nursing (mimeo), Chapel Hill, North Carolina

Latto, S., (1982) *The Coventry Home Help Project — Short Report.* Coventry Social Services Department (mimeo)

Pearson, R., (1981) *An Independent Old Age: Provisions for Pensioners in Scandinavia.* Pensioners Link/Task Force, London

Power, Michael, (1984) *The Home Care of the Very Old.* University of Bristol, School of Applied Social Studies (mimeo), Bristol

Selby, P. and Schechter, M., (1982) *Aging 2000 — A Challenge for Society.* The Sandoz Institute — MTP Press, Lancaster, England (Referred to herein as the 'Sandoz Institute Study'

Slack, G. and Gibbons, J., (1979) *Organising Aftercare.* Centre for Policy on Ageing, London

Stott, Mary, (1981) *Ageing for Beginners.* Basil Blackwell, Oxford

Task Force/Pensioners Link, 1983, (1983) *Task Force Annual Report 1982-83.* Pensioners Link (17 Balfe Street, N.1), London

Troost, H., (1984) 'Altenarbeit/Altenhilfe'. Unpublished paper from the Arbeiter Wohlfahrt, Bonn

White House Conference Staff, (1982) *Final Report on the 1981 White House Conference on Aging.* WHCoA Staff, Washington, D.C.

CONTINUITY OF CARE FROM HOSPITAL TO
HOME

The question of where infirm older patients are to go, when the hospital has finished its care for their illnesses and injuries, has begun to be taken seriously in its own right in Britain during the past dozen years. The topic of the process of hospital discharge, but not particularly in relation to older people, has received a limited amount of attention in other countries. McGuire in 1976 reviewed the rather scant literature on continuity of care up to that point. She concluded that the US had just begun to develop patient-centered care systems needed to continue recovery beyond discharge from hospital. McGuire saw a special need for social-emotional supports. Attention in more recent literature in the United States has been directed to the process within the hospital itself rather than a consideration of discharge in the context of services in the community with an eye on after care. Hinds (1984) in Canada recently studied continuity of care in cancer patients, looking at what problems were encountered by the care-giver at home at the start of her task, and where she turned for help.

The steady stream of studies in Britain of what happens when elderly patients go home from hospital began with the research which Skeet reported in *Home from Hospital* (1970). In addition to statistical findings some thumbnail sketches were presented to show the nature of instances where not only was there no continuity of care — there was almost no care. A few of these cases are presented here; reading them makes it understandable that the book had the effect of mobilizing attention onto the problem of after care. Here, then, are a few of the Skeet sketches:

141. Mrs D. Aet 70 years. Widow. Congestive cardiac failure. Sent home by ambulance to live alone. District nursing service arranged by hospital (by telephone). Patient was put on her bed by ambulance men and was unable to get off again. A neighbour saw the ambulance arrive, so called in. She found that the only food in the house was some eggs and bread bought before Mrs D's admission to hospital and that Mrs D. 'needed everything done for her'. After ten days the neighbour felt she could

not continue to give all the care which was needed. She had sent for the patient's GP who had her readmitted to hospital. The district nurse did not materialise.

143. Mr G. Aet 98 years. Widower. Mitral stenosis. Cerebral thrombosis. Hemiplegia. Doubly incontinent. Sent home to daughter and son-in-law both over 75 years old. No community services arranged. His daughter gave all care for twenty-four hours every day, did all the housework and washing. Had asked 'welfare' for help and had been told it could only be given if patient was bed-ridden. GP had not visited, and daughter 'did not like to send for him'. She said her only need was for 'some respite and someone to wash father down occasionally'.

144. Mrs. H. Aet 87 years. Widow. Hiatus hernia. Acute myocardial infarction. Home help and meals-on-wheels services asked for by hospital medical social worker. Two weeks later, a home help had been two mornings and Mrs. H. had had six meals in 14 days. She was unable to cook for herself, unable to dress and was trying to give herself a wash once a week. Her daughter-in-law had called once but was recuperating from a hysterectomy. Mrs. H. managed to get to the commode and relied on neighbours to empty the pan. She had asked 'welfare' for help, but none had arrived.

146. Mrs. L. Aet 87 years. Widow. Fractured femur. Blind. Sent home to live alone. Bath attendant, meals-on-wheels and physiotherapy requested by hospital medical social worker. Two weeks after her discharge, no one from any service had called on Mrs L. She was paying her neighbour to do the shopping and the laundry. She needed help with dressing and bathing but was receiving none. There were two unemptied chamber pots in her room at the time of interviewing. She tried to cook for herself but found it 'difficult'. She was afraid that she might take wrong dosage of drugs because all bottles were the same size and felt alike. Two months later, a neighbour had called Mrs L's doctor who had readmitted her to hospital.
(pp. 53-4)

Following the Skeet study not only did discharge of patients begin to receive attention from hospital personnel, but further research was undertaken. The Age Concern group in Liverpool (a voluntary organization) supported the first of a group of studies and programs which came to be known as the Continuing Care Project. The experiences of discharged elderly patients was focused upon in an effort to determine what could be done to avoid breakdowns in care of the sort the Skeet study had reported.

Geraldine Amos has directed the work of that project. She presented the view of the problem which emerged from their work and some of the solutions they had investigated in the project's most recent publication, *Home from Hospital — to What?* (1980). Because this project has a long record of careful research and project design directed toward the experience of patients going home from hospital, and because the material is unlikely to be readily available outside Britain, Mrs Amos' report is reproduced at length below:

> Going home from hospital is quite critical to all patients' level of recovery because at this time they are highly vulnerable. They need prompt and appropriate help to enable them to adjust to their situation, and to enable them to remobilise themselves. Help is also essential to avert unnecessary re-admissions and the collapse of the caring relative.
>
> ### The Effects of a Hospital Stay
>
> Loss of self-confidence, reduced mobility, health anxieties, may all follow a stay in hospital. For an elderly patient, confusion and incontinence may be added to the list.
>
> In her study 'Home from Hospital', Muriel Skeet found that 45% of patients of *all ages* had unmet needs, and the Continuing Care Project's study in 1979 found that 65% of *elderly* patients had unmet needs on their return home from hospital.
>
> ### Why do these effects follow a hospital stay?
>
> 1. Hospital admission is seen by staff as an isolated episode rather than part of a continuing care process.
> 2. Hospitals tend to be cut off from the outside world, and most hospital staff lack community experience, which affects their perception of aftercare needs. (A mobility study undertaken by the Project showed that ward sisters were extremely over-optimistic in their expectation of patients' levels of mobility after they had left hospital.

This may be one explanation why ward sisters fail to refer patients — because they do not anticipate the difficulties.)

3. Discharge planning, therefore, has low priority. Hospital systems are not geared for discharge, planning, and the transmission of relevant information about patients is haphazard and chancy.

4. There are pressures on patients to conform. The hospital expects them to act passively and not to take initiatives.

5. The contrast between hospital and home is difficult for patients to cope with because of the dependency fostered in hospital.

The role of the community

The community too is insufficiently responsive; there are often time lags in providing a service. This is discouraging for busy hospital staff who find it very time-consuming to make arrangements for aftercare services (with the exception of community nurses). In addition, community services very rarely send in information before patients are admitted.

The patients

Elderly patients have a higher percentage of unmet needs after leaving hospital than do other age groups, but it is hoped that the St. George's House Consultation will identify remedies or procedures relevant to all age groups.

The characteristics of elderly patients and their caring persons (frequently also elderly) are:

(i) A low level of expectations

(ii) Loss of status which accompanies retirement in our society

(iii) Reluctance to become involved with 'the welfare' or to accept 'charity'

(iv) Fear of pressures, particularly to give up their homes and move into an old people's home or geriatric ward. They fear loss of independence, means tests and 'snoopers'.

(v) Independence, self-respect or 'pride' are very important. They often feel these are the only things left to them.

The Continuing Care Project's recent survey showed that 14 days after discharge from hospital about half of all the elderly patients could not cope with domestic tasks (43%), (11% had no one to help them) nor with personal care (49%), (17% had no one to help them). 84% of these two categories together either had a caring person who could not cope, or had no caring person at all. Mobility levels are important for these patients, yet 46% had not been outside.

By 28 days after discharge over a third, some 39% of the *principal caring persons*, were found to be frail and at risk, and, at that stage, 9% of these caring persons had themselves been admitted to hospital.

Who does care?

(i)   *Before admission.* Community services take little action and communication with the hospital is rare. General practitioners sometimes argue that if they are too honest about a patient's likely discharge needs, the hospital will not provide a bed.

(ii) *In hospital.* Often no enquiries are made and needy patients are not identified. In one study, 62% of the patients had not been asked how they would manage at home. There are variations in the patients for whom enquiries are made, and for whom discharge planning is undertaken. The system seems to favour those who have been in hospital for a long time; waiting-list patients; patients on non-acute wards; patients who are assured. The system is also influenced by the perceptions of staff. The priorities and community experience of hospital staff affect their attitudes to patients' aftercare.

(iii) *After discharge.* Once the patient is back home, it is clear that community nurses are prompt in making their calls. However, these calls are necessarily brief because of the nurse's workload, and in any case she only sees 30% of elderly discharged patients. It cannot, therefore, be assumed that she will undertake the responsibility of dealing with the needs of all discharged elderly patients (especially non-medical needs).

By 14 days after discharge, 29% of patients had not seen any aftercare services (including GPs). Home-help and meals-on-wheels services are often slow in starting. It should be noted that it is the actual service which helps the patient, not the information that it is 'in hand'.

Social workers are rarely involved, although it is more common for elderly patients to receive help from one of the social services.

General Practitioners' calls are delayed, and often they make no calls. 63% of patients in one of our surveys had not received a call from the General Practitioner by 14 days after discharge, yet patients are often anxious about their state of health. In addition, communication from the hospital to the General Practitioner is often poor. The average time for notification of discharge to reach the General Practitioner in this survey was three weeks. We tested the effects of a more prompt and detailed notification of patients' discharge from hospital to GP, but the results were disappointing and we found it more successful to ask the patients to take the initiative themselves in contacting the GP.

Neighbours' calls fell short of expectations though there are variations. Calls by voluntary agencies were extremely rare, even from members of clubs to which patients themselves belonged. Similarly, parishes were seldom involved.

Relatives are noticeably the most supportive — 85% of these patients had received a call from relatives, yet nevertheless it is a fact that by 14 days after discharge 10% of the patients had received no call.

Why should this concern us and the Health Service?

Because the present system leads to avoidable suffering, and to an avoidable expense to community services, where patients are not provided with care when it is first needed, and where they are just left to deteriorate. The burden on the Health Service would be reduced if readmission of patients, and the admission of their 'caring persons' to hospital, as well as the number of 'blocked beds' were minimised.

The Continuing Care Project argues that we should investigate patients' possible unmet needs, and plan early for their discharge home. Services should be given notice in good time (i.e. soon after admission). This must be associated with an updating of information about the patient, if circumstances change.

The Continuing Care Project has investigated a range of alternative solutions, such as:

1. The employment of an Aftercare Co-ordinator
2. Community staff supplying information to hospitals at the time of admission
3. Hospitals identifying patients' likely needs at an early stage (e.g. before admission)
4. Prompt response by the community, e.g. 'Welcome Home' schemes run by voluntary and statutory agencies.
5. Simple alert schemes
6. The employment of a 'Chaplain's aide' to contact patients' parishes.
7. Self-help schemes
   (pp. 13-14)

General practitioners must be notified by hospital of their patients' return to their homes.

Another statement by Mrs Amos in the same report stressed the need for a system for bringing about the hospital-to-home liason needed by elderly patients:

Nearly half our hospital beds are occupied by patients over 65. Technological advances and medical skill mean that most of these patients are treated and expected to return home to carry on their normal lives. ...

To most people a stay in hospital is a disorientating experience — the feeling of being cut off from their usual life pattern can be welcome or unwelcome but it is essentially 'different'. The atmosphere of professional expertise among hospital staff tends to emphasise the feeling of a world apart. Patients accept a dependent role, accept the warmth and regular meals; they do not make decisions, nor ask 'awkward' questions. The contrast between hospital and home can be a shock, particularly for an elderly patient and even more for one living alone in an inner city tower block with no relatives or friends close at hand; or for someone returning to the care of a frail spouse scarcely able to cope with his or her own needs, let alone those of a newly discharged hospital patient. ...

There is no system of ensuring that help is provided where and when it is needed. ...

Help and support should be promptly provided and tailored to the needs of each individual. If Mrs A. arrives home from hospital at 11 in the morning — who will make sure she gets a meal that same day? Who will do her shopping for her? Will someone contact her GP if she needs a reassuring call? Who will move her bed downstairs if she cannot manage the stairs?

It is not wilful neglect nor lack of compassion which leads to patients finding themselves stranded at home without help. Neither can we point to one particular villain and saddle him with the blame.

The emphasis of the hospital system has always been on the efficient treatment of acute illness, resulting in speedy discharge. Hospitals are regarded as the kingpin of the health service and yet their staff do not see themselves as part of a continuous process of care requiring detailed information concerning a patient's domestic situation as well as his medical history. Nevertheless with advancing years a patient's socio/medical problems tend to become more complex and less amenable to fast turn-round methods of treatment. He or she may face a tangle of physical, emotional and social needs, all of which have to be taken into account, but which the hospital, faced with pressure on its beds, may be reluctant to go into.

Understanding

Similarly there is a lack of awareness among staff in general hospitals of the difficulties which are likely to face old people when they return home. This is particularly true for elderly patients discharged from acute wards where a high turnover of patients is combined with an absence of feedback information from the community. ...

All the groups involved in health care are organised differently and this tends to create barriers between them which obstruct the flow of information essential to co-operation and co-ordination. There are few routine channels of communication between professionals in hospital and those in the community. ...

It is therefore essential that there should be a properly organised system to ensure that discharged elderly patients are not left stranded on their return home. Their numbers may not be large but their need cannot be ignored. (pp. 6-13)

The fact that a Health Forum in London was organized to bring together people working with the elderly in health services, social services and voluntary organizations made the topic of hospital discharge planning a topic well-suited for that group to handle. The Forum, organized by Age Concern Greater London, met in 1983 and 1984. Between the two meetings, a working group of the Forum did in fact develop guidelines for hospital discharge of elderly people, noting both public services and voluntary organizations can be of help. The following statement from the guidelines presented at the 1984 Health Forum indicates that, like the Continuing Care Project, they concluded that the several complex entities involved at discharge called for a system with responsibility for liason pinpointed on a particular officer or team:

> *Discharge procedures*: When a patient is discharged from hospital the consultant who has been responsible for the hospital treatment should send information about the patient's condition and any out-patient visits arranged to the GP. A local authority social worker, based in the hospital, is usually the person responsible for arranging for any social service support — e.g. home help — which the patient needs after discharge. Nursing support is arranged through the Nursing Service. Where occupational therapists arrange pre-discharge visits, other disciplines might be involved. However delays in information reaching GPs and community support services are common. One reason for this is that the way discharge is organised is often haphazard, relying on personal relationships rather than systems. Hospitals need to develop standardised discharge procedures, and preferably liaison systems in which there are specific people or teams who are responsible for co-ordinating arrangements for discharge of elderly patients and ensuring that relevant community services are alerted immediately. (p. 1)

The spread of concern over the continuity of care for elderly patients after a hospital stay went far beyond London and other large urban areas where hospital discharge procedures have been highlited by research and conferences. The National Association of Community Health Councils analyzed the 1983 annual reports of Community Health Councils (CHCs) throughout England and Wales with respect to work with older people. In her report of the results, Nicoll (1984) noted that '30 per cent of CHCs were concerned about post-hospital discharge care, a surprisingly high number (40 per cent) aware of the problems of carers and their need for 'holiday' admissions for patients, and a staggering 70.7 per cent emphasized the need for increased community services of all types and descriptions.'

The building of a bridge between the patient's care from professionals in hospital and the care-giving at home has begun to receive attention in Britain from Health Authorities, Social Service departments and voluntary organizations. This has been in the form of some initiatives begun at the hospital, others begun by social service departments, others from community nursing services and still others by voluntary organizations.

Liaison from the Hospital

A scheme set up in an inner-city hospital in Hackney was instituted by the District Nursing Officer of that health authority. It consisted of placing on the hospital staff two nurses who had worked in community services in the area where the hospital is located. One is a former health visitor (who had previously worked as a ward sister in a London hospital); she is in charge and works alongside the former community nurse. Their badges indicate that their work is Community Liaison.

Most of the elderly patients they deal with are located in the acute care sections of the hospital. Their activities are carefully co-ordinated with the geriatric wards, partly because some patients may be moved into that setting from acute care; but the majority of the candidates for discharge go home from the medical, surgical and orthopaedic sections. They are in touch with the very elderly patients throughout their stay, with an eye on discharge, and this individual contact is the center of their work. However, their energies are directed toward creating many ways of developing the staff's own awareness and knowledge regarding after care services. They have identified the need for communication on a two way street between the doctors, ward sisters, social workers, occupational therapists and physiotherapists and the liaison officers; the latters' attendance at case conferences to speak as well as to listen is an important part of their work. The liaison workers also call conferences at the hospital which include the relevant hospital staff, nurses and others from community services relative to the patient's needs, the family members and often the patient him or herself. An activity likely to be discussed at such a conference is a trial home visit by the patient, usually planned to occur during the week before the discharge is scheduled to take place.

The Liaison staff also have organized regular hospital/community seminars of nurses and the other health professionals from hospital and community to clarify roles and make known the kinds of facilities and personnel which can be called upon. Sessions are also held periodically to instruct nurses coming on to the hospital staff regarding the process of hospital-community liaison being developed in that setting. Forms have been developed for written notification giving details of arrangements about medication, services requested, etc., for other personnel to send to Liaison as well as from Liaison to others, and information circulated to facilitate communication. (See Figures 5.1 and 5.2).

Putting hospital and community workers in direct touch with each other has led to several improvements in the quality of after care and in-patient care as well. Ward sisters are learning exactly what information about a patient to give the district nurse when a discharge is about to occur so that the latter can make the arrange-

Figure 5.1: Form to Advise Community Workers of Patient Admission

                                                    Hackney Hospital,
                                                    Homerton High Street,
To: District Nurses/Health Visitors/   London, E.9.
                    Clinic Nurses,   Tel: 985 5555, Ext.
       (Delete that which is inapplicable)

Health Centre:—
       This is to inform you that the following person has been
admitted to Ward ...

       Name:

       Address:

       Date of Admission:—

       We understand this person is known to you and we would be glad to hear of any relevant information which you feel would be helpful for us to know. We look forward to either seeing you or hearing from you. We will contact you prior to the discharge date.

ments actually needed. Generalities like 'Look in on Mrs G now and then, would you?' are being replaced by sending the district nurse information that 'Mrs G is often unsteady when getting out of bed.'

The Liaison worker has also set up communication devices whereby community workers can feed information to the hospital, items which may have direct bearing on discharge planning. On admission of a patient who has been on the list of a district nurse, that nurse is notified of the admission. Frequently the liaison worker or ward sister has then been contacted by the district nurse with information about the situation at home or something special about the patient's diet or care.

The Liaison service has built relationships from the hospital staff not only with the statutory services in the community, but with several voluntary organizations in the community. Especially in a time of budgets, the availability of help from volunteers is essential.

Excerpts from a report describing the first year of the operation of the Hackney project (1983) are presented below in order to demonstrate the many kinds of contacts involved in such co-ordination:

Community Liaison Nursing Service (by Jean Fisher, Nursing Officer)

The Community Liaison Nursing Service based at Hackney Hospital has now been operating for one year. In mid-September the staff involved in the service increased to two which has not lessened the work for the one, but increased the work and scope for both.

A period of introduction and explanation re the proposed service both in the Hospital and the Community took place at the beginning of the year. As the main concern were those elderly being admitted and discharged to and from the hospital, the first involvement was in the Geriatric Unit. Some Consultant rounds and as many of the ward conferences following these were attended, where the planning of discharge arrangements and needs of those being discharged are discussed with nursing, medical staff, social workers, occupational therapists, physiotherapists. Not long after, involvement with other wards occurred where many elderly are placed. Ward conferences are being regularly attended now on nine wards in addition to the

Figure 5.2: Form for Advising Hospital Staff of Community Staff Availability and Information About How They may be Contacted

AVAILABILITY OF DISTRICT NURSES FOR REFERRALS

Nursing Officers / Centres Without GP Sessions	Centres with GP Sessions	Abbreviation in Street List	Morning Session	Afternoon time in Office	Evening Session	Weekend & Bank Holiday
Mr M. M[a] Barton House Telephone:[a]						
	Somerford Grove Telephone:	SG	Mon. Tues. Wed. Fri. 9.30-12.00	Mon.-Fri. 2.00-3.00	Mon: 4.30-6.30 Fri: 4.30-6.30	For All Centres
	Barton House Telephone:	B	Mon.-Fri. 9.30-12.00	Mon.-Fri. 2.00-3.00	Mon: 5.00-7.30	The Duty Officer
	John Scott Telephone:	JS	Mon.-Fri. 9.30-12.30	Mon.-Fri. 2.30-3.30	Mon: 5.00-7.30 Tues: 5.00-7.30	Telephone:
Mrs M. A Lower Clapton Telephone:	Fountayne Road Telephone:	F	Mon.-Fri. 9.30-12.30	Mon.-Fri. 2.30-3.30	Mon: 5.00-7.00 Fri: 5.00-7.00	
	Lower Clapton Telephone:	L	Mon.-Fri. 9.30-12.30	Mon.-Fri. 2.30-3.30		
	Sorsby Telephone:	S	Mon.-Thurs. 10.30-1.00	Mon.-Thurs. 1.30-2.30		Messages for Sorsby may be relayed to Lower Clapton if there are any difficulties in contacting Centre.

Figure 5.2: continued

Mrs N. G Elsdale Street Telephone:	Richmond Road Telephone:	R	Mon.-Fri.	
	Elsdale Street Telephone:	E	Mon.-Fri. 2.30-3.30	
	Wick Telephone:	Wick	Tues.-Fri. 10.30-11.30 Mon.-Fri. 2.30-3.30	Messages for the Wick may be relayed to Elsdale Street if there are any difficulties in contacting Centre.
Mrs Mc Shoreditch Telephone:	City & Goodwill Telephone	city G	Mon.-Fri.	
	Shoreditch Telephone:	K	Mon.-Fri. 2.30-3.30	

A Designated Sister is On Call each weekend and Bank Holiday and the Duty Officer at St Bartholomew's Hospital has the Rota for this.
Mrs B. H, Senior Nursing Officer (District Nursing) Tel:
Note: aNames and Telephone Numbers are Included on the Actual Form.

Geriatric Unit. This includes six medical wards and three ortho-paedic wards. Some Consultants rounds are attended also when possible. There is regular involvement with the Day Hospital and the reviews are attended whenever possible. ...

Calls are received from the community staff in increasing numbers. Where appropriate we encourage direct communi-cation with those involved with clients, but most calls are per-tinent. Especially useful have been calls concerning patients being referred to the Accident and Emergency department which have given valuable background information which has prevented an inappropriate discharge or confirmed the need for admission. Again direct calls to the department are encouraged.

Personal contact with colleagues in the community is valu-able and attempts are made to visit the centre and discuss some aspects in person. We have access to a desk at Lower Clapton Health Centre.

From the wards, there is direct referral to the District Nurs-ing Service. Advice is given with regard to these and areas being worked as concern the following:-

(a) The actual information given - more detail and back-ground needed.
(b) Getting the information out earlier.
(c) The role and skills of the District Nursing Service.
(d) The composition and role of different members within the team i.e., nursing auxiliaries rather than 'bathing attendants'.
(e) The assessment done by a District Nurse on her first visit and therefore the need for her to know all the details and then make her own decision regarding the home management. There is a tendency to dictate when 'she should visit' and the frequency without the direct know-ledge of the home set up. This should also lead to wiser information being given to patients regarding when the District Nurse will visit etc..

If a District Nurse is asked to supervise medication, she needs the signature of the prescribing Doctor. Letters have been sent to those responsible for proposing a new discharge letter/form intended for the GPs. It has been requested that a copy could also go to the District Nurse. It would also give a brief medical summary which would be helpful in addition to the nursing form.

Introduced on to the wards has been an 'admission notification' form which is designed to be completed during the admission procedure. It is simply to inform the appropriate Community Nursing Services as soon as possible if one of their clients are admitted. It will take time for this to be fully utilised but a start has been made.

Likewise, from the wards we have introduced a Health Visiting Service form designed to notify the service of those over 75 years being sent home. These forms are being sent through to us in order that we may monitor them. These are then sent through to the HNS Health Visiting for future visiting. If this can be accomplished — health surveillance of a vulnerable group will be either initiated or continued.

Work is being done with the staff on the way these forms are completed. The additional work that this puts on the community staff is appreciated but I am sure it is a needful part of the service being offered to clients.

We aim to be preventive in our work and therefore are especially concerned to be where discussions are initiated re the discharge of patients. This therefore restricts our desire to do some link follow-up-visit. However, in some instances, these have been done and likewise some 'bereavement' visits where families have not been known to community staff. The pre-discharge visits home with patients are valuable and where a nursing view is thought to be pertinent and the District Nurse is not available, we like to join the occupational therapist or social worker on some of these. These visits are one of the surest ways of ensuring a safe discharge. Visits have also been made where there have been specific complications or where an impartial visitor seems appropriate.

We aim to bring to the wards a knowledge of facilities in the community and to draw on these as required — these include voluntary agencies (FA), Crossroads, Task Force, specific associations etc. We have been in contact with a number of these on behalf of patients/clients.

We liaise closely with different departments including social services, occupational therapy, physiotherapists in addition, nursing and medical staff and we liaise with their counterparts in the community. In many ways we are a link for the patient between the two aspects of the same nursing service, and the back up services and other professional staff.

It is our purpose to facilitate direct contact wherever possible and not to take on the role of a third party, which however must sometimes be the case.

At the commencement of the service I attended Unit meetings at the Hospital to explain the service and likewise in the community. I continue to attend HNS meetings; both Hospital and community. Discussion and talks have been given to some groups for the elderly including HEADS and a group at Chelmer Road. ...

So far two seminars (afternoon) have been held for trained nursing staff with the aim of clarifying roles of the Community Nursing Staff. The last one was followed by a small group including two ward sisters and two District Nurses which was particularly helpful and perhaps gives a lead for the future. ...

The overall purpose of the service is to achieve good comprehension, continuity of care and surveillance of the patient/ client. The work has escalated enormously and our problem is knowing where 'to draw the line'! We have received distress calls from all quarters but we are keen to prevent these rather than to be spending this time in coping with crises, but the latter have also to be dealt with. We aim to channel these through the correct avenues but on occasion need to respond ourselves.

Concern for the future includes the building up of a good 'follow up' service for the elderly on their discharge home where the care of the District Nursing Service is not required. Referrals are being sent to the Health Visiting Service although we recognise that this is increasing the workload in a particular area. If this can be continued the ultimate aim would be for wards to make direct contact but this will take time.

We feel that to orientate hospital personnel into thinking in terms of a prevention service and promotion of health attitude will take time. It will have to be seen to be believed but there is a tremendous opportunity and need for this.

The Community Liaison service will need to continue as it has started and expand as opportunity and time allows. We recognise afresh that the best means of educating and enlightening staff about new concepts and policies etc., is either on a one to one basis or in small groups. (Fisher, 1984)

Of many instances of communication and relationships is the bridge created so that the patient's progress toward recovery is enhanced, not threatened, by his transfer from home to hospital as well as hospital to home. The thorough integration of this new service of liaison into both hospital and community service systems after only a year and a half of operation indicates that it has indeed become a bridge getting a great deal of traffic.

In another borough of London a nurse researcher is working together with the nurse liaison officer on a hospital-based liaison scheme. Hunt (1982) described that project in a paper which makes it clear that there are differences as well as similarities in the two hospital-based situations. The goals of the second are similar to Hackney's. 'To open up lines of communication on a two-way basis between hospital and community in order to improve the transfer of elderly patients into the community' (p. 283). The difference comes in the methods proposed: 'The objectives were to educate hospital and community staff about the need for communication and what was required in planning the transfer of care' (p. 283). The emphasis was placed upon the hospital personnel and bringing about institutional change there. To do this, they set about introducing an assessment tool so that patients' needs for care on discharge could be assessed, recorded and this record serve as the basis for planning the transfer from hospital to community. A copy of the form is shown in Figure 5.3.

The nursing staff 'found the scoring form of assessment simple to use and not time consuming, but they were uncomfortable and ambivalent about is use' (p. 289). The decision was made to withhold its use 'until the nurses had a chance to learn more about the use of the scoring system' (p. 289). Since then, discussion groups of some community and hospital personnel have been set up, in an effort to promote learning about methods of recording and their interpretation, and uses of recorded information.

The tenor of resistance from staff reported in Hunt's article about that project suggests that this arose in part because the liaison work was directed at changing hospital staff's way of functioning in their own bailiwick. This places that approach in contrast with the Hackney operation which attempts to set up all possible interactions (in person and written) between hospital and community staffs as well as between the liaison workers and the full staff (not only the nurses) in each of those two settings. The reports of these two hospital-based projects suggest that it has been

Figure 5.3: Form Developed by Hunt for Assessment of Patient Level of Dependency

ASSESSMENT OF LEVELS OF DEPENDENCY
TRANSFER OF CARE BETWEEN HOSPITAL AND COMMUNITY

PATIENT'S NAME ....   DATE OF BIRTH ....   WARD ..

HOME ADDRESS ....   HOSPITAL ....

PROGRESSIVE SCORING ASSESSMENTS OF CAPACITY TO COPE WITH DAILY LIVING ACTIVITIES

Low Dependency
0-15
Medium
16-30
High
31-45

Total score of 30 indicates cause for concern as does any single score of *2 or above.*

Assessments should be carried out at regular agreed intervals.

A COMMUNICATION	B SOCIABILITY	C HEARING	D SIGHT
Always clear, retains information, indicates needs 0	Alert/Sociable 0	Has good hearing without aid 0	Has good sight, does not wear glasses 0
Mostly indicates needs, retains information 1	Forgetful/Vague 1	Has some loss of hearing 1	Sees well wearing glasses 1
Cannot indicate needs or retain information, retains some expressive ability 2	Apathetic/Withdrawn 2	Hears only with an aid 2	Sees poorly with glasses 2
No effective contact 3	Very Confused 3	Is completely deaf 3	Is completely blind 3

Figure 5.3: continued

E MOBILITY

Walks unaided	0
Walks with help	1
Chairbound	2
Bedfast	3

I BATHING

No help needed	0
Needs aid (rail, stool etc)	1
Needs some help from one person	2
Needs blanket bath	3

M HOME FACILITIES

Special Housing/Warden	0
Bungalow/Grd Floor Flat	1
Flat with lift	2
Bed/Bathroom upstairs	3

F STAIRS

Climbs unaided	0
Manages with aid (e.g. stick)	1
Needs help of one person	2
Cannot manage at all	3

J DRESSING

Manages unaided	0
Needs aid (e.g. long shoe horn)	1
Needs some help from one person	2
Must be fully dressed	3

N LIVES WITH

Spouse/Companion	0
Daughter/Son	1
Others	2
Alone	3

G CONTINENCE (URINE)

Full control	0
Occasional incontinence	1
Regular incontinence	2
Catheter	3

K FEEDING

Eats unaided	0
Needs aid (e.g. special cutlery)	1
Needs some help from one person	2
Has to be fed fully	3

O FAMILY/CARERS' CAPACITIES TO COPE

Can manage without help	0
Needs some help	1
Need much help	2
Unable to cope/no family/Carers	3

H CONTINENCE (FAECES)

Full control	0
Occasional incontinence	1
Regular incontinence	2
Colostomy	3

L PREPARATION OF FOOD

Can make full meal	0
Can make a snack	1
Can get hot drink	2
Unable to get any food/drink	3

Figure 5.3: continued

ASSESSMENT PRIOR TO ADMISSION/REFERRAL

Ability to cope before admission/referral — Scores may have to be estimated from patients or carers' accounts

Date	A	B	C	D	E	F	G	H	I	J	K	L	M	N	O	Total	Nurse's initials

PROGRESSIVE ASSESSMENT SCORING AFTER ADMISSION/REFERRAL — BY DIRECT OBSERVATION OF PATIENT

Above score to be used as baseline comparison with scored assessments after admission/referral —
When possible by direct observation of patient doing activities.
For each single assessment put *one number* in appropriate column below.

DATE	A	B	C	D	E	F	G	H	I	J	K	L	M	N	O	Total	Nurse's initials

MAURA HUNT, SOUTH EAST THAMES REGIONAL HEALTH AUTHORITY

the Hackney approach which has succeeded in building bridges within a short period of time. Both projects are relatively new; with more time they may reach similar results.

It is notable, however, that conclusions regarding the difficulty of directing efforts toward liaison at 'educating the hospital nursing staff' were reached in a project described by Watson (1982). Watson feels that the answer lies not in starting with paper work and not with placing responsibility on hospital-based staff, but on having community nurses, who work in the outside world and know the community, as the persons responsible for liaison, working from a base in the hospital. She states that plans for after care must begin with talking with patients and their family members about what their problems of care at home will be.

Hospitals in other parts of the country have set up several means to bring about better care, some of them very simple ones. Dr John Knox (1982) has reported that the use of the Going Home form (Figure 5.4), a tool developed in the Continuing Care project, had proved to be of great value when a copy was given to patients to take home for use by themselves and their care-givers. It reminded them of drugs and dosages as well as arrangements made for services at home. While designed and used to go from hospital staff to general practitioners and community nurses, the patients' receipt of a copy of the form was particularly beneficial, according to Knox.

Hospitals in three cities in the north of England, with the help of the local Age Concern groups, now have the Aftercare Co-ordinator recommended by the Continuing Care project. They find that one Co-ordinator can deal with 100 discharges per month, working through arrangements for aftercare.

The publication entitled *Organizing Aftercare* (Slack and Gibbins, 1979) included as one of its examples of good practice an arrangement for 'home trials', a form of preparation for discharge planning which was mentioned in the Hackney activities:

This Health district has a policy of 'home trials' for geriatric patients, and also for any patient from acute medical or surgical beds who has been hospitalised for more than six months, provided the geriatrician accepts responsibility for their care. A home assessment is carried out before a date is set for a home trial. The community social worker, health visitor and district nursing service are notified and invited to help. Relatives and

Figure 5.4: The *Going Home* Form Developed by the Continuing Care Project (Referred to by Knox, 1982)

GOING HOME

This form is to be given **unsealed** to in-patients or their relatives on the day of discharge to remind them of arrangements which have been made for their transfer out of hospital to continued care at home. The General Practitioner and Community Nursing Services will receive similar information.

PATIENTS COPY

Name ....

Address ....

....

Unit No............................ Age.....................

(Fix Patient's Information Label here)

Address to which discharged if different:

....

....

....

Consultant..................................... G.P...

Hospital ....

Ward... Date of Discharge..............................

Treatment in Hospital ....

....

Dressings supplied ....

Drugs - Name   **Dosage**

....

....

....

Diet ....

The following services have been arranged. (tick)

With Hospital and Community Nursing Services	Via Hospital Based Social Worker or the nearest Social Services Area Office
District Nursing Sister	Home Help
Health Visitor	Meals on Wheels
Nursing Aids	Sitter Up (night)
Incontinence Aid	Sitter In (day)
Chiropody	Day Centre
Physiotherapy	Personal Aids
Limbfitting Centre	Adaptation to Home
Day Hospital	Social Work Support

Instructions re appliances and exercises ....

....

Out-Patient Appointment ....

Special Instructions...

....

....

....

Signed... Sister/Charge/Staff Nurse neighbours are asked to give *only* the help they will be able to offer on discharge.

During the day at home the patients do the following, under supervision from a member of the team — dressing; undressing; transferring from bed to chair to commode; preparing a simple meal; washing up; drawing curtains; putting on lights; TV; inserting plugs into sockets; putting out milk bottles. The patient is left alone for a while. A full report is made to the hospital team. Any necessary further rehabilitation is now undertaken on the ward. Services for discharge are arranged. Three day trials are also used, to include overnight self or relative care. The GP is notified, home help laid on if appropriate, and the hospital bed kept vacant. Members of the team monitor the patient at home. At all stages, re-admission and further rehabilitation are available, and the hospital team is kept fully informed both during the trial and after discharge, as to the patients progress. (p. 10)

Liaison from District Nurses

One program for discharge planning originating from the community nursing service was described by Thursfield (1980).

Liaison Between Hospital and Community (Mrs P. Thursfield)

Nursing aftercare for patients in the Kidderminster Health District is arranged by the District Nursing Liaison system.

The Care of the Elderly team has special responsibility for elderly patients at home.

If discharge planning is to be effective, patients' needs and the aftercare required must be identified on admission. The ward sister, the hospital social worker, the liaison sister, the leader of the Care of the Elderly team, and the consultant are all involved in this process. However, it is vital that the ward sister first identifies patients' likely difficulties as soon as the patient is admitted to her ward. She has the major responsibility for determining what aftercare should be arranged. Liaison nurses and social workers participate in consultant ward rounds. The ward clerks inform ward sisters and liaison sisters of all admissions of patients over the age of 65.

Social workers visit the wards regularly (including Friday

afternoons to avoid weekend problems). They read through the nursing Kardex, which is an important source of information, with the ward sister.

The liaison nurse may arrange a district nursing sister's call; the provision of special equipment (such as cradles or walking aids); or a linen service which helps patients whose families cannot cope with laundering bed linen and nightwear.

The District Nursing Liaison system cares for patients from acute wards including surgical, medical and minor 'day'.

The Care of the Elderly team consists of a leader who is a district nurse and clinical assistants (SRNs). This team visits elderly patients as a matter of routine.

The team leader visits medical wards daily; she discusses ongoing problems with the ward sister and/or the social worker, and sends in reports on home assessments to the hospital. She also receives referrals from the liaison sister.

Patients are visited at home within 24 hours of their discharge from hospital. Problems may then be discussed with the General Practitioner, neighbours or the social worker, as relevant, and a report is made to the General Practitioner.

The Care of the Elderly team provides immediate support which might not otherwise be provided, because the notice of discharge often reaches the General Practitioner too late.

There is no overlap between different professions because of the close working relations between liaison sisters, social workers and ward sisters.

Psychiatric patients are usually discharged on a weekday, the GP already having been notified of the coming discharge. The patient is then visited on the following day.

There are problems too in Kidderminster, for example there are shortages in certain services, particularly home helps and meals-on-wheels. A regular review of clients might assist here.

There are other valuable services in the area, including:

— Warden-controlled accommodation
— A half-way house where patients are assessed, in self-contained ground-floor flats, for the most appropriate accommodation
— Cross-boundary visiting of nursing staff, which was negotiated in 1975.

The advantages of the discharge planning schemes, i.e. liaison sisters and care of the elderly teams, are that district nursing staff feel totally involved, and are using their knowledge and training in acute work, whilst hospital staff are becoming much more aware of the needs of the patient as a whole, before and after hospital treatment.

Extra funding has not been provided for this system. Any necessary changes have been brought about by examining existing services, and redeploying money when it becomes available. (pp. 33-6)

Like the hospital based Liaison officers in Hackney, the Kidderminster project also brought about new experiences of direct contact between the health professionals in hospital and community and forged relationships needed for continuity in the care of their patients.

A Health Authority in a predominantly rural district in northwest England contains a well-functioning scheme for liaison between hospital and home (Watson, 1982). Planned originally to be carried out by hospital staff, it is in fact carried out by community nurses based in the hospital. Watson, the project's originator, described its evolution from the beginning blueprint to the present system. Community nurses were selected as the staff for liaison rather than hospital-based staff because knowledge of the community services and access to them is essential for aftercare. The work of hospital staff does not include opportunity to gain this knowledge. The pace of work in acute care settings allows little time for taking responsiblity for planning what will take place after patients depart. The liaison nurses, being based at the hospital, are readily in touch with the staff caring for elderly patients as well as the patients themselves, and written, as well as oral information exchanges take place with staff of community agencies as well as those in hospital. The liaison workers regard their task as 'complementing the work of our hospital and community colleagues'.

Watson explained that planning aftercare is done with the patient first, and secondly with the patient's family. The liaison nurse at the outset of contact with an elderly patient's admission, on the basis of information from records and conversations, finds out what community services the patient has already used and what services might be available. From this, she makes a sketch of what aftercare arrangements might look like. Then, says Watson, comes the most important step: she goes to the patient to talk over this question 'What do you think your problems are going to be when you get home?'. They are convinced that no starting point is possible for planning aftercare other than whatever problem may loom large in the patient's mind. The next step is to go in the same spirit to the relevant member of the family: 'How much of a caring role do you feel you can undertake? How can we help you?' The plans beginning with patient and carer are the ones which materialize, is the lesson they have learned in their liaison work.

Daatland's concept of a care system, with the patient and his family carer at the center — described in the chapter on Community Services — seems to be embodied in the approach this liaison project has adopted.

They have indeed developed a number of aids to inform patients, families and some for the community at large. The text of a form describing the service is reproduced below. It is given to patients and their relatives.

Hospital Community Liaison Service

Information for Patients and Relatives

Your GP will be informed by letter of your discharge home.

You can make an appointment with the *Consultant* to discuss your or your relative's case if you have any worries or queries.

On discharge, your *District Nurse* will visit you at home to assess the situation and visits will be arranged as necessary.

A Laundry Service is available if incontinence is a problem. Ask the District Nurse.

Occupational Therapist advice can be given to assist in the problems of daily living activities; e.g. Bathing; Dressing; Personal hygiene; Cooking; and many others.

Aids can be supplied to help with all these activities. The patient will be assessed before going home. We would be grateful if these aids could be returned to the Hospital when finished with.

Physiotherapist. Rehabilitation for the patient and advice on how to cope with a disabled person. Relatives will be involved with care before the patient's discharge.

A Social Worker can be contacted if help is needed from the Social Services Department; e.g. Financial help; Home help; Day care.

The McMillan Nurse is available in the Community (Allerdale only at present) for help and counselling of the terminally ill and his/her carers.

There are also many *Voluntary Agencies* which can give valuable help.

If you have a problem, please contact your GP or District Nurse.

(Signed)

Watson, like Knox, reports that patients find special value and reassurance in the simple matter or taking home with them a card giving their medication schedule. Figure 5.5 is a copy of the card currently in use:

Liaison from Social Services

Still another approach to aftercare is the program set up in a community on the edge of London, in Greenwich, consisting of a combination of social workers, occupational therapists and specially-trained home-helps. It is based in the local department of social services, and its goal is to give intensive help to patients judged to be ready, with such help, to regain their ability to func-

Figure 5.5: Medication Schedule Card

NAME	ADDRESS		D.O.B.	
DRUG	MORNING	AFTERNOON	EVENING	BEDTIME

tion independently at home. The objectives and scope of the service are described in the following statement:

London Borough of Greenwich Directorate of Social Services

Short-term Domiciliary Care Scheme

1. Purpose of the Scheme
The scheme is intended to provide intensive short-term help, normally of up to 4 weeks duration, in the following circumstances:
(a) To mainly, though not necessarily exclusively, elderly people discharged from hospital or sent home from the Accident and Emergency Department without being admitted, who need a considerable amount of help in order to reach their former, or maximum level of functioning.
(b) To mainly, though not necessarily exclusively, elderly people whose caring relative has to enter hospital for a short period and the client is in need of substantial care but does not wish to go into an Elderly Persons' Home for the duration of the relative's hospital stay; also, if staffing allows, to enable the client if he/she so wishes, to stay in his/her own home instead of entering an Elderly Persons' Home when caring relatives go away for a break.

2. Aims and Objectives
(a) To achieve maximum client independence.
(b) To reduce the numbers of emergency re-admissions.
(c) Possibly allow the discharge of clients previously considered impossible.
(d) To respond rapidly (on day of discharge) to all eligible clients.
(e) To assist in the rehabilitation of those facing radical changes to their life style e.g. following a stroke or an amputation.
(f) To provide a flexible service to Accident and Emergency patients who require a few days close-supervision to restore confidence in themselves.

3. Scope of the Service
The service is to be available at short notice during the evenings and at weekends, as well as during normal office hours. It will

operate, as the need arises, between the hours of 7.00 a.m. and 11.00 p.m. It is not intended that staff should undertake any sleeping-in duties as this would absorb a disproportionate number of hours of service, and would also probably mean that the client was more confused and/or disabled than the service is intended to cope with.

Although it is hoped that referrals made out of office hours will be kept to a minimum, a number of Domiciliary Care Assistants will be recruited on the basis that they may be called out, out of office hours. These staff will have their telephone rental paid by the Council. These emergency referrals will be dealt with through the existing stand-by Social Work Team.

The emphasis of the service will be on meeting clients' personal care needs (assisting with getting-up, washing, dressing, toiletting, putting to bed etc.) although other, more traditional home help type tasks like preparing meals, shopping, collecting pensions, laundry etc. will also be included.

It is proposed that the service will be available, in the main, to those people not previously known to the Home Help service, unless they are being discharged in circumstances drastically different to those existing prior to admission, i.e. following a major operation and requiring a high level of personal care.

In many cases, particularly where there is a need to support someone being discharged from hospital, it is expected that there will be a joint assessment by the service organiser, a member of the Community Nursing Service and/or OT. The purpose of this will be to ensure good decision-making about the degree of help to be given to the client and to enable the resources of each discipline to be allocated as efficiently as possible.

It is also expected that the Organiser will be included in Home Assessment visits with OTs and SWs when plans are made for the discharge of long-term patients, and it appears likely that the patient will need the intensive help supplied by the service. This will allow an advance check to be made on home environment and facilities. It will also give the opportunity to advise on practical changes in household arrangements.

In general, the service may be provided for a period of up to 4 weeks. Obviously in some cases, the need will only exist for a shorter period. In others, the need may be for a longer time, in which case the period over which the service is given could be extended, having regard to the extent and priority of demand on behalf of other clients.

A regular review system will be operated to monitor the progress of each client and to adjust the level of service given according to changing needs. The ability to achieve a planned reduction of the service to each client will be necessary, in order to be able to accept new clients and to maximise the limited resources of the service. The short-term nature of the service must be maintained. Towards the end of the agreed period of help, an assessment of the client's abilities will be essential to determine which services will be required after withdrawal of DCA.

This will allow sufficient notice to be given where necessary to the Home Help service etc. to facilitate smooth transfers and perhaps give the opportunity for joint visits by organisers or Care Assistants and Home Helps. Other clients will have achieved a level of independence enabling them to manage without further support and the remainder will return to the care of relatives, friends and neighbours as appropriate.

In terms of the number of hours of service provided per day, clients may be allocated up to about 6 hours, although the normal provision may be less than this, or in some exceptional cases, a little more may be allowed. Every effort will be made to give continuity of workers involved and also to limit to the minimum the number of different workers calling. This will, however, be dependent upon the hours of work of the staff recruited, the number of clients needing the service at particular times etc.

It is intended that the service should be able to respond swiftly to the demands made upon it, so whilst clients may be provided with the optimum level of service, there may be at times a need to reduce this so that others may be helped, whilst ensuring a minimum level of care. Unless a minimum level is achieved the purpose of the scheme will be negated. This may necessitate our asking for the delay of a planned discharge patient on occasions in order to maintain our swift response to emergency situations.

4. Charging Policy
Although some clients of the normal home help service are

required to pay, those receiving the short-term Domiciliary
Care Service will not be asked to pay. This will ensure that the
appropriate level of service will be allocated, depending on the
client's needs, not their financial circumstances.

The two weeks of training for the staff taken on for the project
included input from occupational therapists, physiotherapists,
community nursing staff, social workers and various other workers.
The project director explained that one of the most important
aspects of the training had been to create team spirit within the
group of workers. There is, incidentally, great similarity between
this project and its services/training program of low-paid workers,
most of them working part time, and the program involving training a new level of assistants for home care of older people in
Germany, described in Chapter 2.

The emphasis of the Greenwich project (Short-term Domiciliary Care Scheme, 1984), on working with patients to increase
their regaining of skills for their own personal care, as rapidly as
possible, is in direct contrast with custodial care of patients in nursing homes where the work of the staff is to 'wash, bathe, feed and
dress the patients'. Obviously, this new project is one to watch to
see how much and how often success is possible.

The survey by the WHO Office for Europe (1982) entitled
*Epidemiological Studies in Social and Medical Conditions of the
Elderly* included a summary of a study which would lend some
support to this project based upon rehabilitation potential.
Aniansson, as a part of the Gothenburg Study of 70 year olds,
studied their ability to cope with activities of daily living. The
research went on to examine the potential for increase in muscle
strength by training, affecting such activities as stair climbing and
walking fast enough to cross a street safely. 'The study suggests
that it is possible to train the elderly, and that such training results
in an improved capacity for oxygen utilization as well as an
increase in muscle strength.' (p. 21)

There will be value in comparing the costs and benefits of the
Greenwich project with costs of care in a nursing home after some
period of time. Its projected costs appear to be low; £76,000 is the
amount of the annual budget for 1984. The ten persons employed
as care assistants are serving 14 patients at a time, and the plan is
to move on to a new set of patients as soon as independent functioning is achieved. Their goal calls for the work with the patient to

average four weeks. If their achievement comes close to reaching that goal, they will have served 100 patients and more in a year. And if the workers in this project are able to provide help which will enable people to function independently and live at home rather than becoming increasingly dependent in an institutional setting, they will be providing the benefit everyone wishes.

Self-Help and Kinship in Aftercare

Finally, Malcolm Johnson (1980) has proposed that consideration of aftercare should include the ways in which it is realistic to involve patients and relatives. He has outlined an approach to this topic as follows:

> *Involvement of Patients and Relatives in Discharge and After-care. (Malcolm L. Johnson)*
> Untapped resources is one form of an increasingly familiar view of how health and social services can be extended. But it will need a more sophisticated approach to mine the resources of self-help and kinship, and perhaps some new techniques.
>
> 1. *Some well-known factors*
> — About half the hospital population is over 65.
> — Over half of patients at any time are suffering from long-term illness.
> — Most of the long-term illnesses of later life are irremediable.
> — Up to 70% of nursing staff in geriatric, psychiatric and long-stay wards are untrained. Even more true of social workers.
> — Hospital regimes generally generate dependency, loss of function, loss of independence and high levels of anxiety.
> However, most of the sick community is cared for at home.
>
> 2. *The process of being ill and getting better*
> Recent studies of doctor-patient communication generally conclude that patients feel they get insufficient information. This is not entirely the fault of the doctors, but they are not trained to do it.
> Even so, there is insufficient recognition that episodes in hospital are only one segment of a continuing process of illness.
> Patients need to plan their recovery, to timetable and order it. They need to know how long they are likely to be in, and

most patients are anxious to get out as soon as possible. If sick people are to return to 'normal' functioning, it is important that they are not first debilitated by institutional routines — self-help needs to be nurtured in hospitals in a transferrable way.

In a good ward, discharge planning (which includes patient, relatives and friends) begins at the time of admission and must include:

    (i)   Treatment
    (ii)   Information and timetabling
   (iii)   Self-help in the hospital
   (iv)   Support in the hospital by relatives and friends
    (v)   Embellishment of self-esteem
   (vi)   Rehabilitation must *not* be a series of short episodes
  (vii)   Assessment of patient and supporter capacity for caring
 (viii)   Planning of support for the supporters
   (ix)   Patients and carers must be part of the rehabilitation team

3. *Growth potential of informal care*

Most care is informal care (only $2\frac{1}{2}$% of over 65s are in hospitals). However, there is a vast variety of human groups encompassed by the term 'family', and they are successful to greater or lesser degrees in providing for the otherwise socially ummet needs of their members. Variations can be mediated by supporting the supporters, sometimes by money and sometimes by relieving them.

4. *Practical procedures*
— Early discharge planning allows provision of aids, changes at home, etc.
— Information about benefits and services
— Social work support
— A wider range of 'community fixers'

Conclusions
— Self-help must be encouraged and developed.
— Supporters need information and practical help.
— The caring capacity of carers must be assessed.
— Further increments of care are not cost free — they will need a supportive framework of professional and voluntary skill.

Table 5.1: After Care Problems and Solutions and their Counterparts in Long-term Care

After Care Problems identified by the Continuing Care Project	Long-term Care Problems encountered as endemic in long-term care
1. Hospital admission is seen by staff as an isolated episode rather than part of a continuing care process.	1. (a) Management of episodes of acute illness and injury is the strong point of hospitals and medicine, not management of disability due to chronic illness nor incapacity. (b) Professional services are categorized by certain diseases or disorders at the expense of regarding the patient as a whole person over a human life span.
2. Hospitals tend to be cut off from the outside world, and most hospital staff lack community experience, which affects their perception of after care needs. (Nurses have been found to be over-optimistic regarding the mobility levels patients will be able to reach when they return home from hospital.)	2. Specialization has meant that doctors and other health professionals have gone deeper into the procedures and technology of one aspect of the profession, at the expense of familiarity with their patients in other settings. Home visits by doctors have virtually disappeared in many countries. Nursing homes, where long-term care is often carried out, are isolated from the medical profession and all else that goes on exclusively in medical centers.
3. Discharge planning has low priority. Hospital systems are not geared for discharge planning, and the transmission of relevant information about patients is haphazard and chancy.	3. (a) It is not surprising that the management of acute, life-threatening events dominates the work of people in hospitals. Dealing with emergencies and crises is their business. (b) Hospitals are managed by different administrative systems from primary health care, and social service departments are run by still others. Collaboration among professionals from different bases is almost impossible. (c) All of this, when research is showing medical and social problems and care often to be interrelated.
4. There are pressures on patients to conform. The hospital expects them to act passively and not to take initiatives.	4. Persons experience subjugation in the role of patient. Any person in an institutional setting loses autonomy and control. This is responsible for dissatisfaction with nursing and residential homes as well as hospitals.
5. The contrast between hospital and home is difficult for patients to cope with because of the dependency fostered in hospital.	5. This is especially likely to be true of older people who are dependent upon others for care, and because capabilities deteriorate from lack of use, long-term stays in institutions can be especially destructive. The loss of self-confidence becomes part of the problem.

Table 5.1: continued

After Care	*Long-term Care*
Solutions	
1. Hackney puts hospital staff in touch with community staff for in-patient care matters as well as after care. Mechanisms have been set up by which each side communicates with the other, and on occasion persons from each side plan and carry out a home trial visit together. This process tends to give opportunity to place the hospital episode into a wider context in the patient's life situation.	1. Collaboration between in-hospital and community workers over the care of the patient in both settings builds up an acquaintance (and hopefully mutual respect) for the two settings, and the longer term perspective on health, illness and disability which is needed for management of chronic disorders.
2. The Greenwich project calls for intensive at-home care and rehabilitation to enable the patient to recover and re-learn coping skills.	2. Long-term rehabilitation may come to receive the same input of professional skill and creativity as curing acute episodes, once professionals become better acquainted with the problems and solutions necessary for management following discharge.
3. All of the liaison schemes meet face-on the fact that the hospital puts low priority on discharge planning. Additional staff with knowledge of community services are needed to take responsibility for building the bridge between hospital care and after care at home.	3. The designation of special coordinators to pull together different services at the point of discharge from hospital puts into motion a process which gradually increases the amount of interaction between hospital and community service personnel. Neither of the latter has time nor means of setting up the collaboration from one side — a third party devoted to the establishment of liaison is able to make a beginning to which the others can add as time goes on.
4. The Watson project begins the planning for after care with the patient and the family care-givers.	4. Involvement of patients and their carers has been pointed out by Johnson as a resource for after care planning and for long-term management of recovery.
5. As experience develops in programs like Hackney and others, involving physiotherapists and occupational therapists from the start, it is likely that rehabilitation necessary for home activities will begin to occupy more of a place during the hospital stay.	5. Progressive practices in hospitals — with patients up and dressed during the day, and with opportunities for a variety of activities — are already showing the way to counteract the creation of dependency and inactivity in institutional settings.

— Part of that cost will be in the professional skills model to assess caring capacities.

Lessons from After Care

A great deal of space has been given to the topic of continuity of care from hospital to home. In part, this has been done because there is a sense in which this topic encapsulates much of the macro problem of long-term care for infirm and disabled elderly people. Successful attempts to solve the rather limited problem may indicate ways in which problems with larger dimensions can be taken on.

The accompanying Table 5.1 represents an attempt to 'test this hypothesis', as it were. A list of some of the conditions creating aftercare problems noted by the Continuing Care Project in an excerpt on page 82, is put in the left-hand column. In the right-hand column, opposite that after care problem is the form in which that same condition is encountered in many areas of long-term care.

Following the problems are some types of solutions for aftercare arrangements which have been presented in the preceding pages. Beside these, on the right, are proposals for matching larger scale solutions for the larger scale problems. Numbers are co-ordinated: solution 1 is related to problem 1, and problem 1 in After Care is related to problem 1 in Long-term Care. It is possible that work on after care may prove to be a lever for eventually moving the problems of long-term care toward solution.

References

Amos, Geraldine, (ed.) (1980) *Home from Hospital — to What?* Continuing Care Project, Birmingham, England
Health Forum, (1984) *Hospital Discharge of Elderly Patients.* Age Concern Greater London (mimeo), London
Hinds, Cora, (1984) 'Families' knowledge and use of resources in meeting needs of patients with cancer at home.' Paper presented at the International Nursing Research Conference, Imperial College, London, April 12-15, 1984
Hunt, Maura, (1982) 'An action research approach to promoting planned discharge of the elderly from acute wards to the community'. *Proceedings of the Royal College of Nursing Research Society, XIII Annual Conference,* University of Durham, England

Johnson, M. (1980) Involvement of Patients and Relatives in Discharge and Aftercare, in Amos, G., (ed.), *Home from Hospital to What?* Continuing Care Project, Birmingham, England

Knox, John, (1982) 'Community nurses attached to a geriatric department'. *Demonstration Centres in Rehabilitation,* No. 27, pp. 35-40. January, 1982

McGuire, Helen D., (1976) 'Continuing health care'. *Hospitals 50* pp. 87-91

Nicoll, Linden, (1984) *A profile of the work of Community Health Councils in England and Wales in Connection with the Elderly.* National Association of Community Health Councils (xerox), London

'Short Term Domiciliary Care Scheme,' (1984) Directorate of Social Services (mimeo), Greenwich, England

Skeet, Muriel, (1970) *Home from Hospital.* The Don Mason Research Committee of the National Florence Nightingale Memorial Trust, London

Slack, G. and Gibbins, J., (1979) *Organising Aftercare.* Centre for Policy on Ageing, London

Thursfield, P., (1980) Liaison between hospital and community, in G. Amos, (ed.), *Home from Hospital — to What?* Continuing Care Project, Birmingham, England

Watson, Felicity, (1982) Discharge procedures. *Nursing Times 78,* (26), p. 1107 June 1982

WHO Regional Office for Europe, (1982) *Epidemiological Studies on Social and Medical Conditions of the Elderly.* EURO Reports and Studies 62. Copenhagen, Denmark

6 BUILDING FOR INDEPENDENCE

Several countries have recently been bringing together these factors: the dislike of the isolated long-term care institution represented by the nursing home; the possibility of bringing services to disabilities, rather than the other way around; and, housing complexes which contain a wide range of living quarters for older people, purpose-built to match wide variations in mobility and potential for self-care. These new developments in housing include a range of accommodation, from ordinary flats through 'sheltered' flats to 'assisted flats' to a nursing home with 24-hour care from the nursing staff. The provision of hot meals; alarm systems for summoning help; and a staff of physicians, nurses, physiotherapists, social workers and home-helps are the very necessary elements. Additional services may include chiropody, hairdressing, a library, laundry service and a few shops. An important feature is that flats can be fitted with a variety of special adaptations for a wide variety of disabilities.

The guiding principle of these housing-service complexes is to provide an environment where maximum independent functioning is possible, no matter what the existing disabilities may be. After substantial pioneering work by Denmark and Sweden, other countries — notably Britain — have begun to undertake to follow the principle in their own ways.

Housing developments of this kind were called for by one of the elements in the Sandoz Institute Study's list of 'a complete geriatric care system: Versatility of health care and residential facilities to permit a variety of uses, depending on the changing needs of patients' (Selby and Schechter, 1982, p. 76). The Sandoz Institute experts like the working group of the European Community countries repeatedly called attention to the desirability of a mix of care provision, from no assistance to much assistance, so that residents 'do not have to go through another move if they become unable to care for themselves' (Collot *et al.*, 1982, for CLEIRPPA, p. 34). The *Bulletin on Aging* (1983) reported a similar recommendation in a document prepared by the 33 countries (largely European) who met in Vienna in April 1982:

Provision should be made for: housing for the fully independent aging; small group housing for those interested in co-operative living; and housing with congregate services for frail older people who can live independently despite disability. The guiding principles of housing policies should be reasonable price, appropriate design and suitable location. (p. 10)

The building of housing of these kinds has not been entirely confined to European countries. Some life-care communities have been built in the United States which combine housing for people after retirement with substantial primary health care services and a nursing home where residents can receive long-term care when needed and as long as it is needed. So far, their construction has depended upon private investors and often on initiative from voluntary organizations. The Society of Friends, for instance, has developed some of the well-known communities of the kind described above. Costs have been so high that this option has been available for only a very small number of elderly Americans. This same situation has been true in West Germany.

Scandinavian Developments

Scandinavian countries have developed many such complexes for several years, partly as private, but usually as public ventures. The Scandinavian models provide, in addition, the broad range of in-home services, special aids and (often custom-built) adaptations for the living area, very elaborate alarm systems and, perhaps most important, integration into non-elderly parts of the community. They have noted the unsatisfactory nature of even the most desirable elderly communities when they are segregated from the remainder of the population and become 'golden ghettoes'. Care has been taken in many instances to locate a complex for elderly people near a day care center for young children, a high school or a shopping district.

A good account of the Swedish complexes already in operation in the early seventies was given by Kane and Kane (1976):

The old age home is gradually giving way to the new sheltered housing, the Swedish version of which is the residential hotel. ... with telephone and alarm system, help with the domestic chores—cleaning and laundry, and medical care, chiropody, hairdressing, and physiotherapy services. Residents are visited weekly by a physician and each hotel has a nurse on duty during the days. The newer units also have special rooms set aside for more intensive care as in an old-age home, the idea being that patients can move to such rooms when they need more care without having to leave the building. These special units have 24-hour nursing coverage. There is a restaurant on the premises which can also deliver meals to housebound residents. Although most apartments are designed to allow the residents to do their own cooking, the newer hotels are built with some 'compressed apartments' for those who prefer to rely mainly on communal dining. Each complex also has a leisure center with facilities for recreational and social activities both for the residents and the other elderly in the area. The hotels are designed to be located near shopping areas and with easy access to public transportation (which is itself subsidized for the elderly).

The residential hotels vary in size from those with just over 100 apartments and accommodations for 140 residents to those with over 300 units for some 400 individuals. Four new hotels are scheduled for construction in Stockholm between 1975 and 1977, with 250-300 apartments each; this seems then to be the size most favored. Increasingly these hotels are viewed as the nucleus for a pensioners' service complex, with varying levels of self-care living and supportive services that include day-center activities for those living in the area. (p. 66)

Sweden's Country Report for the WAA included an expression of the philosophy regarding housing and the elderly population which underlies the efforts they have devoted to this:

The aim of the government housing policy is to promote an adequate supply of housing. Public engagement in this sphere is prompted by the fundamental importance of the home for family life and for the individual's health and working capacity, rest and recreation. The goal is that the entire population shall be offered sound, well planned and properly equipped dwellings of ample size and good quality at a reasonable cost. The main object is to provide for the fundamental human needs for communion with one's fellow beings, stimulance, variety, self-esteem, and possibilities for the residents to influence their own environment. The qualities of a residential area depend largely on who lives there. It is important to counteract tendencies to one-sidedness in the population structure; one-sidedness in the age composition, in particular, would be a negative factor. An all-round household and residential structure is therefore important both from social aspects and from the point of view of the national economy.

A guiding principle in the housing policy is that elderly people shall be able to live in self-dependence and lead an active and meaningful life in fellowship with others. The responsibility for housing lies largely with the local authorities. The local authority shall make efforts to ensure that elderly persons have satisfactory dwellings and shall give support and help in the home and other easily accessible service to those who need it. For elderly people needing special support the local authority shall arrange dwellings with common service. The main interest is in improvements to existing buildings, since most elderly people wish to live on in a well-known environment. Important measures to enable them to do so are adaptation of buildings and the local environment to the special needs of the elderly, and municipal and other services in, and in connection with, their dwellings. Good living conditions have a prophylactic effect and often reduce the need for other service.

Today nearly 90 per cent of all elderly people live in ordinary dwellings, roughly equally divided between small houses and multi-family houses. The others live in service flats, service flats with full board (former old-age homes) or in nursing homes/hospitals (p. 25).

A report from the British group Pensioners Link/Task Force was written by Pearson (1981) on the basis of an investigation of

Figure 6.1: The Range of Housing for Sweden's Older People in Terms of Increasing Amounts of Care

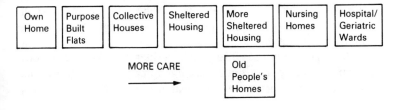

Scandinavian housing for elderly people. She presented the range of housing for Sweden's older people in terms of increasing amounts of care, in Figure 6.1.

Pearson commented that in both Norway and Denmark sheltered housing and collective housing projects built by voluntary organizations are sometimes financed by central or local government. Collective Houses, built for pensioners requiring only a little assistance, have only a few services available for those who want and need them. The flats are small ones, but specially adapted and designed so that people with disabilities can manage the tasks of daily living independently.

The sheltered flats, offering services for a higher level of care as needed, were described by Pearson in the following paragraphs:

Within certain statutory requirements the design of sheltered housing varies from individual single-storey flats to large high-rise blocks. Sheltered units can be constructed as independent buildings, part of a housing estate or as separate terraced houses provided this does not impede the provision of collective services or the summoning of prompt assistance. Discussions flourish about the type of sheltered housing to be provided, but it is clear that pensioners have the same wide preferences as any other section of the population and sensitivity to their choice should be exercised in the allocation of places. Pensioners who wish to remain in a familiar environment should not be rehoused in another area; those who prefer a noisy environment with children should not be removed to a quiet, segregated setting. Insensitivity on the part of planners, housing and social services officials to the effects of relocation has often led to more upset and depression amongst pensioners than any other factor in the removal process.

Generally, in Scandinavia, sheltered flats and very sheltered flats are replacing the traditional role of old people's homes as a form of housing for those in need of care and attention. The reason for choosing a sheltered flat will usually be the need for attention as a result of a physical disability or mild mental confusion, or because of feelings of insecurity, depression, loneliness and isolation.

It is generally recognised that residents should have some form of twenty-four hour security, often alarm systems, with staff on hand within walking distance or a short drive away.

Obviously, this varies between the countries. Norway and Denmark are still researching and piloting alarm systems, whereas Sweden has a highly sophisticated alarm system in operation in many sheltered units and residential specialist housing. Often, this comprises push alarms in each room at a low level for easy accessibility should you fall and be unable to get up, a pull alarm beside the bed, and a 'passive' alarm — often taking the form of activating an alarm if the toilet is not used for 24 hours. All the alarms are electronic and flash outside the room, on each floor level indicating which floor and in the reception area and office. Although the alarms may not be used frequently it is thought that the security factor is very important to the person who lives alone.

Home Helps and home nurses are generally available for those who need them. In Sweden, they often meet daily in the sheltered housing complex and are allocated only to that building.

Generally, in Scandinavia, there is an attached day centre and restaurant with low prices which can also be used by pensioners living in the surrounding area. This is a requirement in Sweden and the facilities and restaurants are 'drop-in' with no requirement to be allocated a place. Other facilities in the sheltered housing complex will include a doctor's surgery, chiropody service, hairdressing and library.

The flats themselves usually comprise living room, bedroom, kitchen, bathroom with shower and toilet, and sometimes a balcony. (p. 20-1)

A particular complex in Denmark was described by Pearson as an example of the combination of a nursing home, a day center and sheltered flats:

Omsorgscentret Møllegården (2800 Lyngby, Denmark)
This is a nursing home with a day centre and sheltered flats in rows close by. The whole of this complex is in a very attractive setting on the outskirts of Copenhagen. It is beautfully designed and landscaped, and was built two and a half years ago.

Sheltered housing working in co-operation with a nursing home is considered to be a good practical arrangement in Denmark. The staff on call can be located in the nursing home and thus on hand for those pensioners living in the sheltered houses. The serving of meals, laundry service, chiropody, hair-dressing and day centre can be run jointly in co-operation. Residents in the sheltered blocks can participate in the occupational therapy and welfare activities arranged for those in the nursing home. It is also considered an effective means of overcoming the difficulties that can arise if someone from a sheltered flat needs to move into a nursing home. The move will no longer be such an upheaval, and will not necessitate leaving familiar surroundings and friends.

The Nursing Home. The Nursing Home has places for 58 residents. Each has a separate room with a bathroom and shower. Pensioners can take their own furniture except for the bed, since a safe standard bed is required. The rooms are light and airy with sliding windows opening onto their own sun terraces, next to the garden. There are alarms in each flat with a member of staff on call for 24 hours. A shop is also based in the reception area.

The convivial atmosphere and the friendly staff with the design and tasteful decorations encourage a cosy, non-institutional flavour to the building.

A new director has recently been appointed to the home. She is a former nurse. The policy of employing nurses to run nursing homes has been encouraged in Denmark since it is believed by some that a knowledge and understanding of medical matters is the most useful asset. Others argue that if members of the medical profession run homes the tendency is to view pensioners' problems as medical rather than social. Nonetheless, it has been equally contested that those with little or no medical knowledge tend to view pensioners' problems as all stemming from social origins.

The nursing home is attached to the *Day Centre.* The day centre is for the use of pensioners from both the nursing home and the sheltered flats. A wide variety of activities can be pursued here — weaving, lace making, painting, carpentry, pottery etc. There is also a pool table. The physiotherapy department is incorporated into this pleasant and airy centre. In general all nursing homes have provision for physiotherapy as well as occupational therapy. Besides the many aids and training facilities in the physiotherapy area, there is also a physiotherapy garden. This has plants in raised boxes so that no bending is required to tend them. The sun terraces of the nursing home overlook the physiotherapy garden so that people can chat to each other while they garden or take advantage of good weather.

The Sheltered Flats. These are built in rows close to the nursing home and day centre. There are flats for both single pensioners and couples, providing places for 50 people. Each flat has a living room, bedroom, kitchen and bathroom with shower. The rooms have large windows and a living room door which gives onto a garden and a sun-terrace. Access to the adjacent complex is either through tree-lined paths or through an underground tunnel which has different coloured printed lines leading to the nursing home, day centre or administration.

Pensions and any earnings are retained when living in all sheltered accommodation in Denmark. There are no means tests for admission and couples can also qualify even if only one partner needs this form of housing. Allocation of sheltered accommodation is through the social welfare department in the same way as admission to nursing homes.

The charge for rental, electricity, heating and care is assessed at 25 per cent of income. (p. 23-5)

Probably the ultimate in demonstration of what can be done to provide independence for people with disabilities is a center in Göteburg, Sweden. It serves as a center for short-term rather than long-term stay. Pearson's description includes many of the features which make this a unique development.

Dalheimers Hus. Göteborg
This building was completed five years ago, financed mainly by a legacy in 1922 from Fritz Potens Dalheimer who asked that the money be kept in trust for 40 years and then be used to benefit people with disabilities. It houses 14 organisations for various disabilities who work closely together. They do not in fact wish to see another building like this as they believe that all people are different and those with disabilities should not be segregated from the community and these facilities should be a part of everyday life. Nonetheless, the building provides some remarkable features. Below is a description:

The outside appears to be a fairly ordinary tower block with seven floors surrounded by a few trees. On arrival at the main door access is gained through wide automatic doors and in addition, all levels have a car park adjacent so that people can drive to each floor and if help with access is needed there is a telephone outside each door in the car park.

Once inside the building all floors have handrails and no steps and a straight line of lights for the partially sighted which they can follow leading to the entrance or exit. Lifts buzz and light up on arrival and have large buttons at low levels so that those in wheelchairs may travel alone. There are bright colours everywhere and telephones on all levels with large numbers and loudness adjusters.

The Lower Ground Floor. Here are the offices and consulting rooms of the Blind Association 'Hope' which also has its own entrance. Study circles of blind and partially-sighted people meet here. There is also a 'practice' kitchen where they can develop their ability to manage in their own kitchens at home. Many people participate in the popular sport of shooting air-rifles in the specially designed gallery, using rifles with electronic sights. This conforms to international competition standards and the members here have reached a very good standard in their competitions.

The Ground Floor. This is the main entrance and contains the offices of the supervisor and most of the disability organisations. There is a large notice board which shows the daily and weekly activities. A swimming pool, sauna and sun room for people with varying disabilities is also housed on this floor. There are special dressing rooms and bath tubs with lifts where baths can be taken at specially adjusted temperatures. After bathing people can relax in comfortable chairs by the pool or in one of the rest rooms. This is open from 9-8 weekdays and 1.30-6.00 at weekends.

First Floor. Here we find the restaurant which provides lunch, dinner and refreshments. Meals are 9 kroner (90 pence). The open plan area provides space to sit and chat, watch television or listen to music. Other rooms provide table tennis, pianos and sewing machines. In addition there is a physiotherapy department and a gymnasium plus a large hall for plays, dances and films. In the open plan area there are exhibitions such as ancient pottery with descriptions in braille, and wall pictures which are made to be touched.

Second Floor. This accommodates the library which provides ordinary books, large print books, talking books and a machine which enlarges print onto a television screen. There is also a tape of the 'West Coast' which is a spoken newspaper.

Each Monday the librarian reads aloud and the book is discussed in the study circle.

There is a reading room, a chess area and a music room where people can relax and listen to records.

Third Floor. The occupational therapy department provides training for people with disabilities. Equipment includes lathes, planes, looms, and potters wheels. Anyone can have remedial treatment lasting for 30 days if they apply with a doctor's certificate. There is also a training kitchen for using specially adapted kitchens in your own home with adjustable working surfaces, sinks and cookers.

A beautiful spacious roof garden wth tables and chairs overlooks the harbour.

Fourth, Fifth and Sixth Floors. Here we have 15 single rooms and 2 double rooms where people with disabilities can stay for up to a month at a charge of 40 kroner (£4) per day for those from Göteborg and 120 kroner (£12) per day for those from elsewhere.

All rooms are equipped for the physically handicapped with special toilets and showers, adapted telephone, handles and rails, no carpet to slip on and nothing to trip over, and with a view of the harbour and the Alvsborg Suspension Bridge. The door flies open when a key is inserted into a lock on the wall next to the door. There is an emergency alarm cord next to the bed. Meals will be provided in the room if the guest does not feel like going down to the restaurant. There is also a communal area where people can sit and chat. It has an adjustable level kitchen and a television.

Anyone can apply for a place if they would just like a break, or if their usual helper goes on holiday or if they have recently become disabled and wish to learn how to manage.

Dalheimers Hus is run by the social services department and is funded annually £800,000 by the local authority who also pay for 30 staff.

Sheltered and More Sheltered in Britain

The British have been gradually working toward the Scandinavian type complex. They have built 'sheltered housing' since the early sixties. There is a long precedent in Britain for provision of a great deal of housing through a combination of local authority initiative and management, and central government money. Local authorities had been involved in some house-building since the early 1900s. To meet the national crisis in housing needs after World War II, so-called 'council estates' — usually groups of semi-detached houses and small blocks of flats arranged in rather small neighborhoods — were built all over Britain, in towns and cities alike. This set a strong precedent for local government provision of housing available for rental.

The present status of sheltered housing has been surveyed carefully by Goldberg and Connelly (1982). They have defined it as:

The term 'sheltered housing' is used to refer to specially designed or converted houses, flats or flatlets — grouped, and with a resident warden; there may or may not be an alarm system and communal facilities such as a common room, laundry or eating facilities. Local authority provision of such dwellings rests with housing departments, and those who live in them are tenants, like other people renting local authority housing. Social services departments may take responsibility, however, for the provision of warden services or their costs. (p. 189)

Its original shape and growth were described in these terms:

Sheltered housing schemes were originally envisaged as a useful form of house midway between an elderly person's ordinary dwelling (perhaps now unnecessarily large or inconvenient) and care in a residential home. A number of Acts and Circulars in the late 1950s and early 1960s gave power and encouragement to housing authorities to provide special housing for the elderly, and to welfare authorities to provide warden services. A 1969 Circular classified such housing as category 1 (self-contained dwellings) and category 2 (grouped flatlets for the more disabled, with certain common facilities) — the assumption was that more mobile elderly people would inhabit the former, the less mobile, the latter.

In 1963 only about 36,000 people were thought to be living in sheltered housing. Subsequently this form of accommodation has grown in popularity — at least partly as a reaction against the institutional nature of much residential care; about five per cent of the elderly population, roughly 300,000 people, were thought to be living in such schemes by 1976 (Hunt 1978), with a more recent estimate of 400,000 (Butler and Oldman 1980). Most sheltered housing is provided by local authorities, with a growing proportion — perhaps now 20 per cent provided by voluntary organisations or voluntary housing associations (Butler 1980).

Originally it was thought that tenants would need only a little special care. A London working party on the role of the warden agreed in 1970 that the aim should be 'to re-create for old people a kind of family life with opportunities for neighbourliness, but offering always maximum privacy and independence' (Greater London Conference on Old People's Welfare 1970). (p. 190)

In a recent survey the average age of tenants in sheltered housing was found to be 75. Because the populations have of course been aging in these dwellings which have proved to be popular, the present situation in many of the sheltered housing complexes is a logical development:

However, once people moved into such dwellings they were reluctant to leave them, and increasing age and infirmity of existing tenants has meant a growing dependent population, with the boundaries between tenants of the two 1969 categories becoming blurred. In addition, recent emphasis on delivery of domiciliary services to people in ordinary domestic housing has meant that by the time tenancies are sought for special housing, the people involved may be more disabled than had originally been envisaged. Attempts to deal with this have contributed to a vicious circle: as greater responsibilities are shouldered by wardens, relief wardens appointed, and more domiciliary resources allocated to schemes, so these services become an expected part of sheltered housing. Those nominating elderly people from the community, and to be responsible for intake and discharge from hospitals and residential homes, assume a high level of care in sheltered housing, and tenancies are requested for more severely physically or mentally disabled people. Tenants may be sent back to such schemes from hospital sooner than they would be otherwise; tenants may be refused admission to residential homes on the grounds that they are too frail. Those younger and more active elderly people whose presence could in many ways ease the problems of the older schemes may refuse tenancies, considering the atmosphere too similar to that of a residential home.

There has been a range of reactions to this situation — the severity of which, of course, varies from one area to another, depending on when schemes were built, what other resources are available, and so on. The impression received by Bytheway and James in their study of allocation policies (1978) was that while both housing and social services departments recognised the 'drift', the former tried to fight it while the latter accepted it as inevitable. One response has been the substitution of 'very sheltered' for 'sheltered' housing: accommodation designed without stairs, with rooms and door openings large enough to ease use of wheelchairs and walking aids, and with specific commitment to high levels of staffing. Another has been the deliberate choice of 'fitter' candidates from the waiting lists when vacancies occur: elderly people whose bad housing conditions might be exacerbating a health problem, but who are unlikely, at least initially, to generate many demands upon the resident warden, and who seem likely 'to make a contribution towards the life of the community' (Thompson 1981). (p. 191)

The high level of domiciliary service provision enables tenants to stay on in sheltered housing despite severe disability. Goldberg and Connelly present some details about the services received:

Tenants of sheltered housing are generally thought to receive more care than those of equal disability in ordinary housing. Although this seems inequitable to some observers, it is perhaps inevitable, given the greater 'visibility' of such concentrations of need, the greater knowledge among tenants of possible aid when they observe their neighbours receiving such help, the role of the warden in liaising with the agencies involved, and the possibility of more efficient use of, for example, home help time when no travelling is necessary between clients. The Leeds University study has found that of the 600 tenants studied, 16-17 per cent were receiving meals-on-wheels and approximately 30 per cent home help; in a study of 129 tenants in ten schemes in Hillingdon 20 per cent were found to be receiving meals-on-wheels and 59 per cent home help (Hillingdon Housing Department 1978). The relative intensity of this provision may be seen by comparison with the proportions found in Hunt's 1978 study of *The Elderly at Home*: overall, 2.6 per cent had received meals-on-wheels within the past six months, although the figure was 8.5 per cent for those aged 85 and over; overall 8.9 per cent had received home help services, with 15.8 per cent of the 75-84 age group and 27.3 per cent of those aged 85 and over receiving such help. (p. 194)

There have been several studies attesting to their popularity. One important finding which matches the Scandinavian ideas is the importance of their locations.

The design of a scheme as a whole has been looked at from the point of view of optimum number of units (see especially Griffin and Dean 1975), location, views, noise levels, security of premises, and so on. As might be expected, a range of views usually emerges. All these aspects undoubtedly have some influence on how satisfactory tenants find the housing overall, but location is now recognised to be of special importance on a number of counts. If maintenance of independence is to be the aim, there must be easy access to shopping facilities and pub, church, library, and so on. The Warwickshire study found, for example, that the majority of tenants in the six schemes left the complex at least once a week, and 'shopping' was the destination most frequently quoted; most of the schemes were near shops and village or town centres (Reed and Faulkner 1980). (p. 193)

Care Housing is a relatively new type of accommodation in Britain, designed to meet needs for care for infirmity and disability. It exists in different forms in different locations. A pilot project, The Abbeyfield Pilton, was opened in 1982 in Edinburgh, Scotland. Duncan (1983) in a booklet describing the project, distinguished this type from its predecessor, sheltered housing: 'Sheltered housing is designed for people who are still able to run their own homes. Frailer people may not be able to do this and their need is for alternative accommodation where care is provided without taking away the choice and independence of the individual. One such alternative is "Care Housing"' (p. 1).

The points made by Duncan to provide a definition of care housing are these:

Definition of Care Housing
Care Housing consists of a small number of bedsits grouped together with a communal sitting room and kitchen and an adjacent flat for a resident warden/housekeeper. It has the following features:

— It is *small* — not more than eight to ten bedsits to keep the personal flavour and prevent it becoming an institution.
— It is *anonymous* — as far as possible it is indistinguishable from other houses in the road, and can in fact consist of a number of ordinary flats or houses which have been adapted for the purpose.
— It is *part of the local community* — it is situated as near as possible to shops, buses and other facilities. The tenants are people who have lived locally or who have relatives living in the area.
— It *aims to encourage maximum independence and individuality* among its tenants. Each bedsit is completely furnished by the tenant and has its own lock and key. Tenants receive the normal services, like home helps and district nurse, if they need them. They are encouraged to do as many domestic tasks as they can including keeping their rooms clean, setting tables and washing up.
— It *provides a degree of care* — each room is linked to the housekeeper's flat by an alarm system and although 24 hour care is not guaranteed the housekeeper or home help is usually about during the day and there is always someone on call at night. Two meals are provided but residents make their own breakfast. Arrangements can be made to provide

breakfast for those who cannot make their own. A relief housekeeper sleeps in the building on the housekeeper's days off. When, because of the frailty of the residents, extra help is needed this can be provided by increasing the number of hours worked by the relief housekeeper or by the use of volunteers. Nursing care is provided by the district nursing service.

— It is *flexible* — each development of Care Housing will adjust to the needs of those who live there and will reflect something of the character of the local community. Local people will play some part in the life of the tenants and may be able to give extra help in times of need to those who require it. (p. 2-3)

Duncan's booklet describes the setting up of Abbeyfield Pilton with details of the actual building used, the adaptations and the capital costs; the staff members (housekeeper and home help); relationships with the community; and how the project was launched and the residents located and selected. Here is the description of the residents themselves:

Of the first ten residents six were women and four were men. All of them had medical problems in varying degrees including rheumatoid arthritis, asbestosis, poor sight, depression, angina, cancer, muscular deterioration and mild confusion. Three had considerable mobility problems, one caused by a road accident, another by a fractured femur and a third by a broken leg. Many of the old people had been living in badly vandalised areas and were frightened, isolated and unhappy. Several had been housebound. Two had been living with relatives and had to leave because of family tensions. Another had a drink problem. Two had been in hospital for over a year and two more were being considered for admission to an old people's home. Six of the residents were 79 or over on admission and the oldest resident is now 89. The average age is 78.5 years of age. (p. 12)

The weekly charge was met by the residents' state pensions plus Supplementary Benefits, for which almost all of the first group qualified. Each has part of the pension for personal use, but the majority pay for their living expenses in the project.

The response of residents has been enthusiastic, and more

projects are to be opened in the district.

The Centre for Policy on Ageing has recently published a report dealing with residential homes rather than shared housing. It is entitled *Bricks and Mortals* (1983). However, one point it makes is relevant to all housing schemes involving care-givers for infirm elderly people. The announcement from the Centre about the publication included this:

> Design is only one factor influencing the quality of residents' lives. Thus, the study looks at the quality of life in the home and assesses the extent to which residents are free to choose their own furnishings and decorations, eat meals where and when they like, control their own medicines and pension books, and come and go at will. Such aspects of residential life may be subtly influenced by design, but they are primarily related to the principles and practices adopted by the staff.

Norway has come to view appropriately designed housing as the basis for providing for long-term care of elderly people outside of institutions. (There is also substantial institutional care in nursing homes and residential homes (old people's homes) provided through the public sector.) Their developments and financial assistance schemes in housing for older people in Norway were described in the Country Report for the WAA:

4.2 Housing and Environment

Housing policy for the elderly has become an important link in the planning of services outside institutions. This policy covers partly special flatlets, partly schemes to improve the technical standard of the aged person's own house or flat, and partly housing grants to compensate for high house-rent and heating costs. Moreover, residential homes are also regarded as part of this housing policy.

4.2.1 Flatlets for the aging

Flatlets reserved for pensioners (retired or disabled) are usually concentrated in independent houses or in buildings linked to institutions. Some flatlets are also spread geographically and integrated into ordinary housing projects. Most old-age flatlets are municipal, whereas a few are operated by the municipality and private organizations in collaboration. Generally, these flatlet schemes for elderly are intended for couples or single persons who are able to help themselves. Collective service is only available to a very limited extent in these blocks. However, today the tendency is to build the blocks near to social service centres. In 1981 there were about 21 000 special flatlets for elderly persons in Norway, financed by the State Housing Bank. This represented 2.7 per cent of the dwellings financed by Housing Bank schemes since 1946. In postwar years about 80 per cent of all dwellings have been based financially on loans from this State bank. If calculated on the basis of the figures for total annual construction of dwellings in recent years (between 35 000 and 40 000 units per year) the proportion of flatlets for elderly persons amounts to about 3.7 per cent. The number of rooms in residential homes financed by the State Housing Bank come in addition ... Most of the operational expenses are usually — but not always — paid from the municipal budgets.

4.2.2 *House improvement and repair*
The Improvement and Repair Scheme falls into two categories — loans and grants.

Favorable loans may be given by the State Housing Bank on a social basis for repair to houses, insulation etc., thus making it easier for the elderly person to remain at home. The loans are granted to persons having reached the age of 60, but in certain cases persons below this age may be eligible. For the first six years, no instalment payments are required. The rate of interest starts at 5 per cent and is later increased by one per cent per year, up to the regular interest rate for Housing Bank loans, 10.5 per cent.

Grants for repair of older dwellings is an arrangement for the benefit of elderly disabled persons and others with particular social requirements. The grants, which are not liable to repayment, are earmarked for dwellings with unsatisfactory sanitary equipment and insulation. The grant arrangement is run by the State Housing Bank, and covers the whole country. It is subject to means tests. The maximum subsidy in each individual case is NOK 10 000 with the possibility of a higher limit if the applicant is disabled. The grant can be given independently of improvement loans from the State Housing Bank.

4.2.3 *Housing subsidies*
The Housing Subsidy Scheme — current subsidies — is operated

not only for the elderly but also for disabled persons and families with children. However, as far as the elderly are concerned, the scheme should be regarded as one of the basic instruments which enable — or make it easier — for an elderly person to stay at home. The scheme is administered by the State Housing Bank and the municipalities.

The aim of the housing subsidy is to reduce the housing expenses for households with low incomes and/or high housing expenses. The basic principle is that the scheme should cover 80 per cent of the difference between real housing expenses and the appropriate housing expenditure for the individual household, the actual income considered. Governmental housing grants can be made both to old people's dwellings and old people's homes, provided that flatlets or rooms can be regarded as 'independent housing units'.

For the year 1982, the State Budget provides for NOK 285 million for the housing subsidy scheme for elderly and disabled pensioners. Eligibility is determined by the Social Welfare Office of the municipality. (pp. 23-6)

Is This the Light at the End of the Tunnel?

Elderly persons who meet with disabling episodes like strokes, heart attacks and injuries are fortunate indeed when they live in housing complexes built on the Scandinavian model. When they have lived there in a sheltered flat before the illness, they can return from hospital to a familiar community. Full nursing care will be available if needed, and help is there from the rehabilitation professionals. Flats are fitted with the appropriate adaptations to make possible independent activity when patients are ready to get around on their own. They have the security of knowing that a call for help will be answered should it be necessary.

Such an environment provides what is needed for the 'caring spouse'. It would even be adequate for a person living alone, with a minimum of nursing care, daily visits from a home help, and the possibility for having meals brought in until the patient can manage to go to the restaurant.

The range of possibilities for disabled persons has moved a long way from the two options of the standard nursing home, with its dependence-building institutional character, or the home, where there is only the unprepared, untrained family member. There is new promise in the complex of flats *cum* built-in aids *cum* social and health professional services *cum* a unit providing full nursing care, all of which provides needed care plus rehabilitation for independent activity plus the assistance for independent living when ready for it. In the next chapter we will call attention to the supportive environments where these new developments have taken form.

References

Butler, A. (1980) Profile of the Sheltered Housing Tenant, *Housing 16* no. 6, 6-8

Butler, A., Oldman, C. and Greve, J., (1983) *Sheltered Housing for the Elderly*. George Allen and Unwin, London

Bytheway, W.R. and James, L. (1978) *The Allocation of Sheltered Housing*, Medical Research Centre, University College, Swansea

Country Reports for the World Assembly on Aging (1982)

— *Aging in Norway: Humanitarian and Developmental Issues*. Royal Norwegian Ministry of Health and Social Affairs, Oslo

— *Just another Age: A Swedish Report to the WAA*. The National Commission on Aging, Stockholm

Collot, C., Jain-LeBris, H. and Ridoux, A. (1982) for the Centre de Liason d'Etude, d'Information et de Recherche sur les Problèmes des Personnes Agées. (1982) *Toward an Improvement in Self Reliance of the Elderly. Innovations and New Guidelines for the Future*. The Commission of the European Communities, Brussels (Referred to herein as CLEIRPPA)

Duncan, Isabel, (1983) *Care Housing* Lothian Regional Council Social Work Department, Edinburgh, Scotland

Goldberg M and Connelly, N., (1982) *The Effectiveness of Social Care for the Elderly*. Heinemann, London

Hunt, A., (1978) *The Elderly at Home* Her Majesty's Stationery Office, London

Kane, R. and Kane, R., (1976) *Long Term Care in Six Countries: Implications for the United States*. Washington, DC: The John E. Fogarty Center, National Institutes of Health. DHEW Publication No. (NIH)76-1207

Norman, A. (1983) *Bricks and Mortals* Centre for Policy on Ageing, London

Pearson, Rosalind, (1981) *An Independent Old Age: Provisions for Pensioners in Scandinavia*. Pensioners Link/Task Force, London

Reed, C.A. and Faulkner, G.J. (1980) *Your Own Front Door: A Study of Very Sheltered Housing in Warwickshire, 1979-80*, Warwickshire Social Services Department

Selby, P. and Schechter, M., (1982) *Aging 2000 — A challenge for society*. MTP. Published for the Sandoz Institute for health and socio-economic studies. Lancaster, England (Referred to herein as the Sandoz Institute study)

Thompson, L., (1981) 'Hammersmith's Initiatives: Housing Management in Practice'. *Housing Review 30*, pp. 98-9.

United Nations (1983) 'Summary of Selected Governments' Statements on Aging Presented to the Third Committee of the General Assembly of the United Nations at its Thirty-Eighth Session, in Vienna, 1982', *Bulletin on Aging*

PART TWO

THE LAYERS OF CARE BENEATH THE SURFACE

7 THE ROLE OF GOVERNMENT

It is proposed in this book that the nature and effects of all of the programs and services for long-term care of older people are heavily influenced by a layer of the society's beliefs which lies beneath the surface. It is further proposed that differences from country to country in this layer may be larger than the visible forms on the surface. This layer has already been described as consisting of the attitudes and beliefs held in a nation about the proper role of government, both central and local, in relation to the population's needs and national resources. At one extreme, it is regarded as a proper governmental function to take responsibility for gathering and holding resources to provide for people when they find themselves in certain conditions of need. At the other, the government is not trusted to be capable of discharging this responsibility, nor would it be good for the citizens if it did, and governmental involvement should be kept to a bare minimum.

Providing for Individuals in Conditions of Need

Different perceptions of the role of government result in great differences at the gate behind which lie the resources to be used for the population finding themselves in a condition of need. The differences in the gatekeepers have been described as quite like those between two departments of a bank: the trust officer and the loan officer. In a nation like Sweden, where one finds on the outer layer several different provisions and calls it a 'welfare state,' there is an unequivocal assignment to government to provide for certain conditions in which people may find themselves, and to do this through common resources, namely taxation. Unemployment, sickness, single parenthood, being very young and being very old — all of these are such conditions or 'entitlements'. The proper role of government is believed to be to see to it that individuals in those conditions can go to claim the resources to which their condition gives them the right. This is the trust officer perception of the role of government.

All industrialized countries set aside resources for certain conditions of need, but some require an individual to go to some length to make the case that he or she has the need to receive the help. Help is available only if one can show that one has no other means available, and thus help is available on a means-tested basis. Behind this stance there is frank distrust — of people or of government, or of both. Hurdles and obstacles are put in the way of obtaining a share of the resources. This is the 'loan officer' conception of the role of government.

The distribution of resources is in one case a perfunctory paying out, in the other, a grudging release. Dependence of the recipient enters in, no matter what, but the distinction between the attitudes of the gatekeepers make a big difference in the recipient's feeling of powerlessness: indeed this is an intended result on the part of the loan-officer approach, according to Phillipson (1982) describing British history of a different era, at the time of the Poor Law Amendments. In the FRG, the recognition of the vulnerability of human dignity under these conditions of need is called to our attention by Flamm (1974), who tells us that the first sentence of the Basic Law (constitution) is this ' "The dignity of man shall be inviolable. To respect and to protect it shall be the bounden duty of the State authority." ... It is incumbent on the State not only to respect and protect human dignity by repelling all encroachments on it; rather the State regards it as its foremost task to uphold the dignity of man by means of laws which provide for welfare benefits and assistance so as to enable everybody to live a decent life' (p. 9). But the West German government has not yet brought its means-tested program to pay for nursing home care into line with these dicta.

There are several good reasons for putting the spotlight on governments' positions with respect to responsibility for providing long-term care for the elderly. The most important is to require each nation to take a careful look at what its position actually is at the same time that it takes an equally careful look at the population this position is affecting.

The position actually taken by countries is, unfortunately, quite clear. Very few nations have taken the 'trust officer' position toward needs of the elderly like the Scandinavian countries where this attitude does extend even to long-term care. A comparison can be made between two of them, Norway and Sweden, and West Germany, at a very basic level by looking at their development of nursing home beds in relation to the size of their population likely

Table 7.1: Populations Over 75 Years Old and Beds Available in Nursing Homes[1,2,3]: Comparison of Norway, Sweden and West Germany[4]

	Norway	Sweden	West Germany
Number of persons over 75 (in thousands)	230	508	3,334
Number of beds available in nursing homes (in thousands)	30	40	102
NH beds as percentage of the over-75 population	13%	8%	3%

Sources: [1]*Aging in Norway, Humanitarian and Developmental Issues,* 1982. Country Report for the World Assembly on Aging.
[2]*Just Another Age: A Swedish Report to the WAA,* 1982. Country Report for the World Assembly on Aging.
[3]Dieck, M. (1981) *Social and Medical Aspects of the Situation of Older People in the Federal Republic of Germany.* The German Center of Gerontology, Berlin.
[4]Skeet, M. (1983) *Protecting the Health of the Elderly.* World Health Organization, Regional Office for Europe, Copenhagen.

to be in need of them, those over 75 years of age. (See Table 7.1). Figures from the WHO reported by Skeet (1983) show the numbers of persons over 75 in the three countries in 1980. Numbers of beds available in nursing homes were reported in their Country Reports for the WAA. (In the case of the FRG, they came from a companion volume from Dieck, 1981.)

Even more important than the mere presence of facilities is this: not only are the places more apt to exist in the Scandinavian countries; nursing home places are provided by the locality without charge, while the cost must be borne by the individual in West Germany. And as we have seen in the previous chapter, this is only one type of facility and service the Scandinavians provide.

The more common condition is that a nation will be ambivalent with respect to needs of the elderly, on some measures adopting one stance and towards other needs another stance. The care of persons disabled by long-term chronic illnesses is one provision which most countries have so far held back from financing.

The impression of a generous welfare state is created by such measures as the provision of medical services and hospital care without charge through the National Health Service in Britain. West Germany's indexing of pensions to keep the incomes of pensioners in line with inflation certainly suggests an attitude of generosity. Thus, provisions for long-term care covered by national insurance schemes might be expected, but they are not there in either country. Long-term care in nursing homes appears to be the likely cop-out point for some welfare states.

It seems that most governments regard such care as too expensive for all individuals to be able to handle on their own — and they have set up sources of funds which can be drawn upon when the individual has 'spent down' his or her own resources. But they also perceive this care as too expensive for the government to supply open-handedly. This is clearly the case with the United States, where Medicaid, a program available *for the poor*, paid one-half of the 16 billion dollar annual bill for nursing home care at the end of the seventies. The fact that individuals in Britain and West Germany also must spend down their worldly goods to become eligible for this resource is examined in the next section of this chapter.

Perhaps most countries would have to admit, as did the Israeli delegate to the Sandoz Institute study group (Selby and Schechter, 1982), to 'a lack of commitment in dealing with problems of the elderly' (p. 36). Or, perhaps more to the point, it is because in most people's minds, including the minds of decision-makers, providing health care for long-lasting chronic diseases compounds the heavy expenses societies associate with their health care systems, with the heavy expenses associated with their elderly populations. Even Sweden may be growing wary: in an article in a recent book about the Swedish Health System, Speck (1980) referred to 'the "trap" we are walking into, i.e. the economic constraints in combination with the demographic trends we must face up to' (p. 182). He made this observation also: 'The general attitude of the state towards the growth of medical care expenditures has shifted from indulgence and approval during the greater part of the 1960s to concern and disapproval during the 1970s' (p. 201).

Nevertheless, Sweden has by no means renounced the responsibilities they, like the other Scandinavian countries, had assumed toward the elderly; in their Country Report to the WAA in 1982 they referred to increased resources 'to care for the chronically ill, especially the elderly, both in their own homes and in local nursing homes' (p. 19). Denmark apparently remains firmly committed to the trust officer position, as it was stated in the CLEIRPPA (Collot *et al.*) report of 1982:

The medical and social facilities, whether institutionalized or not, are financed virtually in their entirety from taxes and administered by Local Authorities. Both domiciliary services and services provided in an institutional environment are free of charge for the majority of the elderly population, while the minority who have high incomes are required to make a small contribution. (p. 214)

Norway, in their Country Report for the WAA, has presented a clear statement of that nation's assumption of responsibility to see that the care needed by elderly people is provided, administered and paid for. Various public bodies have their roles to play:

A number of public bodies are engaged in community action for the elderly, and co-operation between them is a major issue.

1.2.1 The municipalities and the counties

According to the Social Care Act, services for the aged are the responsibility of the municipalities, with the Social Welfare Board as the main organ. Fields of work in the foreground are residential homes, as well as various social services in the non-institutional care of old people living at home, such as schemes for home nursing and home help, building of flatlets for the aged, and other measures for the welfare and well-being of this group.

As regards old people who need treatment in somatic or psychiatric nursing homes or assistance in related day care centres, the responsibility is placed with the County. As mentioned above it is the responsibility of the counties to plan, build and operate health institutions, including nursing homes. Expenses are covered partly over the County's own budget and partly through 'block grants' from the National Insurance Budget. By and large the block grant to each County covers about 50 per cent of the costs of all health institutions that are included in the County's health plan. The health plan is subject to approval by the Ministry of Health and Social Affairs.

1.2.2 Responsibility of the Government (the State)

Within the care of the elderly in its broadest sense, the Government's obligations — financial and administrative — are carried out by various bodies.

The National Insurance Scheme under the Ministry of Health and Social Affairs covers expenses in connection with old age pensions, nursing homes (50%, the remaining 50% being covered by the County), home nursing (75%, the remaining 25% covered by the municipality), and telephone subsidies.

The Ministry, via its regular budget, subsidizes municipal home-help schemes (50%), whereas the Ministry of Labour and Local Government supports housing schemes for the elderly, through the State Housing Bank. The new 'block grants' to stimulate municipal service for the elderly and the handicapped are incorporated in the annual budget of the Ministry of Health and Social Affairs.

Administration, including planning and legislation, in the field of health and welfare services to the elderly is the task of the Ministry of Health and Social Affairs. The relevant agencies are two departments and three advisory bodies:

— *The Department of Social Services* has a specialized division for services to the aged and the handicapped. The division concentrates its activity first and foremost on legislation, central planning and coordination.
— *The Health Directorate* (organized as a department of the Ministry) is responsible for administration and supervision of the home nursing scheme, and the Director-General of the Health Service is authorized to approve nursing homes.
— *The National Council for Care of the Aged* is appointed by Royal Decree, and has its secretariate in the Ministry of Health and Social Affairs. The Council has an advisory function, and is a common denominator for the interests connected with the care of and the services for the elderly in the community (questions of old age pensions are outside the mandate of the Council). The Council is a body for co-operation between State authorities, municipalities, pensioners, voluntary agencies and personnel organizations in the social and health services.
— *The Norwegian Gerontological Institute* became a State Institute in 1973. Primarily, the task of the Institute is applied research, but it also participates in planning, education, guidance and advisory services. (pp. 6-7)

In that same part of the Country Report, it is pointed out that non-governmental organizations have had a special role as pioneers and innovators in the field of aging in Norway.

The Country Report also furnished an account of the evolution in Norway of public care of the aging:

Public Care of the Aging. Historical Trends

The first step towards a scheme for public provision for the 'poor' was taken in 1845, when State and municipalities introduced regulations with a view to providing assistance to 'old and infirm citizens' — and by the provision of municipal poor-houses.

At the end of the same century the Church as well as a number of different religious organizations became involved in the care of the elderly, first of all by establishing old people's homes.

From the turn of the century — and up to World War II — the municipalities became increasingly involved in the care of the elderly, which till then had been synonymous with old people's homes. An increasing number of municipalities supported the old people's homes run by the parish. The next step — municipal institutions — was soon to follow, and in the 1920s and 1930s, a number of municipalities established municipal old people's homes and nursing homes.

During this period a number of privately funded institutions for the aged were also started, financed by charity drives, donations and legacies.

Financial difficulties prevented the municipalities from expanding other services for the aged. Prior to World War II, services like the home help service were unknown in the municipalities, and economic benefits to the aged could only be provided by a few relatively prosperous municipalities.

The first statutory old-age insurance was introduced by the Act of 16 July 1936. For its time, it was a fundamental social reform. Although the pensions were small and subject to a means test, the scheme allowed for a pension to any person who had reached 70 years of age.

Gradually the old-age pension was increased, and in 1957 the means test was abolished. A number of reforms in the social field were introduced in the course of the following decade, implying marked improvements in economic security, not least as far as the aging population was concerned. The last — and most important reform was the National Insurance Scheme, which came into effect on 1 January 1967. (pp. 16-17)

Note: it was the National Insurance Scheme which provided from the national treasury for nursing home and home nursing care.

General Avoidance of Government Support for Long-term Care

It is worthwhile looking further into the fact that most governments have managed to avoid the running of nursing homes and extending insurance coverage to cover their cost in the way hospital costs are covered. This has been true in the UK and the FRG as well as in the US, as was noted earlier. Insurance schemes which pay hospital bills amounting to billions each year do not cover nursing home costs in the FRG or the US. There is the safety net of means-tested assistance in all three of these countries, but the older person has a long and scary fall before reaching the net.

Of course, all governments — even the US which talks about self-reliance and private initiatives in connection with long-term care as well as medical care — are aware that they are faced with a dilemma. The costs associated with the care of disabilities due to chronic illness in a population with more and more of those illnesses each year are increasing just when their economies are regarded as in poor shape or, at best, shaky.

It is no wonder that a hodge-podge of solutions have been attempted as governments have switched back and forth in their postures regarding the government's proper role. Sometimes there has been a move, or a look, in the positive direction. In the previous chapter it was noted that a German newspaper carried an announcement in 1984 that a bill is to be brought to the Parliament to provide insurance coverage through the constellation of health care insurers for the nursing care needed for those who are disabled. The measure is to be financed by an additional payroll tax of between 1 and 1.2 per cent. The bringing of this bill represents the trust officer finally reaching to include the long-term care problem in the FRG. But the ambivalence which will meet this bill in Parliament in days of economic stringency, is a certainty. It is said that this type of bill has been proposed and promoted in the

FRG for the past ten years so far to no avail.

In the same Germany which wants to bring about that reform, there are older people who need supplementary benefits for their pension incomes to pay for the visits they need by the community nurse. They are prevented from applying for the benefit by the policy which requires contributions from their children and their grandchildren if they make application for Social Assistance. Many of them would and do go without the nurse's visits, and in fact go without food, rather than to suffer the shame of having someone from Social Assistance go to collect money from their children and grandchildren. This means that the care which might keep the older person in reasonably good shape is not received, and in a short time, the condition will grow so serious that an expensive hospital visit will be required. That will be covered by insurance.

Similar false economies occur in Britain, where the government is willing to support the private nursing homes and provides Supplementary Benefits up to well over £150 per week for a patient's care. On the other hand, the same government is cutting down on the budgets of the Health Service and grants for local authorities to supply home care services at per-patient costs which would reach about one-fifth of that amount.

In the US there has been a rush to develop home nursing care, in the hope that this will prove to be cheaper than institutions. Though so far no dramatic differences in cost have been shown to exist, more experience needs to be brought in on the matter. As with the examples from the other countries, the real problem is the lack of rational problem solving and deliberate planning in this matter where so many human concerns and so many resources are involved.

Another result of governments' assuming a little more responsibility here, only to relinquish it there, is a condition commented on in the Sandoz Institute report in one of its understatements: 'Old persons and their families are perplexed about their rights and opportunities' (p. 86).

In virtually every country, the condition in this layer with respect to services needed by patients who suffer disabilities is one of uncertainty, wavering and interim measures to avoid the assumption of responsibility. The Sandoz Institute report includes 'Dodging Responsibility' as a heading and outlines various reasons why each government must face up squarely to exactly what the dimensions are of its needs for long-term care provision.

Realistic Assessment of the Need

Decision makers must take care neither to underestimate what is needed to provide for an acceptable quality of care, nor to over-estimate the quantity of patients who will need to be cared for. Overestimating numbers may occur because the rate of increase of the very old has often been referred to and is indeed a large percentage figure, but it must be remembered that a 50 per cent increase may mean a change of only 10 to 15: a large percentage may be associated with small numbers!

Accompanying this is the tendency of some to associate the very large numbers of people reaching retirement age with numbers needing long-term care. But, as one of the Sandoz Institute study experts (Selby and Schechter, 1982) has stated, 'those aged 60 and over comprise two generations, a younger and generally fit group and an older group that is especially vulnerable to health impairments'. The line between the two is put at various points, but for the Sandoz Institute working group, the older group began at age 80. Table 7.2 is taken from their report, and from this we see how relatively small a portion the over-eighties are, of the over-60 population. In the US in 1980, of the total population of 223.2 million, there were 33.9 million persons over 60 (a little over 15% of the nation's total), while in the entire country there were only 4.4 million persons over 80 (just under 2% of the total population).

By no means do all people over 80 need care for disabilities. For France it was estimated that of its 1.5 million persons over 80, one quarter will be entirely autonomous (CLEIRPPA Collot *et al.*, 1982). The *Chartbook on Aging in America* (White House Conference Staff 1981, p. 81) reported that only one-third of people over 85 in the US in 1977 reported a need for help with one or more of these daily tasks: bathing, toilet, eating, dressing. An Oslo study reported by the WHO (1982) found that 54 per cent of those between 70 and 74 were able to manage without any outside help; for those between 75 and 79 the percentage was 34 per cent; for those over 80, it was 12 per cent. Notice that these percentages refer not to presence or absence of *severe* disability, but to any need for help whatever.

Data from another source regarding elderly disability in the US came from Branch (1982) who testified before the Special Committee on Aging of the US Senate about his evaluation of the program

Table 7.2: Population in millions (total, aged 60+, 70+, 80+) (1980-2000)*

	Total population			Population 60+			Population 70+			Population 80+		
	1980	2000	Increase %	1980	2000	Increase %	1980	2000	Increase %	1980	2000	Increase %
Australia	14.5	17.8	23	1.9	2.7	38.7	0.8	1.3	58.7	0.2	0.3	61.4
Brazil	122.3	187.5	53	7.5	14.0	86.7	3.0	6.0	100.0	0.7	1.6	117.1
Egypt	42.0	64.4	53	2.4	4.6	91.7	0.8	1.7	112.5	0.1	0.3	146.9
Federal Republic of Germany	60.9	58.8	-3	11.4	13.3	16.9	6.0	6.1	1.1	1.5	1.7	12.8
France	53.5	56.3	5	9.1	10.8	19.4	5.1	5.6	10.4	1.4	1.5	4.9
India	684.5	960.6	40	33.9	65.7	93.8	11.1	22.4	101.8	2.0	3.6	80.0
Israel	3.9	5.6	44	0.4	0.6	38.2	0.2	0.3	50.0	0.04	0.08	100.0
Italy	56.9	59.1	4	10.0	13.5	34.6	5.0	6.9	38.0	1.2	1.9	55.5
Japan	116.6	129.3	11	14.8	26.4	78.4	6.4	11.9	85.9	1.5	3.0	102.5
Kenya	16.5	30.4	84	0.7	1.3	85.7	0.3	0.5	66.7	0.04	0.1	150.0
Nigeria	77.1	150.0	95	3.1	6.4	106.5	1.0	2.2	120.0	0.2	0.4	155.3
Philippines	49.2	77.0	57	2.2	4.6	109.1	0.7	1.7	142.9	0.1	0.3	114.5
Poland	35.8	41.2	15	4.7	6.8	44.7	2.3	3.2	39.1	0.5	0.7	50.0
Sweden	8.3	8.1	-2	1.8	1.8	-1.8	0.9	1.0	11.1	0.2	0.3	36.9
United Kingdom	55.9	55.2	-1	11.1	11.3	1.3	5.4	6.0	11.1	1.4	1.8	28.6
USA	223.2	263.8	18	33.9	40.1	18.3	15.6	20.6	32.1	4.4	5.8	31.8
World	4,432.1	6.118.8	38	375.8	590.4	57.1	168.3	252.3	59.5	35.3	59.6	68.5

Source: Provisional projections of the United Nations Population Division, New York, 1980.
Note: *Table is from the Sandoz Institute report, page 199.

of the State of Massachusetts to provide home care services
to its 'vulnerable elders'. Five per cent of those non-institu-
tionalized elderly — over 65 — were found to be 'vulnerable'. With
the five per cent of those over 65 who are in institutions, largely
nursing homes, that study would indicate that ten per cent of persons over 65 need some degree of care for disability.

With admittedly a group slightly younger than 80 — and that is
important in just such matters as this one — the Swedish WAA
Country Report had this hopeful report:

> An extensive health survey of 70-year-olds with follow up five
> years later shows that many persons aged 70 and 75 years may
> in many respects have the same functional ability as, for
> example, the average 30-year-old. There are, of course, many
> whose functions are very much impaired. As regards many
> functions, the fact is that the older the population becomes, the
> greater the variance in functional ability. (p. 19)

Of course, the costs of running nursing homes as they are currently operated are very high, because the staff ratios for patient
care are necessarily very close to one-to-one for the very disabled
and about 1:4 for the 'lightly disabled'. Those were estimates
resulting from the staff studies of the Kuratorium in Cologne. The
fact that there are alternative ways to provide care in models which
would have lower staff costs has been explored extensively in a
previous chapter.

Robert Butler's article on 'The Economics of Aging' was
referred to in the first chapter. He referred to the frequency with
which 'big money "scare" tactics' appear with reference to older
people in the popular press and in serious literature as well. Butler
referred specifically to an article which, by adding up every possible pension scheme and benefit, had calculated and announced
that $152.7 billion was the amount 'spent on the elderly' in one
year. Butler regarded the throwing-around of these big figures as
preventing people from giving aging policy questions the careful
consideration they must have:

> Amounts like $152.7 billion may cause taxpayers to wince auto-
> matically. This kind of figure is natural ammunition for those
> who wish to argue that the elderly are getting 'enough' out of
> Uncle Sam's revenues. The amount even has been used to argue

that 'too much' is being spent on the elderly, to the detriment of other groups. An unintelligent debate will promote conflict among groups that depend on government for support because they are deprived or sick or unfortunate.

The economics of aging involve more than these dollars. The issues are more complex. They involve what we want to do for ourselves as a society through governmental and other mechanisms. Obviously, resources are limited and we want to get the most for our money. But we must guard against big money 'scare' tactics. (p. 65)

The Case for Change

Surely it is time to put an end to the wavering which makes for the hodge-podge of arrangements, none of them very satisfactory, because none is taken on with the general acceptance which governments and insurance firms have displayed in the case of acute care in hospital.

Because of the frustration arising when governments do not assume this responsibility, and yet cannot avoid it, they (we) then blame the victim. A special kind of pity and disgust is held for the poor recipient of Medicaid for nursing home care in the US and for the pensioner in the local authority home in Britain or West Germany. The Sandoz Institute Study report tells of a UK comment that 'social services administrators seem to take a punitive attitude towards applicants' (p. 86). We may describe the attitude in that instance as 'the loan officer who is about to foreclose'.

Let it be clear that the holding back of provisions for long-term care typical of nearly all countries is not consistent with the attitude expressed in many of them about the role of government in other kinds of services for the elderly. There is real dissonance with the fact that in capitalist democracies, and perhaps in every country but the few exceptions noted, long-term care is perceived, in almost unique fashion, to be beyond the limits of how far the government responsibility will reach in a generous way.

Important segments of public opinion would like to see this changed. The delegates to the United States' White House Conference on Aging in 1981 made clear calls for government to take responsibility for long-term care provision. The WHCoA Final Report gave a summary of issues contained in the 42 recommendations most favored by the delegates. 'The most frequently addressed topics in the qualitative analysis (of the delegate survey) were long-term care/home health care (7 recommendations), Social Security (6 recommendations), employment (4), rural transportation (3) and crime (3)' (p. 15).

The content of the recommendations for long-term care/home health care: 'Two types of recommendations fall in this category: those that seek to improve conditions for those in long-term care facilities (Recommendations 163-168) and those that stress deinstitutionalization from such facilities whenever possible. The latter group emphasizes expanding in-home care and stresses that families should be encouraged to take care of their elderly relatives' (p. 15).

The recommendations themselves made it clear that these improvements were to be brought about by redesigning the provisions contained in the Medicare and Medicaid programs, the national schemes covering the costs of medical care of elderly people.

A statement related to Recommendation 214-A gave a description of the continuum of care which is needed and ended with a statement of the governmental responsibility they envisioned:

That every older American should be guaranteed access to a continuum of care which enables them to function in the environment of their choosing and in the least restrictive social and physical setting that can sustain their total well-being. A full range of home health and in-home services should be developed and should be accessible to rural and urban elderly in every community. These should include, but not be limited to, mental health and social services, physical, speech, and occupational therapy, nutrition, homemaker and transportation services. The ultimate responsibility for guaranteeing access to this continuum of care should be that of the federal government. (p. 120)

The tough position toward providing care for disabled old people only when they have spent their savings and become poor can hardly be a position which governments would knowingly defend. The position is not justifiable on the basis of cost when the large amount already being spent through the means-tested programs is admitted. (The government's portion for nursing home costs for 1981 in the United States was 11.3 billion dollars).

Despite the size of current expenditure, serious planning of new models of care has not yet been undertaken. Neither is the tough position defensible from the standpoint of logic. Can any case at all be made for what the hard line with respect to care for disabled old people is supposed to accomplish? Can any case be made for paying open-handedly for expensive surgery and high technology procedures in hospital, while refusing to pay for nurses and therapists to go to the homes of patients to assist their rehabilitation and recovery of mobility and speech?

As matters now stand the future is grim for the typical older person whose disability prevents him from doing much about what he is faced with. Unless he lives in a Scandinavian country, or unless he can be cared for by his religious denomination or his lodge, or unless he is so wealthy that the cost does not matter, he must become poor — undergo the indignity of admitting to having 'fallen to this' — to receive what is necessary and available to him for survival. No wonder, then, that many countries notice that a sizeable portion of the eligible population — reportedly about 25 per cent for the elderly in a recent British study (Kerr, 1983) — do not 'take up' benefits for which they would be able to qualify.

In a period of relatively poor economic conditions, nations and their governments are not apt to make any general change toward a more open-handed policy for population groups in need. We have attempted here to raise the question as to whether nations do not wish to examine what they are doing in refusing to take responsibility for the proper care of their very elderly disabled people. However strongly citizens may believe that the governmental role in general should be small, it seems likely that experiences with their own families would convince them that here is a rather special case. Those in need of long-term care are not the persons one wants to see confronted with a tight-fisted government role. The size of the population with this need will never be overwhelmingly large. Keeler and Kane (1982) reporting on the Rand Corporation study in the US stated: 'with our national wealth, we should be able to afford decent care for those in need of long term care' (p. 95). It seems likely that most citizens in the industrialized countries would feel that it is possible and appropriate to supply what is needed in the dignified way in which a trust officer serves his or her clients. Denmark does it every day!

Government's Indirect Supporting Role

The readiness of government to involve itself with certain conditions of need is not limited to the provision of or payment for services directly to clients. There is a potential role, carried out in some countries more than others, for supporting other groups for everything from very large to very small roles in activities which are designed to meet needs of persons in those conditions of need. The largest instance must surely be the delegation to religious and other voluntary groups by the government of the FRG, as described in an earlier section. There is much development of initiatives in that situation, one of them having been the development on the part of one of the voluntary groups of the neighborhood 'social service center' which now has been put into general use.

The governments of Norway and Great Britain have given a great deal of support, from both the local and national levels, to voluntary organizations ready and willing to offer services to elderly persons. The WAA Country Report from Norway described the relationship between the pioneering role played by the non-governmental organizations and the subsequent assumption of responsibility for the new services by governmental bodies. Material from the Country Report presented in chapter 4 described the process by which this partnership has resulted in many of the services important for long-term care for Norwegians, and for involvement of elderly persons there in providing services for elderly persons.

Voluntary group initiatives supported by government have developed many of the services enabling infirm older people in Britain to go on living in their own homes. Local authorities as well as central government have supplied funds to subsidize projects of Age Concern groups at the local, regional and national levels, to name one outstanding example. This co-operation has made possible the development of a multitude of services, from transport to home-delivered meals to day centers to neighborhood wardens. It also has resulted in a large body of very valuable research into topics affecting elderly people. It was Age Concern Liverpool which supplied funding for the first of the Continuing Care studies which have provided so much documentation of the needs of elderly patients when they leave hospital. The CLEIRPPA report called attention to the value of the British example of partnership

formed by public financial support and private agency development of services:

> The principle of the multiple financing structure is especially
> attractive: it provides a means whereby the health authorities
> can make allocations to social services programmes, thus reliev-
> ing the demand on the health services. Since its introduction in
> England in 1976 and in Wales in 1977, this structure for co-
> operation has been used to finance many projects of benefit to
> the elderly.
>   The voluntary organizations work closely with the Local
> Authorities and many of them receive subsidies from the State.
> (p. 257)

The mechanism of joint funding referred to by CLEIRPPA was
explained in some detail for the 1984 Health Forum organized by
Age Concern Greater London. The leaflet containing that material
has been adapted to present it in Figure 7.1. The directions
given to local Age Concern groups make clear the opportunities
for participation by private organizations in the public decision-
making process. These opportunities are brought about by the
British joint planning-joint funding approach to service development.

Another form of the indirect supportive role of government
with respect to provision for needs of older people is its support of
research. The allocation of funds from the Department of Health
and Social Security at the central government level for a multitude
of local as well as national research projects into the needs for and
the operation of services for older people has provided a wealth of
information for use in planning and information exchange from
one part of the country to others and from one type of service to
others.

It seems extremely important to regard the readiness of government to subsidize the efforts of voluntary organizations, and of
government services operating at other levels and in other departments, as an important part of the governmental role in responsibility for providing for people in conditions of need.

The underlying spirit of a government's willingness to take substantial responsibility for providing resources for elderly needs is
an important factor in efforts which require collaboration between
and among departments. Britain has for a long time supported the

Figure 7.1: Leaflet to Inform Voluntary Groups About Joint
Funding and Joint Planning Opportunities in Britain

HEALTH
FORUM
JOINT PLANNING
of Services for Elderly People in London

WHAT IS JOINT PLANNING?

JOINT PLANNING has been established
as a policy since the 1970s. It was
initiated by central government in order
to encourage Health Services and local
Authorities to collaborate in the
provision of better community services
for such groups as mentally ill, mentally
handicapped, disabled and *elderly
people*.

JOINT FINANCE has also been introduced
as an incentive to joint planning. Under
this arrangement, funds are available to
health authorities to spend on
community projects initiated by either
health services or local authorities for
the support of the particular care groups.
Voluntary organisations can now also
apply for funding for such projects.

SPECIAL JOINT PLANNING MACHINERY
has also been established.
Representatives from various levels of
health and local authorities meet
regularly in formal working groups to
discuss plans relating to the care of
these groups. They also consider the
distribution of joint finance monies.

JOINT PLANNING can result in *improved
services* for elderly people, avoiding
duplication or patchy coverage and thus
ensuring more appropriate and
accessible facilities.

WHAT CAN AGE CONCERN GROUPS GAIN FROM JOINT PLANNING?

Recently, the concept of joint planning
has been widened to *include the
Voluntary sector*. This is in recognition of
the considerable contribution made by
Voluntary services to the care of such
groups as the elderly. Voluntary
Organisations such as Age Concern can
now participate in joint planning groups
and become more generally involved in
the joint planning process.

An opportunity to contribute ... by
participating in joint planning groups
your organisation can have an important
opportunity to see and to contribute to
plans and policies of your local health
authority and local authority concerning
services for elderly people at the *Crafting
stage*.

Understanding of Age Concern's work ...
In addition to your day to day working
contacts, you would be able to develop
new links at a policy and planning level.
In turn, Health and local Authority
planners will gain greater knowledge
and understanding about the work of
your organisation and about the
potential and limitations of services you
can provide for elderly people.

Wider consultation ... Through this
involvement in joint planning, your
organisation is more likely to be
consulted over a variety of planning
issues affecting services for elderly
people. Your group can also participate
in the formal consultation procedure
concerning draft plans.

A chance to improve services ... From
daily contact with elderly people, your
organisation can provide valuable
information to the joint planning groups
concerning health needs of elderly
people. You could also convey the views
and wishes of elderly people about the
kind of services they require in their
area.

HOW CAN JOINT FINANCE HELP?

Age Concern organisations are eligible to apply for *Joint Finance* from the Health Authority for the support of projects. This can be a vital additional source of financial support.

In order to attract such funding, projects would need to be innovative in nature, perhaps offering a service which neither the health authority nor local authority currently provides. Projects could be based on more personal or individual care by volunteers, or the support of carers or even the provision of specialist advice on health care matters to elderly people.

Finance could cover paid workers, administration and accommodation costs. Projects can be operated solely by your organisation or can be jointly managed with the health and/or local authority. However, like most other sources of funding, there is a maximum period for joint finance support.

The process for the allocation of Joint Finance is quite long and complex and is part of the joint planning cycle. Proposals pass through the various levels of joint planning groups for consideration. It is therefore to your advantage to have a representative from your Age Concern group on these joint planning groups in order to gain interest and support for your application.

A number of Age Concern groups have already successfully gained Joint Finance support for particular projects. Write to your District Administrator or Director of Social Services for further details of Joint Finance in your area.

The Health Forum was established by Age Concern Greater London in May 1983. Representatives from health and social services and voluntary organisations throughout London meet to discuss the issues concerning the health needs of elderly people in London. For further details contact the Secretary of the Health Forum, ACGL, 54 Knatchbull Road, London, SE5 9QY. Tel: 737 3456.

HOW DO WE GET INVOLVED IN JOINT PLANNING?

By *using working links*: There could be opportunities to form or join a multidisciplinary group where you can meet colleagues from both health and social services to discuss how to improve working relations or to experiment with new methods of service delivery. Or you could jointly carry out small surveys into the health needs of elderly people. The resulting information could be passed for consideration to one of the formal Joint Planning Groups.

By *participating in a CHC*: You or a member of your Age Concern group may already be a member of your local community health council. This can be an important means to gain sight of health service documents and to comment on draft plans upon which the CHC has a statutory right to be consulted.

By *formal consultation*: Age Concern groups can ask to be formally consulted by the district health authority or local authority concerning plans for services for elderly people in the area. There may be short-term operational plans or longer-term strategic plans. Planning documents can be sent to your organisation for consideration by your committee and comments sent direct to the Authority.

By *joining one of the joint planning groups*: These are arranged by your local health district. There are a variety of stages in the joint planning process at which you could participate: in Working Groups or Joint Care Planning Groups specifically on services for elderly people; and Joint Care Planning Teams; and the Joint Consultative Committee. From 1 January 1985 voluntary organisations will have the right to appoint 3 members to their local JCC.

This guideline has been produced by the ACGL Health Forum as a result of a study carried out by a Working Group on Health and Social Services Policies and Practice. Other guidelines are available from ACGL.

work of non-profit Housing Associations, where capital grants have been made for remodeling and building costs, resulting in low rents. Some of the associations have joined with a Department of Social Services in Scotland anxious to develop assisted flats. We have seen a description of those in the previous chapter, as Care Housing. Without the government support for housing associations, the provision of a new kind of long-term care in that city could not have materialized.

It is notable that whether through the voluntary organization route or the government services route, or some of both, the innovations leading to perceptions of new horizons in long-term care provision have occurred in the countries where there is, at least in some areas, the generous attitude of the welfare state. In particular, the development of necessary community services and the housing complexes providing for independent living for a wide variety of disabilities as well as for the completely fit have come from Britain, the Federal Republic of Germany and the Scandinavian countries.

The need for creativity and innovations in arrangements for long-term care is so great that it is important to recognize that this type of investment by central and local government in relatively small-scale voluntary organizations for service and research has paid off in the development of new kinds of solutions. This is especially important in the 'cut back' climate brought into every country by slower moving economies. Since the forecasts are generally for continuation of slow economic growth, countries can ill afford to be penny-wise and pound-foolish in this area of expenditure.

Reference was made above to the strong current of opinion reported from the 1981 White House Conference calling for 'opportunities to choose alternatives to nursing homes'. Part of a relevant Recommendation, Number 214, stated:

> The institutional and medical care biases in the Medicare and Medicaid programs should be modified to allow reimbursement for personal care and social long term care services in community and home-based settings. In Medicare, the housebound and skilled requirements for home health care should be eliminated and coverage of home-maker/chore services should be provided; in Medicaid, the states should utilize the new Community Care Waiver. (Final Report WHCOA, p. 119)

Stanley Brody (1979) has published his analysis of expenditures for medical and long-term care which resulted in his conclusion that the federal government expenditure in a single year was 30 billion dollars, while its expenditure for health and social services (community care) was one billion. This is the basis for the reference to the 'institutional and medical care biases' in the resolution.

Obviously, the White House Conference resolution is a call for initiatives to develop the kinds of home-delivered services and the types of housing making it possible for many people with disabilities to continue to live at home. These services are frequently available in European countries. The delegates wondered why not in the US?

It is not that the US has not spent money for elderly care. As well as the billions just mentioned the US Country Report for the WAA stated that 'During the 1970s in particular the Federal and State governments made large sums of money available through contracts with voluntary agencies for the delivery of many public services' (pp. 120-1)

It is exactly this which illustrates the importance of this layer of care: whether the government sees that its role is to take responsibility to face up to a need and do the problem solving and planning to handle the situation. Simply to spend money, while avoiding the taking of responsibility, results in no new solutions. The British and Norwegian governments and the FRG granted money to private organizations who acted in partnership with them to develop programs and use their experience to feed back into the formulation of the next steps the government would take. Their governments supported research and used the results in the same way.

To have the opportunity to choose alternatives to nursing homes spoken of in the White House Conference resolution calls for the US, and any other government, to face the problem and work with organizations interested in helping to find solutions. The European countries have shown the way.

References

Branch, L.G., (1982) in testimony to the Special Committee on Aging, US Senate. In *Long Term Health Care for the Elderly.* Government Printing Office, Washington, D.C.

162   *The Role of Government*

Brody, Stanley, (1979) The thirty-to-one paradox; Health needs and medical solutions. In *Aging: Agenda for the Eighties*, pp. 17-20. The Government Research Corporation, Washington, D.C.

Butler, Robert, (1978) 'The economics of aging: We are asking the wrong questions'. In *The Economics of Aging*, a National Journal Issues Book. Government Research Corporation, Washington, D.C.

Collot, C., Jani-Le Bris, H. and Ridoux, A., for CLEIRPPA, (1982) *Towards an Improvement in Self Reliance for the Elderly: Innovations and New Guidelines for the Future.* The Commission of the European Communities, Brussels

Country Reports for the World Assembly on Aging (1982)
— Aging in Norway: *Humanitarian and Developmental Issues.* Royal Norwegian Ministry of Health and Social Affairs, Oslo
— *Just Another Age: A Swedish Report to the WAA.* The National Commission on Aging, Stockholm
— *Report on the Situation of the Elderly in the Federal Republic of Germany.* The German Center of Gerontology, Berlin
— *US National Report on Aging for the United Nations and the World Assembly on Aging.* Department of State, Washington, D.C.

Dieck, Margaret, (1981) *Social and Medical Aspects of the Situation of Older People in the Federal Republic of Germany.* The German Center of Gerontology, Berlin

Flamm, Franz, (1974) *Social Welfare Services and Social Work in the Federal Republic of Germany.* Deutscher Vereins für Öffentliche und Private Fürsorge, Frankfurt

Health Forum, (1984) *Joint Planning.* Age Concern Greater London, London

Frankfurter Allgemeine (1984) 'Hessen's Draft Law for Nursing Care Insurance' May 12, 1984, Nr III/Seite 3

Keeler, E. and Kane, R., (1982) 'What is so special about long-term care?' In Kane, R. and Kane, R. (eds.) *Values and Long Term Care.* Lexington Books, Lexington, Mass

Kerr, Scott, (1983) *Making Ends Meet.* Bedford Square Press, London

Phillipson, Chris, (1982) *Capitalism and the Construction of Old Age.* Macmillan, London

Rückert, W., (1980) *Organizing Nursing Services in Nursing Homes.* Schriftenreihe der Bundesministerium fur Jugend, Familie und Gesundheit, Bonn

Selby, P. and Schechter, M., (1982) *Aging 2000 — A Challenge for Society.* MTP, Lancaster, England, (Published for the Sandoz Institute for Health and Socio-economic Studies.) Referred to herein as 'the Sandoz Institute study'

Skeet, Muriel, (1983) *Protecting the Health of the Elderly.* World Health Organization, Regional Office for Europe, Copenhagen

Speck, Jean-Erik, (1980) 'Why is the system so costly?' In Heidenheimer, A.J. and Elvander, N. (eds.) *The Shaping of the Swedish Health System.* Croom Helm, London

White House Conference Staff (1981) *Chartbook on Aging.* The WHCoA Staff, Washington, D.C.

White House Conference Staff, (1982) *Final Report: The White House Conference on Aging, 1981.* The WHCoA Staff, Washington, D.C.

World Health Organization, Regional Office for Europe, (1982), *Epidemiological Studies on Social and Medical Conditions of the Elderly.* EURO Reports and Studies 62. WHO Regional Office for Europe, Copenhagen

8 THE LAYER OF HUMAN RIGHTS

Underneath the layer representing beliefs about the role of the government, we have postulated another layer representing the rights of the individual against being shaken up or overwhelmed by the greater power of the government, and certain protections of individual human dignity. If there ever were a place where the importance of this level can be seen, it is in long-term care arrangements. This is due to the particular combination involved. On the one hand, societies seem to perceive that the arrangements necessary for long-term care cause them great expense and trouble, especially when the population-wide needs for these are growing fast. On the other hand is the utter helplessness and vulnerability of the individual who stands in need of the care. Indeed, long-term care represents the epitomy of the tension between 'troubles the state has with provisions for the elderly' and the 'troubles of the older person with what is provided by the state'.

Violations and Protection of Human Rights in Long-term Care

The condition of this layer in the long-term care area is revealed by various facts and comments in the Sandoz Institute report (Selby and Schechter, 1982). Some UK practices were described as 'inducing patients to be passive and submissive, and of little effort to draw patients and families into the process of making decisions about care' (p.93). And, 'The UK experts urge that the elderly be drawn into consultative and decision-making processes affecting health and social services' (p. 96).

About Sweden, this was stated: 'The Swedish systems of care are searching for better forms of co-operation among patients, families and professionals. For example, the potential and limits of geriatrics are explained (and) patients and families are encouraged to participate in decision-making about therapy' (p. 95).

The absence of specifications for obtaining 'informed consent' for admission to an institution and for therapeutic procedures is felt to indicate that this right frequently is neglected by those in the care-giving system. Such neglect and omission have been called into question in the US by health lawyers who have pointed out the poor situation of the older patient to challenge professionals who have determined 'what is best for her' and have experience in making a convincing case to the patient and family in such situations.

An article by Copp (1981) dealt with the special situation for elderly patients with respect to their right to be adequately informed before giving consent. Copp was writing about this in relation to research in nursing and other fields of health. She formulated questions which are appropriate for professionals to keep in mind in order to inform elderly people adequately, when the matter at hand is their participation in a research project. When the decision called for is for a certain type of surgery, or a change of residence from their own home to residential care, the effects are far more lasting than anything likely to result from participation in a single research project. The questions which Copp proposed are, therefore, even more important. They are as follows:

*Questions to be answered regarding reformed consent
procedures with aged patients or clients*

Can he read the informed consent?   Many of the elderly cannot do so because of lack of education or because they do not speak the prevailing language fluently.

Can he see to read the informed consent?   Many of the elderly cannot find, do not wear, and deny having spectacles. Holding the instructions in his hand, he may not be able to see to read them and may not confess the problem or ask for help.

Can he hear the instructions and terms of the informed consent?   Covering up hearing deficits is a precise art for some older persons. They smile, agree, nod appropriately, and fill the silences with appropriate responses. But they do not understand their rights as a research subject because they are not, in fact, hearing them.

Can he understand the instructions given by the informant?   Jargon, technical terms, and scientific concepts which subjects cannot comprehend have no place in consent documents. The onus is on the researcher to be clear and to provide reasonable assurance that the subjects understands, through careful choice of words and definitions of terms.

Can he ask questions? Aphasia, communication blocks, and cognitive impairment may erode mental alertness of the patient's ability to communicate. The loss of previously effective communication tools frustrates and depresses him. An unhurried atmosphere where questions are welcomed is essential. Patients often require composure time.

Can the informant answer his questions appropriately? Informers may be forced to communicate through writing or a third person, an intermediary who brings the consent form to the potential subject. What understandings and authority does the interpreter of the form have? What effect does he have on the subject and those involved in research or in patient care? (pp. 194-6)

It is significant that it was the section on long-term care options in the report of the White House Conference on Aging of 1981 which included this recommendation:

Congress should provide support to the National Judicial College or similar institutions to train judges as to the special legal needs of older persons so that judges would be sensitive to those needs and would influence lawyers and other court officers to keep the court system available and protective of the rights of older persons both within the community and within institutions. (WHCOA, p. 121)

Actual provision for invasion of human rights of elderly people is contained in a British statute. The book *Rights and Risk* (Norman, 1980) points to a section of the National Assistance Bill, passed in 1948, giving power for the compulsory removal of infirm old men and women from their homes. This violation of a fundamental liberty is described by Alison Norman who observes that 'It is a further indication of how lightly elderly people's civil rights are regarded that no national statistics are kept concerning the use of (that) Section 47' (pp. 30-1). Norman points out the regularity with which rights of choice are overriden in the operation of residential homes with respect to meal times, food to eat, keeping their own pension books, being able to lock the doors of their rooms, and even staff present at bathing time! She quotes the Residential Care Association as having said, 'Far too often the attitude remains that when old people come into care they become subject to the system and needs of the staff which involves a massive loss of personal dignity and individual freedom' (p. 40).

The human rights issues involved in the passive patient role often imposed upon elderly people in hospitals and nursing homes were considered carefully by Norman (1980). She described several instances of the use of restraints requiring absolute patient passivity: cotsides (rails) put up along bedsides, chairs with straps for confining patients, locking doors of patient rooms at night. She linked the tendency to use these with what she called the 'safety first policy'. She finds that hospital practices and nurse behavior are based on protection from possible harm, and thus the restraints are employed to prevent falls, the doors or gates locked to prevent 'wandering'.

There is the practical reason, that the institution or health professional want to avoid being sued, or reprimanded by authorities, if harm should befall an elderly patient. Norman described this situation in the following paragraphs:

The whole ethos of nursing care is directed towards protection from harm, and accidents are therefore felt to be a disgrace, especially if they occur in a ward which is not geared to a programme of planned, active rehabilitation where a degree of risk may be accepted. All accidents have to be reported to the senior nurse and an accident form completed in triplicate. If the accident proves fatal, there will be a coroner's inquest and this is especially dreaded. This may not be realistic so far as the actual role of the coroner is concerned ... but it is certainly true that a fatal accident to an elderly person in hospital is likely to produce adverse publicity in the local press and will not promote the career of the nurse in charge at the time. It requires a really positive approach from the consultant and the hospital administrator (who may fear claims from relatives) to militate against a 'safety first' policy.

The consequence is that confused and unsteady patients may be literally imprisoned by the use of cotsides and 'geriatric chairs' and in some cases be physically tied down. (pp. 56-7)

A further point, however, is that restraining devices sometimes themselves bring about physical harm, not to mention the psychological damage they do. When this is the case, rights are violated in the name of lowering a risk, by a procedure which actually increases the risk.

The routine use of cotsides is now widely disapproved of by geriatricians as increasing the danger to restless, confused, or independent-minded patients who will try to climb over them. This opinion is reinforced by the findings of a study of hospital accidents with special reference to old people carried out in a group of Scottish hospitals. This reported:

> Fourteen out of the 43 falls out of bed occurred when cotsides were in place and in all of these, the patient was suffering from restless confusion. Few could question the need for cotsides for ill patients and those recovering from an anaesthetic, who are in danger of rolling out of bed, but their use in restless, confused patients is more debatable. They are easily climbed over and around and the distance fallen may then be greater than it would otherwise have been. To the confused patient, the feeling of being caged in may be an added encouragement to 'escape'. Both Davidson (1975) and Isaacs (1965) have condemned their use in this type of patient. Restlessness in a confused patient is, in any case, a symptom requiring investigation, not restraint, pain, the desire to micturate or defecate, anoxia and the toxic effect of drugs being frequent causes. Perhaps one valid argument in favour of cotsides is that their rattling at night is an effective alarm system where, as frequently happens, only one nurse is looking after a ward.

Nevertheless, many nurses feel safer when they are up and will replace them when they get a chance.

The kind of chair which keeps a patient immobilised, either by making it too low for him to get out of unaided, or by penning him in by placing a fixed tray across his lap, or by tilting him back at an angle, is equally deplored by the experts and in equally common use — even to the point of being advertised in the journal of the British Geriatric Society *Age and Ageing*.

(The writer knew personally one elderly woman who was imprisoned in such a chair for three years and who cried with frustration about it each time she was visited. True, she might have fallen if she had tried to stand and walk unaided though she could do so when she entered the hospital. But would this really have been a worse fate?) (pp. 57-8)

Norman's concern with the British statutory provision for moving a person from his or her home has been noted earlier in this chapter. She considers that this is both a serious and a fairly frequent occurence, and as a basis for questioning the policy, presents the account given by a psychiatrist, Dr Baker (1976), in the following excerpt from her book:

The risks of choosing the 'safest' solution for mentally frail old people are vividly illustrated in an article by Dr. A.A. Baker in which he describes a scene which, as he says, must be familiar to many doctors, social workers and members of the public:

... an old lady lives alone, with a neglected garden and dilapidated house. She has gradually lost her contacts with the outside world, and the circle of friends and neighbours who had helped her with shopping and visits has diminished as she has become increasingly dirty and neglected. She has discouraged home help and meals on wheels services and is now living in squalor and is perhaps incontinent. Her memory is failing and general health becoming frail. She may already be known to the police because of her wandering from the house, and neighbours and others have begun to put pressure on the medical and social services to have her removed. An incident such as a fall in the house, a fire, or another episode of wandering or fear of hypothermia has brought the firm request that she should be admitted to hospital. Admission is arranged, sometimes by simple persuasion of a muddled old lady and sometimes by use of section 25 of the Mental Health Act, or other legal framework. Most of those concerned feel a sense of relief and say to themselves that she will be better off in hospital. There, it is usually argued, she will be safer and have a longer life, a better quality of life, and better medical and nursing care. The facts, however, are not so comforting.

Baker goes on to say that in his psychiatric hospital it had been found that 25 % of patients of this kind died within three weeks of admission, although some of them were physically healthy when admitted. The cause of death is usually a terminal bronchopneumonia, and the pattern of events is often similar:

> The patient is admitted, bathed, redressed, and within twenty-four hours may be hardly recognisable as the same person as the dirty tattered, old woman crouched at home by her fire. On the other hand, the old woman crouched by the fire often had a good deal to say for herself, showed both individuality and determination, and could be self-assertive. In hospital, however, the same old woman may appear bewildered, restless, look around in perplexity and seem unable to express any need other than, perhaps, the desire to get home. The initial restlessness, often with wandering around the ward and looking in vain for familiar places or people, will give way to apathy and dejection. This may happen spontaneously, but it may also be induced by medication. In the phase of apathy, appetite is often diminished, incontinence develops, and physical frailty with falls becomes more obvious. At some point, perhaps after a fall, or because the change in the patient's appearance causes concern, she is put to bed, within a day or two develops chest symptoms, and dies a day or two later. (pp. 10-11)

Norman's investigations of 'Rights and Risk' for the elderly led her to raise several questions which arise in connection with the sacrifice of old people's freedom in the name of their safety or health:

> How far should old people be allowed to live in squalor if they refuse help? What level of danger or inconvenience to neighbours outweighs an individual's right to remain in his own home? What use should be made of compulsion under the Mental Health Act or the National Assistance Act? How does one balance the risks of institutionalisation against the risks of remaining independent? How can institutional care preserve the identity of those being cared for? How can the care of the dying be improved. How can the legal and social rights of mentally disabled old people be protected? (p. 13)

In a personal communication Norman has made an additional point. It has to do with authorities' misuse of statutory powers for removal of people from their homes to institutions, for their own reasons rather than the client characteristics:

> ... Section 47 National Assistance Act (should be used) in deliberate cases of denial of help or self neglect by people who are fully responsible for their actions. The Mental Health Act should be used for people who are at serious risk to themselves or others by reason of mental illness or mental handicap. All too often the Mental Health Act is in fact used (in cases where) Section 47 is the only legal means of compelling admission.

Having said all that, it is important to state that on an individual basis there are instances of exemplary protection to be found in Britain. Some homes for older people have gone to great lengths to promote practices designed to protect the rights of those who live there. Norman has presented the following example of such good practice from one local authority in the form of a declaration of Residents' Rights:

East Sussex County Council
Social Services
BRIGHTON DIVISION

Residents Rights

What you have a right to expect if you live in one of the County Council's homes for elderly people.

I.   Basic rights of residents

1. The main concern of our homes will be the quality of life of their residents.
2. Residents have the right to personal independence, personal choice, and personal responsibility for their own actions.
3. Residents have the right to care for themselves as far as they are physically and mentally able, and willing, to do so.
4. Residents have the right to have their personal dignity respected by others in every way possible, and to be treated, whatever their disabilities or frailties, as individuals in their own right.
5. Residents have the right to personal privacy, for themselves their belongings and their affairs.
6. Residents have the right to take a full part in decisions about daily living arrangements, to be consulted about any changes which may be pro-

posed, and to have a genuine say in social services policies.

7. Residents have the right to the same access to facilities and services in the surrounding community as any other citizen, including registration with the medical practitioner and dentist of their choice.

8. Residents have the right to be given every opportunity of mixing with other people in the community, whether by going out or by inviting other people in.

9. Residents have the right to have their cultural, religious, sexual and emotional needs accepted and respected as well as the whole range of other commonly accepted needs.

10. Residents have the right to expect management and staff to accept the degree of risk that is involved in these principles, and not to have their personal independence unnecessarily or unreasonably restricted for fear of such risk.

(p. 46)

An entirely new development is the code of practice for residential care described in *Home Life*, a publication of the Centre for Policy on Ageing (1984):

Home life: a code of practice for residential care was drawn up by a Working Party sponsored by the Department of Health and Social Security, convened by the Centre for Policy on Ageing, and chaired by Kina, Lady Avebury.

The code is applicable to privately-run homes, and to those provided by voluntary and charitable agencies. *Home life* is an attempt to define 'good practice' in residential care so as to provide guidelines for all those who provide care in homes. It is intended to promote the highest standards of care and quality of life for the many people for whom 'home' is 'a home'. *Home life* takes as its starting point the *rights* of residents — their right to live with dignity, to live a full and normal life, and to have the respect of those who care for them. The section on 'social care' makes recommendations on admission procedures, terms and conditions of residence, general administration — covering, for instance, keeping records, complaints procedures, rules, and resident involvement in decision-making — privacy and personal autonomy, residents' financial affairs and health care.

The questions raised in this chapter suggest the importance of watching over the manner in which this new code is observed and enforced.

It says something about the position of the elderly in American society, that violations occur even despite the constitutional guarantees for citizens in such well known provisions as the Bill of Rights and the requirement for due process. In fact, these are added to by a special Patient's Bill of Rights for nursing homes, a list something like the British statement, which is handed to patients on entrance and posted prominently in the home. Most states have a requirement for this protective measure. Yet, the elderly person in institutional care must receive inadequate help from these formalities. For the Final Report of the White House Conference on Aging (1982) contained the following recommendation, one of the three recommendations receiving most delegate support of those submitted by the Committee on Options for Long-term Care. It was reported along with staff and delegate comments:

Recommendation No. 168 Committee 6 Synopsis

Rights of older persons in need of long-term care must be protected. Such rights include the right to independence, civil and constitutional rights and freedom of choice. To protect those principles and rights the following must be integral parts of any long-term care program: (1) legislation of comprehensive bill of rights including civil and criminal penalties for those in violation; (2) improved access to the community for older persons; (3) development of mechanisms to promote dignity, foster human development, and ensure quality care; (4) legislation to provide advocacy services to protect rights of LTC patients; and (5) legislation requiring service providers to offer care and services on a non-discriminatory basis, without regard to source of payment.

Scores

Total number of responses: 445   Net score: 332
Favorable   358
Neutral   8
Unfavorable   26
Unclassified   53

Staff Summary

(70 responses analyzed). Contending that long-term care (LTC) patients are often exploited, most respondents felt that this is a needed recommendation. The delegates argued that

these patients are unable to protect their own rights and need the government's help in this regard. Those disagreeing felt that this recommendation was marked by unnecessary mandates and excessive regulation.

Excerpts from Responses by Delegates

Pro. 'Implementation of this would improve conditions in many nursing homes.' 'In practice, civil rights are non-existent in a great many nursing homes throughout the country. One of the best solutions to this problem is to step up Home Care on a very large scale.' 'Since some of these people cannot protect themselves they need laws that will do this for them.' 'The rights of long-term care patients should be protected. They should be given the most dignified care and encouragement to be dismissed into a less restrictive society, at the earliest possible time. If they cannot be released from the long-term care facility, they should be in a setting where they are cared for as individuals, with all the rights accorded American citizens.' 'This is especially well-presented and pertinent.' 'Agree — especially with #4.' 'A good statement of the right to a long-term continuum of care.'

Miscellaneous. 'Long-term care should be studied carefully.' 'Family members should be encouraged to assist in support of care for loved ones.' 'I favor the intent of this, but not a "mandate."'

Con. 'Most of these are already in place. This would be impossible to police.' 'I object strenuously with the implementation of civil and criminal penalties as it will unnecessarily criminalize the providing of long-term care when present regulations provide sufficient and adequate protection for patients in long-term care facilities. I object also to the establishment of receiverships and private right of action as it will unnecessarily boggle the system into litigation — to the detriment of the providers and the patients.' 'The majority of those older citizens in nursing homes are there because they can no longer live alone. I am opposed to these patients leaving the nursing home alone.'

The fact that violations of human rights occur despite clear legal protections indicates a failure of enforcement in the case of elderly patients. The similarity is evident between this and the failure to include long-term care costs in the coverage by health insurance. In both cases the population affected is almost entirely made up of very old, very infirm patients. Norman recognized the underlying difficulty, in this statement:

> Careful and detailed attention to necessary reforms will do little to alter the way in which old people are treated unless we can also do something to change the way in which society stereotypes its older members as 'old dears,' OAPs' or 'geriatrics' and then uses the stereotype to treat them with patronage, infantilisation, or barely concealed contempt. (p. 89)

A protective measure with potential for a very long reach is contained in the German picture. There was previous reference made to Flamm's book (1974) citing the opening sentence of the FRG Basic Law: 'The dignity of man shall be inviolable. To respect and protect it shall be the bounden duty of the State authority' (Flamm, 1974, p. 9). The very next section of the Basic Law deals with the right to a free unfolding of personality, and that the very principle of the social state is intertwined with enabling this development to occur. The German law goes on to identify the 'Special Circumstances of Life' (which might be called risk factors) for which assistance of various forms must be made available, to protect dignity and to enable the personality to develop. Being an aged person is such a 'Special Circumstance of Life'. From this come the provision of supplements to pensions, building dwellings adapted to the needs of the elderly, providing home help, home nursing, social centers and advisory centers. All this, and education as well.

These statements — 'that the bounden duty of State authority' is to respect and protect human dignity, and that 'the very principle of the social state' is intertwined with enabling the unfolding of each human personality to occur — would seem to give protection and to demand affirmative action to correct sins of commission and omission against the dignity and free functioning of personality of the elderly. Such 'sins' do in fact occur and supposedly are just as common in the old age and nursing homes of the FRG as they are in the British situations cited by Norman and in France, the US and, indeed, in most other countries. The extent to which any protection takes place depends, again, upon the prevailing perception of the role of government with respect to elderly needs, since implementation of the tenets of the Basic Law depends upon action by the federal parliament and by the government of each Land (state).

People familiar with the possibility for individual recourse through the courts on the basis of the protective measures of the US Constitution through the Bill of Rights and the due process provision, must realize that in German society, the function of the Basic Law is interpreted differently. The provisions of the Basic Law are to provide direction for legislation enacted by either federal or state governments. So far as has been determined in this investigation of provisions for elderly care, individuals have not claimed redress, for instance, when such violations of dignity have occurred in nursing homes as have been reported by the Senioren-Schutz-Bundes, the SSB 'Graue Panther'. Rather, that organization's response is essentially one of attempting to promote legislative action through their own demonstrations and by an agreement with one of the political parties, the 'Greens'. This means that correction of a situation violating, let us say, the right to privacy, depends upon the willingness of the government in power to take action to change an existing standard. The right to privacy might surely be judged to be violated with the present standard allowing 6 persons per room in old people's homes, as reported by the SSB (who had worked to have this brought down from the previous 8-per-room). Changing the standard to a more acceptable number per room would, of course, call for great increases in money for buildings and staff, and this would only be done in today's economy by a government with a very large commitment indeed to providing for elderly people's needs in the 'trust officer' manner. Thus, the violation of rights continues — protection is postponed.

The strongest 'declaration of independence' brought to bear on the condition of the elderly was encountered in the description of the policies of Denmark in the CLEIRPPA report. The traditional high regard for the right to privacy dictated that geriatric patients should not be kept in hospital beyond a brief assessment period, but be moved quickly to one of the nursing homes, publicly financed in Denmark. There, they can have their own room furnished with their own possessions. As to housing, we are told that 'the key considerations are self-determination, independence and equality for the elderly. This means that they must have access to the housing of their choice offering conditions in which they are able to look after themselves, preferably without need for outside help' (p. 215).

The *Plan of Action* of the World Assembly on Aging (1982) spoke of the human rights of the elderly in its paragraph 56 and Recommendations 8 and 9:

> 56. All too often, old age is an age of no consent. Decisions affecting aging citizens are frequently made without the participation of the citizens themselves. This applied particularly to those who are very old, frail or disabled. Such people should be served by flexible systems of care that give them a choice as to the type of amenities and the kind of care they receive.

> *Recommendation 8*
> The control of the lives of the aging should not be left solely to health, social service and other caring personnel, since aging people themselves usually know best what is needed and how it should be carried out.

> *Recommendation 9*
> Participation of the aged in the development of health care and the functioning of health services should be encouraged.

It is clear that long-term care provisions as they now exist in most countries call for careful attention to the extent to which the rights of the elderly are endangered if not actually violated. Not only are there needs for protective measures, but often for affirmative action measures to overcome the effects of practices through which their rights have been compromised for long periods of time.

Protection of rights is likely to be especially necessary in the case of the minority members of any society: blacks and Hispanics in the US, Asians and West Indians in the UK and Turks and Yugoslavs in the FRG, to name some specific cases existing today in large numbers. The position of anyone whose minority status is compounded by being in the less favored position by age, economic status and gender is vulnerable indeed.

People who came some years ago to a new country and raised their families there are likely to be especially isolated when they reach old age. The children will frequently have left the original culture behind and this affects negatively the companionship and care the elderly person might otherwise receive from their families. Compounding other difficulties is the problem of understanding the system of retirement and pension rights (if any exist), the health care system and any special services or entitlements which may exist for older citizens. Elderly people having problems themselves with this system can perhaps understand better than anyone else the situation of those who have the extra difficulty of differences in language and cultural background.

Attention has recently been given to the position of elderly people of minority groups by aging organizations and gerontologists in the FRG, the UK and the USA, but obviously much effort will be needed to protect their human rights, above all when they are in need of long-term care.

Recommendation 213 and its Implementation, as reported in the USA's WHCoA Final Report (1982, p. 118) outlined the several factors needing careful attention for the special case of aged people of minority groups:

Recommendation Number 213:

Due to the significance of cultural factors and of ethnic identity in the maintenance of physical and mental health of the aged and consequently in the care of the aged in general, and especially in the care of most of the Euro-American, families are still largely tradition bound and retain the nearly exclusive responsibility for their elderly requiring long-term care.

It is proposed that the cultural factors and ethnic identity be recognized as a source of support for the elderly requiring long-term care. And that these elderly be given the opportunity to live out their lives in accordance wth their traditional values within their families and that special incentives should be made to ethnic families as to all families taking care of their impaired elderly in the form of: tax deductions or credits, income implements or constant attendance allowance, respite or relief services, adult day care, and improved Medicare and Medicaid benefits for in-home care and families.

Implementation.   There should be general recognition of the significance of cultural factors and ethnic dentity in the care of the elderly in general and especially in the care of elderly requiring long-term care, on all levels of government — federal, state, local.

Americans who identify themselves as members of distinct
ethnic American groups should be fairly represented in federal,
state and local government programs for the elderly as advisors,
administrators, staff.

Any outreach programs aimed at the older population particularly with regard to various major public social programs,
must have appropriate and effective ways of reaching and
informing the older Euro-American population.

All governmental and private agencies concerned with long-
term care for the aged should be sensitized to be able to provide
'culturally relevant services', that means services tuned in to the
culturally defined ways and needs of ethnic groups.

The Sandoz Institute report included a framework for formulating policies and programs on aging outlined by Leo A. Kaprio,
regional director of the World Health Organization's Regional
Office for Europe in Copenhagen. The framework included three
General Principles and ten Specific Principles. There could not be
a more adequate guarantee of the good condition of this layer of
care in any country than to insure that these principles were
observed. This would include not only the services the country
provides, but also the behavior of those who care for the very old
people in their population. So many of the principles flow from the
theme of protection of human rights that Dr Kaprio's WHO,
statement is reproduced in its entirety.

Three general principles and ten specific principles are proposed, as a framework for formulating policies and programs on
aging within overall national plans.

General principles

To establish health and social policies on aging, the key issues
must be brought into the political arena. The following general
principles are directed at political decision makers.

1. Policies for people.　Health and development policies
express the political will of governments to do something for
people, with people. Aging policies reflect the commitment of
governments to maintain the elderly within society in a state
that gives dignity both to elderly individuals and to the community.

2. Triumph of survival. It would be a perversity to consider the results of our increasing success in improving human survival, and in regulating fertility, as problems. Rather, wise and far-sighted statesmen should try to foresee what these twin triumphs of 20th century civilization imply for life on our planet, now and in the year 2000. We are entering an age of aging. The effect of this on societies should be viewed positively, as a triumph and not as a problem.

3. Advancing our humanity. A principle underlying all social policies should be that the whole of mankind is devalued when any group of human beings is devalued on grounds of race, religion, sex, or age. A general consensus on this principle has been established among nations over the past three decades. The sustained international effort to advance humanity passes a further historic milepost with the United Nations World Assembly on Aging. This gathering may mark the beginning of the end of age discrimination in human society.

Specific principles

1. Sharing the benefits of societal development. All human rights and privileges should extend to the elderly. Many elderly people, by virtue of a lifetime characterized by war, struggle, and hardship, have a special claim to a fair share of the benefits flowing from the development of our societies. Beyond material needs, the elderly require at least as much social interaction, emotional support, and care as the rest of society. ...

The well-being of people in old age is determined by the conditions of life during their working years. Inequalities during this earlier phase of life are perpetuated and even aggravated with aging. Thus, policies for the elderly should not be formulated without reference to the needs of other age groups in the same society. In particular, resources must be allocated preferentially to the most economically deprived people, whatever their age. The coming generation of elderly people will benefit from continuing efforts to reduce health inequalities and to achieve 'health for all by the year 2000'.

2. Individuality of elderly persons. The population described as elderly is not a homogeneous group. Indeed, the variation in individual capacities increases with age. From the health perspective, those aged 60 and over comprise two generations — a younger and generally fit group, and an older group that is especially vulnerable to health impairments.

3. Independence.   The keystone of policies on aging is the commitment of all sectors of government, of non-governmental organizations, of the caring professions, and of individuals to programs aimed at the promotion of health and the maintenance of function during aging. Impaired health, aggravated by social and economic disadvantages, diminishes the activity of elderly people, reduces their independence, incapacitates them, and affects the quality of their life.

4. Choice.   All too often, the Third Age is the 'age of no consent'. Decisions affecting elderly citizens are frequently made without their participation. This applies particularly to those who are very old, frail, or disabled. Such people should be served by flexible systems of care that give them a choice of types of amenities and care. In particular, the elderly should not cede control of their own lives to health, social-service, and other caring personnel, since they themselves usually know best what is needed and how it should be carried out.

5. Home Care.   In 1978, WHO member states adopted a policy, expressed in the Declaration of Alma-Ata, of providing primary health care. This is defined as essential health care which is based on practical, scientifically sound, and socially acceptable methods, and which is universally accessible to individuals and families in the community through their full participation. From this policy there stems an unequivocal commitment to supporting and caring for persons of advanced age within their own homes.

Developing countries will be unable to afford the costs of institutional care. They should therefore establish policies of community-based care for the elderly. Home care is the best economic option, and also provides more emotional satisfaction.

Contrary to widespread belief, a considerable proportion of mental disorders in old age are either treatable, partly preventable, or modifiable by means that require neither specialized nor institutional care.

Services should not generate dependence, and paternalistic practices which erode independence should be discarded. An explicit objective of health policies should be to help elderly persons maintain the maximum degree of independent life in the face of increasing difficulty in performing daily activities.

The principle of promoting and maintaining independence applies also to housing, transportation, and social and family-welfare policies.

6. Accessibility. Public services should be accessible to all generations. In addition to health services, leisure, recreational, and educational facilities need to be progressively adapted to cater for all generations, not only for younger people. The early development of leisure, recreational, and educational activities that help people to prepare for retirement is of particular importance.

7. Engaging the elderly. Policies should aim to promote cohesion between the generations. The application of this principle to the area of health means that elderly individuals, their families, and neighbors would share responsibility for adopting health measures aimed at improving the health and well-being of the community as a whole. Another consequence for health programs might be that the elderly would help young or disabled people, as in the 'adopted grandparent' projects of some countries.

Housing policies aimed at re-uniting the generations would help to create better-balanced communities blending different age groups.

8. Mobility. The elderly, particularly in rural areas, are often unable to use public amenities and services because of impaired mobility. A first priority for informal good neighborliness, or for lay and religious volunteer activity, should be to assist elderly citizens to achieve sufficient mobility to enable them to attend local markets, shopping areas, community centers, religious services, and primary health care facilities.

Elderly people who need help to keep themselves mobile would benefit from the advice of caring personnel who are trained to assess functional capacity and to offer guidance on adaptations and aids to daily living.

9. Productivity.   The great majority of elderly people today do not show symptoms of decline in their mental and physical function, but rather enjoy a level of health that permits them to lead a socially and economically productive life. In the developed world, an increasing number of people of all ages are committed to healthier eating habits and life-styles, and to the maintenance of physical fitness, mental alertness, and a stimulating social environment. These future cohorts, of people who retain their health but retire from the work force, represent a vast resource of skilled and experienced people — one which no society can afford to leave untapped. More flexibility is required in the distribution of work over the life-span, while education needs to be viewed as a continuous, life-long process.

Public and private employers, trade unions, educational bodies, voluntary agencies, and elderly self-help groups should organize programs to provide the stimulus and motivation to develop a purposeful life after retirement.

10. Self-care and care by the family.   Elderly people, together with their families, should be more involved in their own care. Information is required on the promotion of health and the prevention of disease, as are simple handbooks of personal care. Knowledge of locally available services and social support systems is also important, and will assist elderly people and their families in seeking health care. Too often the elderly fail to seek care, in the belief that ailments are part of the aging process.

Public authorities should identify and support people who are caring for frail, elderly relatives at home, since this often imposes heavy physical, emotional, and financial demands.

New orientations are required on the part of care providers — to help elderly people maintain independence, to promote self-care, and to prevent disability. Such support to the elderly requires practitioners who are knowledgeable about aging, who are interested in elderly people and their families, who are skilled in working with them, and who are concerned about the quality of care given. (The Sandoz Institute Study, pp. 187-91)

Activist Organizations Of and For Elderly People

The need for organizations of elderly people able and ready to act in matters affecting them is closely related to the protection of their human rights. It is no mere coincidence that Denmark, a country cited above for having strong protection of the human rights of elderly people, has paid close attention to elderly organization. The Danish EGV has been described in the following paragraph from the CLEIRPPA report:

> The broad lines of Danish policy are reflected in the activities of the EGV, a non-profit organization which acts as a spokesman for the elderly. With the support of EGV's 3000 paid staff, its 1000 volunteers and its substantial budget, elderly people participate in the management of clubs, recreational centers, housing schemes and homes; EGV also carries out research programs. The EGV believes that elderly people must be given an opportunity to express their wishes, to play the fullest possible part in decisions affecting their interests and to organize their own lives as far as possible. With these ends in view, the EGV has set up a structure for self-determination by way of elections; the association stresses the importance of creating greater awareness of the elderly in a society which is creating more and more social and legal obstacles to their full participation in active life and political affairs. (pp. 214-15)

Not only the EGV in Denmark, but existing organizations in other countries of and by the elderly as well as for the elderly are important with respect to the maintenance of their rights and their dignity.

Norway has given close attention to the role of elderly organizations with special concern for their promoting the integration of elderly people with the whole society. In the Norwegian Country Report for the WAA, they gave the following argument for active participation by elderly people:

> More energetic action seems necessary in the time to come in order to promote a higher degree of integration of elderly people in society. The importance of their active participation can be regarded from two angles: From a *humanitarian* point of view self-realization through meaningful activity in adequate surroundings is essential for the well-being of the individual. From a *developmental* point of view the resources of the elderly should be utilized — in co-operation with the elderly themselves

— to the benefit of society as a whole.

The participation of old people is essential on different levels: On the individual level, it is important that each person has opportunities to self-determination and influence over one's own situation. On the local level, it is important that the role and function of the elderly, in the family situation and in the local surroundings, is active and meaningful. It seems that the community has been too engaged in questions concerning the local support given to the elderly, and to a very little extent looked into the existing support given and received by old persons in their immediate surroundings, e.g. in the family. On the administrative and political level, it is essential that old people have the same rights and possibilities of participation and influence as younger generations. (p. 57)

The Norwegian Country Report also listed some ways by which elderly interests are represented in decision-making in that country:

— The National Council for the Care of the Aged ... in which the pensioners have a strong representation, acts as an advisory body for Government offices, regional and local authorities and voluntary agencies in matters concerning the care of the aged.
— As part of the State budgetary process, the National Association of Pensioners (together with the organizations of the handicapped) have got a formalized right to carry out consultations with the Government concerning the economic transfers to the aged and the handicapped. These negotiations include both the size of the total economic transfers and the breakdown as to how much should be used on pensions, how much on subsidies, and how much on provision of different kinds of services.
— The Ministry of Health and Social Affairs has launched a project aimed at discovering and changing regulations in the legislation that are discriminating to old people and represent obstacles to their participation. Examples of such regulations are retirement regulations for admittance to official bodies, commissions etc.
— The National Association of Pensioners has launched a Country-wide scheme recommending all municipalities to

establish an 'Old People's Council'. The task of such a council is to act as an advisory body for the local political authorities in all questions of care of the aged and in matters of interest to old people in general. For the time being, the Ministry of Health and Social Affairs is co-operating with other central agencies in an evaluation of the function of these councils. (p.56)

The FRG's SSB Graue Panther organization is said by CLEIRPPA (Collot *et al.*, 1982) to be 'the most spectacular' in that country. There is a committee on domiciliary assistance and one on communal accommodation 'which regularly visits institu-tions and exposes any irregularities that it may find'. They are said also to support individuals' causes where necessary before the courts, 'particularly where they have a bearing on general problems affecting elderly people' (p. 155). Organized 'to promote elderly people's interests by elderly people themselves', an impor-tant SSB objective is 'self defense by elderly people of their rights and interests' (p. 154).

Besides the SSB in the FRG there are various apparently strong branches of an activist organization called the 'Evening of Life Movement'. The declared purpose is 'to involve elderly people in social and political activity in that country, and more particularly to give them a share in responsibility for dealing with problems connected with old age' (p. 162). The Dortmund branch was described as organizing to take their own affairs in hand to reject social and political dominance.

Another impressive group described in CLEIRPPA is the Old People's Unions of the Netherlands, partly financed by the govern-ment. It is said to represent '500,00 people, one-third of the elderly population', and at the national level, 'it defends the inte-rests of elderly people when government decisions affecting them are undertaken' (p. 151).

A relatively poor position of legal protection for human rights of the elderly in Britain has been suggested by the condition referred to, cited by Alison Norman, that British law specifically provides for the compulsory removal of an elderly person from his home. It may therefore be no coincidence that there is not a well-organized national activist group of and by elderly people in Britain. This is not to minimize the excellent strong organizations working on behalf of the elderly: Age Concern, Help the Aged and the Centre for Policy on Ageing; nor to overlook the fact that various trade union leaders and others manage a Pensioner's Convention once a year. Older people in Britain might have reason to feel that their rights as they see them were more secure if they had their own large-scale organization of the order of Denmark's EGV or the Dutch Old People's Unions.

One section of the US Country Report for the WAA described the evolution of political power on the part of older people in the 50 years between the thirties and the eighties.

The Citizen Role

Older people achieved national prominence during the 1930's when large numbers joined the Townsend Movement and other advocacy groups to constitute a citizen lobby for establishment of retirement income programs. As the aging movement evolved during ensuing decades, older people increased in number and became a significant proportion of the electorate. Hundreds of thousands joined organizations created for or by them, became increasingly articulate lobbyists, participants in conferences on aging, political leaders, and members of legislative and program advisory groups. Gradual weakening of negative stereotypes and enactment of anti-age discrimination legislation have enabled many to find staff positions in community agencies and organizations serving older persons as well as other elements of the population. Their increasing involvement has come in response to growing usefulness of their years of experience, skills, and first-hand knowledge of the circumstances and requirements of their peers.

Studies conducted by The University of Michigan's Survey Research Center in the late 1950's revealed that a higher proportion of persons in the 55 to 70 year age period participated in national elections than did members of any other age group. Although participation declines during the more advanced years — because of higher mortality rates among men than among women, and because mobility limitations prevent some from getting to polling places — it was reported that interest in local and national issues is maintained.

A quality of life study conducted by the American Institute for Research in the mid-1970's found citizenship activity to be one of the more significant contributions to life satisfaction among older people. Using participation as a measure of interest, the study found that three-fifths of both men and women at age 50 through 70 keep themselves informed of national and local issues, vote, and have an appreciation of political, social, and religious freedom. The study confirmed the earlier Michigan study's finding of greater interest on the part of older citizens than among those in the early years of adulthood.

Creation of two organizations of older people — the National Retired Teachers Association/American Association of Retired Persons and the National Council on Senior Citizens together with the National Association of Retired Federal Employees, foster State and local chapters, publish periodicals announcing proposed and enacted legislation beneficial to their members and news of local chapters, to seek to influence public policy.

A recent and striking example of citizen participation has been the 'Silver-haired Legislatures' currently operating in 13 States. Facilitated by State agencies on aging, they convene representative assemblies of older persons who meet in simulated legislative sessions in legislative chambers of the State capitol. Legislation is proposed, costed, discussed, and voted on, often with the guidance of members of the official legislature. Success of the silver-haired legislature groups has been measured by a high degree of favorable response to proposals in official legislative bodies.

Statutorily based national policy now directs that older people be named to advisory boards to the several hundred State and Area Agencies on Aging and to the 1,100 nutrition projects fostered by the Administration on Aging. Other agencies at Federal, State, and community levels take similar advantage of the specialized experience and knowledge of older people. (p. 104)

The various groups of older citizens in the US vary in the extent to which they act as strong advocates for benefits and reforms apart from the popular one of Social Security income. The US Country Report for the WAA spoke of:

A growing emphasis on advocacy by and for older adults, and the recognition of the political power of this population segment in the formulation of government policies which directly affected them. (p. 5)

However, championing better long-term care for the infirm, very elderly person, or protecting the rights of the aged members of minority groups are undertaken very seldom, and claim very little attention from the large organizations. Smaller groups like the Older Women's League (the OWLs) and the Gray Panthers are the groups likely to pay some attention, but even they do not give highest priority in a steady campaign to protect the rights of individuals in these situations.

The condition of this layer of care must surely be improved. When we turn to what older people themselves have told us about the experience of being old in contemporary society, and specifically by Miss Newton of being a patient in nursing homes, we see how urgently that improvement is needed.

References

American Bar Association, (1981) *Model Recommendations: Intermediate Sanctions for Enforcement of Quality of Care in Nursing Homes.* American Bar Association: Washington, DC

Baker, A.A., (1976) 'Slow euthanasia or "She will be better off in hospital."' *British Medical Journal* 1976, No. 2: pp. 571-2

Berkowitz, S., (1978) Informed consent: Research on the elderly. *The Gerontologist 18* (3)

Centre for Policy on Ageing (1984) *Home Life: A Code of Practice for Residential Care.* Centre for Policy on Ageing, London

Collot, C., Jain-LeBris, H. and Ridoux, A., for CLEIRPPA (1982). *Towards an Improvement in Self Reliance of the Elderly: Innovations and New Guidelines for the Future.* The Commission of the European Communities, Brussels

Copp, L.A., (1981) 'The Protection of Aged Human Subjects in the Clinical Research Setting.' In Copp, L.A. (ed.) *Care of the Aging*, pp. 192-203 Churchill-Livingston, Edinburgh

Country Reports for the World Assembly on Aging (1982)

— *Aging in Norway: Humanitarian and Developmental Issues.* Royal Norwegian Ministry of Health and Social Affairs, Oslo

— *US National Report on Aging for the United Nations and the World Assembly on Aging.* Department of State, Washington, DC

Flamm, F., (1974) *Social Welfare Services and Social Work in the Federal Republic of Germany.* Deutchen Vereins für Öffentliche und Private Fürsorge, Frankfurt

Kaprio, Leo, (1982) 'A statement from the WHO.' In Selby, P. and Schechter, M., *Aging 2000 — A Challenge for Society.* MTP. Lancaster (Published for the Sandoz Institute for social and economic studies.)

Norman, Alison, (1980) *Rights and Risk.* National Corporation for the Care of Old People, London. (Now known as the Centre for Policy on Ageing).

Selby, P. and Schechter, M., (1982) *Aging 2000 — A Challenge for Society.* MTP, Lancaster, England (Published for the Sandoz Institute for health and socio-economic studies.) Referred to herein as 'the Sandoz Institute study'

Senioren-Schutzbundes, (1983) *Grauer Panther*, No. 2 (June). Wuppertal,

Federal Republic of Germany: SSB

White House Conference Staff, (1982) *Final Report: White House Conference on Aging, 1981.* WHCoA Staff, Washington, DC

World Assembly on Aging, (1982) *Plan of Action.* From meeting of the World Assembly on Aging in Vienna Austria, August, 1982. (Referred to herein as WAA)

9 AT THE CENTER: THE ELDERLY PERSON RECEIVING CARE

The book written by Gladys Elder OAP (1977) is the principal source of information regarding the important matter of the thoughts and feelings of the person receiving care over a long-term. It is especially valuable because there are so few accounts from elderly people themselves. We have her own experiences, for she had various problems with her health and several stays in hospital, and she brought us also the experiences of other pensioners. Her own background held lengthy episodes of poverty, and even homelessness, combined with a great respect for education, especially literature. This placed her in a position to appreciate and interpret the feelings of less fortunate people who often have no voice to speak to the mainstream of society.

The title of her book about growing old today is, *The Alienated.* J.B. Priestly, who at age 82 wrote the introduction, agreed that the title proclaimed the central problem of old people today. In the book, Elder searched the histories of today's pensioners as well as their present living conditions for the various causes of this feeling among them.

She took up the cause of older people in her own later years and became a speaker by radio and TV as well as before clubs and gatherings, and newspapers sometimes carried her articles and letters. All of these served to stimulate many older people to write to her about their own experiences and feelings of growing old. In her book, finished just before she died in 1976, Gladys Elder included excerpts from many of these letters. She felt they made eloquent testimony of the way the lifelong hardships, and society's repudiation of the values which had kept them going, resulted in destruction of their self esteem and left them, in their later years, no recourse but to withdraw.

My generation, in all classes of society, have seen the very foundations of their morality and beliefs collapse. There is a terrible sadness in lost illusions for those of us who had visions. ... Here is the essence of a terrible alienation. We are as strangers from another planet. ... Little wonder if so many of my generation save themselves from the vertiginous effects of change by becoming first anaesthetised, then segregated, finally alienated (pp. 71-2)

The following part of a letter from a 70-year-old to Mrs Elder put it as follows:

Thousands of old people ... gave their all and risked their lives in two world wars for their king and country and now don't even get respect but are treated like muck ... the people of Britain have a lot to thank most of the older people for, but they can't get them underground quickly enough. We know that we are not wanted, that is why we get bitter and go back in to our shell and want nothing to do with anyone. Who can blame us? It makes my blood boil when I see the way old people are treated. (pp. 29-30)

The anger in those words is a tip-off. The picture of old age from so many of Mrs Elder's correspondents is not the peaceful and quiet time which the bystander might imagine it to be if he took at face value the stoic acceptance of their situation, whether in a geriatric ward, an old people's home or their own household. Writing to Mrs Elder they expressed a mixture of anger, pain and fear underneath their strong tendency — a product of a lifetime's conditioning of the poor — to respond with a passive, stiff-upper lip acceptance of their lot.

The pains are both physical and psychological. Arthritis, poor hearts, old problems with feet and backs, very poor dental conditions, poor eye-sight, deafness (one of Gladys Elder's own problems): all of these are painful and common disorders. They go on, and worsen, as acute infections come and go. Probably the greatest psychological pain comes from the disappointed hopes *vis-à-vis* their children. The following statement of this came in a letter prompted by an Elder broadcast:

I brought up two children alone. My husband died when I was 45, my children respectively 4 and 8. I have had several operations and can no longer go out cleaning, and I'm only 63 but I feel a hundred. My children have left me and seem not to care if I'm alive or dead. They are both married ... I can't bear Sundays so on Saturday night I take some very strong tranquillisers

which keep me dazed all day Sunday. I take mild tranquillisers every night during the week, otherwise I couldn't sleep
for vague pains all over. I think it may be protein deficiency as I
cannot digest cheese or eggs. I have literally begged my son for
help ... I have always tried to be a loving person, but now I feel
like a hurt animal and am retreating into myself, away fom the
cold heartless average person. *They* are all right, have husband/
wife, car, fridge, etc. They can go on holiday. I haven't had a
holiday away from my four walls for 16 years. On the few occasions I have seen my son ... he has come out with some very
cruel statements. He says that surely age should have mellowed
me instead of being bitter and 'This is a material world. It's
every man for himself' ... My one prayer is that I don't live to
be really old. (pp. 47-8)

The presence of fear is given us in the appeal which went to an
agency on the point of pursuing with the authorities her case for
repair of the poor plumbing and other conditions in the flat where
she lived:

Please I beg you don't go near them about me. I am terrified of
them. They pushed me around in 1967, and I have not for-
gotten that awful time they gave me. You see, I have high blood
pressure and heart trouble which Dr Winkler of Tachbrook
Street will confirm, and for which I have tablets (9 a day) so you
see I need peace and quiet. So please don't report anything to
them about me beyond paying the rent. I want nothing to do
with them. (p. 51)

Elder referred in the following paragraph to the helplessness
underlying such fear:

The old are resigned in the face of a defeat they cannot possibly
hope to reverse. For their very circumstances make them helpless, as do frustration, the discomforts and disabilities of the
aging process, the economic shackles and the indignities to
which they are subjected. (p. 34)

Beneath the anger and the pain and fear Elder recognized the
special tragedy of the impact of social change on working class
people who have themselves experienced the twentieth century

from its beginning. As we have seen above, she saw this as the source of their alienation. It appeared to be connected with the feeling of rejection by their children and society:

> To many of the old the questioning (today's much wider and harder-hitting version of the ever-present rebellion of youth) is not only insane but intolerable: the old 'know' that certain basic principles are right — the importance of the family unit, patriotism, knowing one's place in society and accepting it unquestioningly. Thus the young completely disrupt their world, and there is no longer any solid ground under their feet ... It is almost impossible for the aged to re-examine terms of reference that have become integrated into their personality. ... For never forget that many of us feel that our social milieu *does not entitle us* to more than a minimal subsistence; that to accept flagrant injustices, a third-class life with sweet resignation in old age is a sign of maturity; that nothing can be done — things will always be the same. All too often, therefore, a rise in the subsistence level is regarded with deeply-felt gratitude. (p. 73)

Elder quoted Jeremy Seabrook's sorrowful observation of today's working class elderly persons:

> They have lived to see their customs and rituals fall into desue-tude, their accredited beliefs spent, their received ideas suddenly used up ... and when they handed on to their children the only life they knew, enshrined in the family treasures now abandoned, the children laughed and refused them and went their ways. (p. 69)

But rather than 'sweet resignation,' Elder sees strong emotions behind the stoic exterior they manage to present:

> I find there is an underlying feeling of loneliness in the aged, of being left behind, of having been cheated (especially in this country where hopes of 'a land fit for heroes to live in' was one of the first broken promises by political parties after the First World War). There is a feeling of bitterness, of helplessness, and in many cases an incredible stoicism displayed in the face of economic difficulties and physical disabilities; a valiant attempt to retain some dignity, in many cases by an *appearance* of not caring. (p. 34)

Problems with Health Care

Hospitalisation

Having had health problems intermittently through her life, it was not surprising that in her seventies Gladys Elder became ill and eventually had to be hospitalized. The terrible time she had was regrettable on every count. At least, however, it produced one older person's account of experiences involving a stay in a mental hospital which, as in other countries, in the National Health Service is the backwater of a system which otherwise serves the elderly rather well. We pick up her account when for the second time in six months she was suddenly overcome by an attack of severe illness and depression.

One evening in the following May I went to bed quite happily, looking forward to a visit to my other daughter. The next day I awoke with the exact repetition of the same violent depression, again accompanied by violent nausea, a bitter taste in the mouth — and a paralysing feeling of lethargy. Because of the suddenness and persistence of the depression I saw my doctor. X-rays, medication and examination revealed nothing physically wrong. At the end of an appalling five weeks the symptoms again vanished as suddenly as they had come.

I took stock. Retirement, a declining bank-balance and an increase in the *tinnitus* (the medical name for unceasing noises in the head) I had suffered for some while, eye irritation, rheumatism and hearing-loss must be taking their toll. Yet, apart from the *tinnitus*, I had more or less adjusted to these various complaints. Only other sufferers know what it is like to be afflicted with this 'noises in the head' disease. Sometimes, after learning to tolerate the incessant cacophony, a new and sudden internal sound can again make life quite intolerable.) Were these all contributory factors to my new and nameless disease?

The following September it attacked again. I was staying with my sister in Swanage and enjoying myself immensely. We had had an enjoyable day at Poole and I sank into sleep with the sigh of satisfaction that goes with pleasant tiredness after a happy and lively day. When I awoke, the burden of intense melancholia once again possessed me. This time it did not go away. I will not repeat the symptoms — the same, only worse. Finally my doctor advised me to see a neurologist and I agreed.

In fact, he made an appointment with a consultant psychologist. The day I saw her I was in the deepest despair, all hope gone, full of loathing and self-hatred, quite unable to talk, think or act. And yet, such was her personality, so bright and cheerful was she, that I suddenly found myself involved in a lively discussion about Tennessee Williams and the actor, Richard Burton! She asked me if I would be prepared to go into Delph Hospital for a short stay. I agreed, only realising later that this was part of the famous Winwick hospital, a mental institution. I suddenly became fatalistic, resigning myself to the inevitable, in much the same way, I imagine, as certain people face approaching death. 'This,' I told myself, 'is the onset of senescence.'

The hospital was badly in need of decorating and refurnishing, the decor resembling nothing so much as that of a public lavatory without the fittings. The ward was cold — a large room with only one fire. The food was terrible. One memorable meal was a portion of flitch of bacon which was uneatable, accompanied by black pudding with the label still on! Another was of whitish stew which reminded me of the joke about the Frenchman who, when presented with a plate of porridge by a Scotsman, asked whether 'it was *to be* eaten or *had* been eaten ...'

In spite of the extreme kindness of the nursing staff, I was treated to an appalling battery of pills. My circulation deteriorated and I was always cold. A friend brought me a hot-water-bottle; but for some inexplicable reason I was not allowed to use it — perhaps they thought I might try to commit suicide by swallowing the stopper! I awoke one morning to find myself covered in diarrhoea. This, I decided, was the end. Not only was I now psychotic — I was also incontinent. I would commit suicide. I saved sleeping tablets, planned to ask for home leave, and with the aid of aspirin and alcohol would finish it all off. But it wasn't so easy. 'Bring me all the tablets you have in your locker!' commanded the staff nurse one day. I asked, 'I suppose you'll never let me out of here now?' To my amazement she replied, 'You could go today — we could not prevent it!' A ray of hope — and another one later when it was discovered that one of the many tablets I'd been taking had caused the diarrhoea. If only they had told me at the time of this possibility, how much suffering I would have been saved! (pp. 100-2)

After Care

Gladys Elder went on to point out 'ways in which after care of elderly patients left a great deal to be desired'. This was not because geriatricians failed to recognize its importance. She quoted the following from Sir Ferguson Anderson:

> A methodology has now evolved, beginning with the ascertainment of or seeking out illness in the old person's home, and one way of doing this is by asking the health visitor to visit every individual in the community of 70 years of age and over. (p. 104)

The practice, however, had not yet reached Sir Ferguson's standards of care; as Elder commented:

> Alas, in practice, the after-care of elderly patients leaves a great deal to be desired. I meet and hear of people who have been sent home to cold rooms, or to poverty, while unreasonable delays occur in follow-up treatment. There is insufficient rapport between hospitals and family doctors — and, above all, there is a severe shortage of health visitors. I myself, living alone, have never *seen* a health visitor, even after coming out of hospital following a cancer operation. Many elderly people fail to report incipient signs of what might become serious health deterioration because they fear the all-too-common accusation of hypochondria.
>
> A vast amount still needs to be done about the diet of patients in after-care. Hospital food seldom caters for the special needs of the aged, and thus, at a time when the patient needs building up, the diet is inadequate or inappropriate. Though Meals-on-Wheels supply an absolutely essential service, dietary needs get lost in the savage demands of our inflationary economy. Protein, for instance, is absolutely necessary to maintain vigour in old age (it will be noticed that those elderly who can afford a sufficient quantity of meat, fish and cheese are not seen shuffling along, wrinkled, bent and twisted). A study by Griffiths and Brocklehurst revealed that 41 % of old people admitted to hospital were deficient in Vitamin C and 50 % in Vitamin B. (p. 105)

The Need for a Progressive, not Regressive Patient Role

The great difference made to the patient when the patient role is regarded with some hope for rehabilitation was noted by Gladys Elder in the following paragraph:

> But even when after-care — and indeed the care of the aged generally — is of a high calibre, I feel that there is a great danger of treating patients as children, thus encouraging them to accept this regressive role. Instead of being kept immobile, whether within hospital or without, skilled treatment, physiotherapy and the supervision of qualified geriatricians would ensure that a number of those previously confined to bed or a wheel-chair should be able to live a more normal life. (p. 105)

Old People's Housing and Hypothermia

A report from the Centre for Environmental Studies was noted by Elder, where hypothermia had been cited as a reason for their finding that in England 60,000 more people die in the six cold months than in the six warm months. She went on to describe the very poor condition of heating in the housing of elderly people, according to a survey carried out just a few years before she wrote.

Of the houses of 1000 elderly people visited in a 1973 survey, those of 754 had temperatures at or below the 65 degrees Fahrenheit recommended by the 1961 housing study. For 537 of the 1000, the temperatures were at or below 60.8 degrees, the figure established as a minimum; in 106 cases (more than one-tenth of the total), the temperatures were below 53.6 degrees! Few of the persons surveyed were in receipt of a fuel allowance, hardly surprising since 74 per cent did not know that in certain circumstances old people could get extra money for heating.

It is hard to imagine more cruel treatment by their fellow men than to be left to die of cold. Elder described some actual victims of such abandonment and cruelty:

> Des Wilson, lately of *Shelter*, has brought the attention of the public to a number of such cases: the elderly Portsmouth woman who had been dead in front of her television set for over two months before being found; another man dead for three weeks before anyone discovered him. It was reported that four different men had died this lonely death in one block of flats in one year. An eighty-one year old woman died in her home of

exposure and frostbite, weighing only five stone at her death. (p.
45)

The Ultimate Fear.

The demands on the health care system to be brought in the next
few decades by the number of very elderly people caused Elder to
voice the fear that the shadow of euthanasia may loom even larger.
'Legalized euthanasia', she said, 'is merely an escape from the
responsibility of caring for the sick and infirm'. She felt that this is
a not uncommon fear among elderly people.

Gladys Elder was not alone in raising this subject in connection
with the necessity for providing medical care for elderly people.
The Sandoz experts, (Selby and Schechter, 1982), looking forward
to changes in the provision of services possible by the year 2000,
included these observations:

> The outlook in many countries is for larger populations of
> elderly persons, with the most rapid expansion at ages above 80.
> Costs of care will be up, not only because more people will be at
> ages where dependency rates are high due to illness, especially
> with senile dementia, but also because of the expense of better
> trained manpower and technological advances. ...
>
> Sensitivity to costs may encourage insensitivity to quality of
> care for the elderly: institutions for long-term care may become
> warehouses. Moreover, the American (experts) expect that the
> issue of euthanasia for the most feeble, institutionalized elderly
> may be raised. (p. 76)

Attention: Caring Professions

What the older population thinks and feels about their life needs to
be heard by the whole population, but very especially by those
whose professions and vocations involve older people as their
clients and patients. Gladys Elder herself felt that there was reason
to expect some change away from subservience and resignation to
their impoverished state, as 'the elderly' include people who grew
up in a different age from her own group, born at the turn of the
century. But there is reason to believe that the conditions which
gave rise to the feelings of anger, fear and pain of which Elder
wrote, especially the underlying conditions of poverty, loneliness

and alienation, will continue for some time. There is also reason to suspect that conditions in other nations are not too different, for the elderly in the USA, the FRG, France and most other countries are also likely to be the population with high poverty, the poorest housing, poor nutrition and with health care more lacking than it is for Elder's British elderly.

Alienated people respond negatively, if at all, to would-be service providers, including medical and nursing care. The failure to 'take up' what others in the society offer, thinking it will meet their needs, has been noted with respect to the provision of help with fuel. Kerr (1983) has studied very recently the failure to take up supplementary benefits as well as tax and housing reductions in Britain. The Country Report for the WAA from West Germany stated that many who are entitled make no claim for benefits under their social welfare programs because of the shame attached to the persistent memories from the far-off days when Poor Laws were in effect there as in Britain. This avoidance of benefits and services is a signal to us of the elderly who 'opt out', and an indication of their negative reactions. It means that we 'haven't got it right' at all. Does this not suggest the need for dramatic changes toward having the elderly themselves present in all stages of service planning?

Perhaps much of the costs which bother our economists so much could be avoided if we get rid of the waste, for instance, of medical and nursing care where patients fight, rather than involve themselves, in attempts to get better. This means that professionals must learn to respect their elderly patients. Gladys Elder taught us this. She recovered from the serious illness of depression when she was cared for by a doctor who respected her so much that he encouraged her to write her book. And when he had to leave for another post, he wrote her a letter ending 'May I say that I consider it a privilege to have met and conversed with you?'. She credited this letter with having helped give her back her self esteem. She said 'I had gained much confidence from having met him and this enabled me to go on from where I had left off (before the illness). Now, whenever I feel discouraged or depressed, I re-read that letter.' (p. 104)

The curative value of the care from that doctor did not depend upon investment of more money, but on his responsiveness to the particular needs and value of his patient, built upon respect for her as a person. Such care is perhaps all that can reach the alienated, fearful, sometimes angry feelings of elderly patients and put them on their way to self confidence to achieve some degree of recovery as well as some degree of self respect. While especially important to a doctor or a nurse, this message is by no means confined to those professions. It is necessary for all who deal with older people of this generation to realize some of their underlying feelings: for social workers, grocers, bus drivers, neighbors and members of their families.

Likewise it is necessary for those who plan and administer the programs and services 'for' the elderly to realize why they must always be 'of' and 'by' the elderly if their goals are to be realized. Perhaps many alienated older persons will, like Gladys Elder, respond to an invitation to 'come in'. There is no substitute for their own advice and directions regarding what the elderly population needs.

From Inside the Nursing Home

The other book containing information from an older person herself is entitled *This Bed My Centre,* and the author is Ellen Newton. It exists because she kept a diary of her experiences as a very ill elderly person during the six years when she was taken to a succession of nursing homes in Australia, her country. She experienced long-term care in these institutions until she finally rebelled and discharged herself. She explained why: 'Long years of unnatural waiting in places surrounded by death threatened to overwhelm me'. She was just barely well enough and did manage in a small flat after leaving the last of the nursing homes. Her illness was a serious heart problem, angina, and she was very frail indeed.

The main theme in her tale of the drab life, lacking in creature comforts as well as stimulation, was the powerlessness she felt. Miss Newton's book is a testament about the neglect of human rights protection, starting at the beginning of the book, when she was told by her doctor that 'they decided' to have her enter a nursing home — the next day. And when she was in the midst of the institutional nursing home life, she could do nothing but accept the regimentation and the abject loss of her identity, her dignity and control over her life.

We begin with the scene in hospital when she was told what 'they had decided':

We've decided it will be best for you to live in a nursing home where you will get the expert care you need! *We've decided.* Angels would have trodden more warily. So would Matron. And clever downright Sister Mead could have told this highly qualified young doctor that they might at least have given me a small voice in their decision to wrap up my life forever. There were things I might have said, too, if I hadn't suddenly felt tired, and as cold as buried stone.

'It will be better if you do not go home,' he says, just like a clerk at a tourist bureau saying you'll do better travelling in the Southern Aurora, than in the Daylight Express. Home is your peculiar treasure. For your GP it is just another address.

You are no longer an average human being, alive with joys and doubts and fears. Hope is not for you, either. From today you are a Patient.

'We've arranged for you to go straight from here on Thursday to Haddon — the nursing home where we've booked you in.' As quickly as that, he had stripped all brightness from the day. 'It will be better, you know, if you don't go home at all from here.' 'Yes, Doctor.' He left me — with my future foretold. Without another word. When he closed the door, it was just like the finality of death. (pp. 4-5)

We have noted several times the isolation of the nursing home from the rest of the health care system. A few days after entering her first nursing home, Miss Newton tells us of its segregation from life:

Because there is so little coming and going from outside, and no communication worth mentioning inside, living in a nursing home is an odd kind of segregation. It's like being lost in a fog that closes down more heavily, just as you think you can see your way out. ...

The sense of segregation is so palpable, you feel as if at any moment you will be tightly enclosed in a cocoon of isolation. Except for the milkman, before dawn, there's no sound of traffic passing by. Everything is negative. You never hear young people singing, speeding recklessly home from late parties, or even the stereophonic calls of philandering tomcats. Never the sound of children's voices, laughing and calling to each other as they race down the street. Only spasmodic screeching a few

doors away, that would send cold shivers down anyone's spine.
Yet they tell me nobody here ever has severe pain. It's like living in space. But it has its own grim kind of permanence, for we
are all here for the term of our unnatural lives. Unless you are
'away with the fairies,' the lasting anguish of being uprooted
from your own kind must destroy you. And there's no speaking
of it to anyone. Not to Helen — above all. Never to Helen (pp.
18-19)

(Note: The sister with whom Miss Newton had made her home
before her illness and hospital stay is Helen. It was Helen who
was her attentive visitor and, generally, her confidante.)

Miss Newton spent many months in the second home to which
she went. It was in an entry there, much later on, that she returned
to the sorrow of being away from the mainstream:

Although it's Sunday, there does not seem to be much visiting.
When you are outside the mainstream of living, ties are broken.
This sense of solitude is one of the things that the *haves* do not
escape. Nor do the *have-nots* in these little nursing homes,
which as Daisy Ashford said of Edward VII's crown, are 'small
but costly'. In one way all handicapped people are alike. They
will never live again as average men and women do. That is
what bring us to havens of doubt and shadowy despair like this
same Dawson Towers. Already there's an end-of-the-road feeling all round me in this small room. At least when the bell tolls
there's nothing under this roof that will make it hard to leave.
Pretty thought for a grey day ...

A recurrent theme in her description of the several nursing
homes was the drabness, the tiny room with nothing to warm it.
Apparently no notice was taken of the fact that a resident might
need some beauty, some space to accommodate personal possessions and keep them at hand. They arrived at the home:

We go inside, past a small lounge, its end wall almost filled by
the biggest television set I've ever seen, and a couple of windows that do not exactly sparkle in the afternoon light. Along
each of the other two walls, there is a row of vacant, unsmiling
faces facing each other. Their owners sit in big chairs, wedged

leg to leg, with not an inch to spare, as if they have all been drilled into keeping those two straight, inflexible lines for ever and ever.

My room has about as much humanity in it as a parallel-ogram — no mirror, no shelf or table of any kind to hold a book or a single flower. Not even a hook or a rail where one could hang a print. But there is a small cupboard for hanging clothes. Beside the bed there is just enough space to open the door into the shower room and toilet. They call this a duplex and it is shared with the patient next door. In it there is a cupboard, the door of which is a mirror. It is placed so high on the wall that if you are of average height you have no hope of seeing anything below your eyebrows reflected in it. The towel rail is broken at one end.

Helen says she will bring my bookshelves and some books as well. There will be a place for a small bowl of flowers then. Possibly a print, too. It may be the complete absence of the faintest hint of colour that lets a rank mist of stark isolation lie over this room.

Life there was an affront, from the hour of rising, right through the day, with much noise, partly from TV's, and — by far worst — the cries at night.

Day begins here at 5 am. No early morning cup of tea. Breakfast at 7.30. The main meal is at midday. There is afternoon tea poured into your cup as your nursing-aide of the moment likes it, and handed to you from a trolley in the hall.

Thursday — Television in the lounge sounds non-stop at undreamt-of decibels from nine o'clock in the morning till final bedding-down time comes at half-past seven in the evening. Besides this, TVs are often tuned, in private rooms along the corridor, on three different stations. Even an iron door could not shut out this hideous uproar. These poor fellow-travellers must be all but stone-deaf. Yet noise, like a football match and races, seems to be relished for its own sake. It should be possible to turn on my own TV softly at night. Helen has had it tested and the verdict is that it is performing perfectly, on all stations. It must be this power-point that is at fault. As this is something entirely in the hands of God and the proprietor. I've a feeling nothing will be done about it.

The staff are mostly kind and considerate. Except last night.

The storm-trooper of a sister on duty tramped ceaselessly up and down the uncarpeted corridor in heavy, outdoor boots every time bells and loud, mindless cries called for her attention. She and her equally raucous nursing-aide, kept shouting to each other all through the night, from one end of the hospital to the other. Probably on the principle that if all their patients were not stone-deaf, they should be.

Wednesday — More than an hour since Helen went. It seems like a day. Soon those cries, that wound more senses than just your hearing, will begin. For some unfathomable reason my door cannot be tightly closed against them.

The next nursing home Miss Newton described as a very small one, with only five residents. She met with the discomfort of a very cold room upon her entrance, and a failure to provide the hot water she needed to accompany her bedtime medication. Here as elsewhere there were many times when she was hungry, the food was so sparse. There was nothing she could do about being hungry, nor the deprivation of heat in her room, nor of the hot water needed at bedtime — she was helpless. On arrival at the new home:

Monday At three o'clock, as requested, we arrive at Vere de Vere House. Matron opens the door, picks up one suitcase and takes it into my room.

'Tea is at five,' she says and leaves us to unpack.

This morning's temperature was 5°C and is probably only two or three degrees higher now. Helen finds a power-point, but there is no sign of a radiator. She takes my electric blanket out of its box, and turns back the bed covers to put it in its place, then realises she needs help to lift that good heavy mattress and adjust the tapes. 'This room is absolutely perishing,' she says, still buttoned up in a coat and scarf, as I am, too. 'I'll have to get help with this blanket.' It is some little time before she manages to make contact. She comes back with Matron, who eyes the blanket with distaste. But she helps Helen put it in place and remake my bed.

'Matron, we've found the power-point, but there doesn't seem to be a radiator in here. Will you give me one, please?' I dare to ask.

'There is no radiator for this room.'

Helen, with that enchanting smile of hers, quickly takes over.

'Never mind, Matron, my sister has her own radiator. I'll slip over with it early tomorrow morning.' But —

'I do not allow radiators in my Ladies' rooms. They are too dangerous.' Helen and I look at each other and smile. We are both freezing, still buttoned up in our coats and scarves. And my two suitcases are still unpacked. But just what escape is there for me, *anywhere?*

'There is a heater in the lounge,' says Matron, then departs.

' "The ice was here, The ice was there, The ice was all around," — in more ways than one,' I murmur to Helen.

'There is no hot drink by way of supper. So I take my thermos, knock on the kitchen door, and ask if I may have it filled with boiling water, explaining a hot drink has been prescribed for me with my night issue of pills. The thermos is brought to my room later, by someone who is a relative of Matron's, and is also our cook-housekeeper. She seems a pleasant woman. But no, she couldn't possibly give me a cup and saucer and spoon. 'They are all needed.'

'Perhaps a glass then.' Eventually a glass arrives.

A couple of hours later, warm at last, and desperately tired, I opened my thermos. It holds a scant cup of lukewarm water. It probably never was boiling. To hold the heat for several hours, most people know a thermos must be filled. How to melt Helen's chicken cubes, without even a spoon to stir them, is a problem. Suddenly I remember the versatile little fruit knife that was given me as a souvenir of the second Elizabeth's coronation. I manage to unearth it, and it performs well. But my night cap is very nearly stone-cold.

Miss Newton's helplessness was epitomized by this situation:

'If you should ever be ill at night be sure you ring for Matron, darling,' were Helen's parting words. There is no bell.

The worst aspect, however, was the passive role into which the residents were cast. At more than one point, she likened the social atmosphere to boarding school. Residents were expected, as school children are expected, to keep to the rules of 'bedtime' and 'time to get up'. And not only were they reprimanded as a school marm might reprimand, but they themselves obeyed! Miss Newton herself followed instructions, with a 'Yes, Matron'. That was the worst of all for her.

The lounge is also the diningroom. Tonight the evening meal is three sticks of pencil-thin asparagus on a square of toast. There are also ample servings of a solid-looking milk pudding, with cream. There is no substitute for me, but there is one slice of bread for everyone, and butter and jam to go with it, on the table that is completely covered with all-over synthetic lace. My seat is at the end facing the kitchen door. There are two doors into this loung-diningroom, as well as a wide-open archway opening on to what I imagine are other bedrooms. There is a space-heater at the far end of the room, half on, 'so that the room will not get overheated'. Matron waits at table. On my left is a charming, very old lady, Mrs Dermott-Smith. On my right two characters who do not speak. Nor do they, unless asked, pass anything this very big table holds, to anyone sitting near them. Five chairs with ample cushioned seats and backs of blue corduroy are ranged on blue-green carpet along one wall. Their bare, wooden arms all touch each other, like sardines in a tin. You are allotted one of these chairs, just as you are given your desk at school. The chairs are not uncomfortable, but any casual grouping is forbidden. And easy, informal talk is discouraged. My chair is between Mrs Simpson and Miss Joskin, my right-hand neighbours at table.

The meal is soon over and all ladies retire to their chairs. The table is cleared and there is silence, again like boarding-school.

At half-past six the television set is officially turned on. This is especially for Mrs Dermott-Smith. There's a football replay, and she is a keen follower of the game. The TV blinks and stutters for several minutes.

I don't think it's quite tuned to the station,' I venture. And being the most alert and able-bodied of the Ladies present, I move towards the set.

'Oh no,' comes a chorus, '*no* one is allowed to touch the T.V.' Whereupon, Mrs Dermott-Smith, whose corner seat is almost on top of the set, leans forward and quickly makes the necessary adjustment. The news session follows.

By eight o'clock Matron appears. On the wall opposite me is a large coloured print in blues and greens, to match the carpet. Above what must be a big fireplace, now partly hidden by our space-heater, is the twin of this misty landscape, with a slight difference. The colouring is the same. In other respects it is a poor relation of Landseer's *Dying Stag*. From colour schemes and art, my mind is wrenched back to the facts of life. There is a general movement, and without a word being spoken, it is subtly conveyed to me that Ladies are expected to retire at eight o'clock.

Early morning is not my most brilliant hour. Besides, bed is warm, and the rest of the room is still icy. It is well after nine when I amble towards the shower. When I return to my room Matron has just finished making my bed. In words that fall like chips of ice she says, 'I want you to be out of the bathroom, *always* before half-past nine, Miss Newton, so that I can shower my Ladies.' Well. There is a second bathroom. And she obviously can't be 'showering' her sundry Ladies in both at the same time. Her problem must surely be a very temperamental hot water service which has just frozen and frizzled me by turns. Too meekly, I reply, 'Very well, Matron'. Trailing her little, brief authority, she departs.

The dust jacket of her book tells us that in fact, Miss Newton must be considered one of the lucky ones:

Articulate, literate, with a devoted family, her nursing homes were expensive, privately owned. Yet she was sometimes cold and frequently hungry; sometimes ill but her bell went unanswered. She had no real privacy yet no hope of normal life with her geriatric, often seriously disturbed fellow patients. And, she was powerless to change her condition — except by writing about it.

Miss Newton's 'caring institutions' in fact gave considerably more discomfort and defeat than care. The conditions she met are a vivid illustration of health care institutions isolated and away from the mainstream of health care with its standards of practice. In her experience they were clearly more interested in making a profit than in making people well.

References

Country Report for the World Assembly on Aging (1982)
— *Report on the Situation of the Elderly in the Federal Republic of Germany.* The
    German Center of Gerontology, Berlin
Elder, Gladys, (1977) *The Alienated: Growing Old Today.* Writers and Readers
    Publishing Cooperative, London
Kerr, Scott, (1983) *Making Ends Meet.* The Bedford Press, London
Newton, Ellen, (1979) *The Bed My Centre.* McPhee Gribble Publishers,
    Melbourne, Australia
Selby, P. and Schechter, M., (1982) *Aging 2000 — A Challenge for Society.* MTP
    Press, Lancaster, England. (Published for the Sandoz Institute for health and
    socio-economic studies.) (Referred to herein as 'the Sandoz Institute Study'.)

PART THREE

LOOKING AHEAD

10 QUESTIONS TO GUIDE THE PLANNING OF CARE

The interests of the very old in most of the industrialized countries are suffering to a greater or lesser extent the effects of an attitude which would place limits on the role of government to assume responsibility for their needs for care for infirmity and disabilities. We have seen this to be true in Britain as well as in the USA and West Germany. The study we have made here leads us to put to these nations this question: 'Do you really intend to do the damage which results from dodging responsibility for the needs for restorative and ameliorative care of those very elderly people among you who are disabled and infirm?' For the means-tested programs for care provision which these countries persist in offering cost governments very large sums of money — 11 billion dollars each year for nursing home care in the United States at the start of the eighties — and they are being spent to purchase care of a generally poor quality. 'Poor quality' because long-term care in institutions like nursing and residential homes keeps the very old disabled and dependent, and in the process often violates their rights as human beings for dignity, privacy and independent choice.

The refusal of governments to take a position of responsibility for facing the needs for care of this group also produces long-term social damage. It results in the failure to make progress toward more satisfactory and, in fact, more economical care provision. The development of improved approaches in long-term care — like those which, in fact, exist in the countries of Denmark, Norway and Sweden — requires government involvement and some financial support of initiatives from the private sector. The advances in care of very elderly persons which have taken place have occurred very frequently when government has acted in partnership with small independent efforts of private organizations to provide care, conduct research and develop new kinds of vocations, combinations of services and housing suited to the needs of very elderly people.

This final chapter presents a short review of the examination of layers of care contained in the preceding chapters as a basis for estimating the chances for positive movements on the part of these nations in the future.

The purpose of this book has been to propose a framework for examining in depth the provisions made by a nation for long-term care of its very elderly people, many of whom are disabled and infirm. We have looked at the approaches taken by various industrialized countries in order to have a broad perspective on solutions for providing care in appropriate amounts and forms.

More is needed for this than a photographic impression of the features visible on the surface. Countries differ in ways more far-reaching than whether they build large nursing homes or organize more domiciliary services. As a way of understanding the complexities of our subject, we have introduced the metaphor of a sphere, with layers of attitudes and beliefs beneath the surface features, and at the center, the reactions of older people themselves to infirmity and care.

The layer beneath the surface is said to contain beliefs and attitudes about the role governments should take in using resources to meet special conditions of need. There are great differences in this from country to country. The nature of this attitudinal layer affects not only how much money is spent, but the fundamental matter of the older citizen's self esteem. Older people share these same attitudes toward what governments should and should not do — indeed, they have lived with them longer than others in their nation. When there is some stigma attached to receiving help to afford medical and nursing care needed for survival, the personal cost is a drop in one's sense of self worth. This means lowered self-confidence for coping with necessary activities of daily living, activities which become increasingly difficult for everyone progressing from 75 to 85 and to 90 years of age. Given the high prevalence of chronic diseases and impaired sensory functions at advanced ages, it is not easy to keep going as an active individual even in a nation which provides generously for needs for basic care.

There is still another layer of attitudes and beliefs of equal importance beneath this one. It has been labelled human rights protection which, again, differs from nation to nation. Older people experience many threats to such rights as dignity and privacy and control over decisions about where they are to live and what they are to eat for dinner. Very old people who are infirm tend especially to possess little power and to be seen as powerless and incapable. Thus, it is inevitable that others will tend to 'take over' — sometimes with the best of intentions.

This position with respect to human rights is affected dramatically by institutional living of any kind, and very old people are more likely than the rest of us to live in an institution of some kind: nursing home, old age home and, in some places, in a hospital or mental hospital. It is not surprising that threats to human rights are being addressed in many different countries by organizations of older people themselves. The encouragement and support of such groups is important on this basis alone. And it is notable that Denmark, with its very active protection of the rights of infirm elderly people, has the Ensomme Gamles Vaern, the EGV, an active organization of, by and for older people.

Under these layers lie the reactions of the infirm old people themselves to their situation and to care-giving. Our metaphor places this at the center, because it is the reason for it all. It is unfortunate that so little information exists about the reactions and feelings of the recipients of care. A few sources have been searched, and the messages obtained call for close attention to what they say. It is important that older people in the Scandinavian countries be heard from: do they, in fact, feel better off?

In the preceding chapters the proposed framework has been followed and several countries' actions investigated accordng to its terms. The findings may be used for indicating the future directions for a nation to take as it considers the long-term care to be provided for its very old people.

The Questions

The elderly Gertrude Stein was asked by her friend about the meaning of life, 'What is the answer, Gertrude?' Miss Stein's response is well remembered: 'But, Alice; what are the questions?'

The findings of this study can be said to call for each nation to find its answers about long-term care by facing up to these questions:

— Will long-term care be recognized as a national responsibility?
— Will the rights of citizens in long-term care be protected?
— Will the disabled and infirm elderly be given a voice in that future?
— Shall we be ready to welcome the guests? To be the guests?

Each one of these is a major question and only some of its dimensions can be touched upon here. Obviously, each nation must face up to the questions in its own terms, but there are some general points to be made.

Will long-term care be seen as a national responsibility? This question is by no means directed only to the fiscal matter of who pays the bill for nursing home care, as important as that is. We have seen that housing arrangements are directly related to the ability of elderly people to manage independently. Will local communities give high priority to the housing needs of infirm elderly people, and to an assessment of what it has and what it needs by way of appropriate stock? We have seen that most infirm elderly people are cared for at home. It is evident that governments everywhere are giving care by the families of old people a great deal of rhetorical praise. Will those governments believe their own statements and give needed supports for family care-giving? The thoughtful examination which the concept of care is finally receiving may lead to quite different ideas as to what family care must consist of, especially in view of the fact that so many women follow careers outside of their homes. If the older person, like the rest of us, can never accept as *care* the help she receives from a stranger, perhaps contacts with the family members when possible and desired will need to be seen as contributing the emotional content of care, while the necessary caring tasks are provided by people for whom this care-giving is the paid employment they need. That may be the 'care system' which can be managed with today's family by structure and roles. The development of new vocations and career ladders in the field of elderly care gives promise in this regard. There is an important place for volunteers in care, as it is coming to be viewed.

We have seen that provision of care for very disabled, very elderly people in the ordinary nursing home setting is unpopular almost everywhere. This is in part because of the degradation required when people have to admit that they are poor and helpless to qualify for payment for this care. In part it is due to the inappropriate nature of the life in institutions for older people whose lifestyles have been so very personal and private up to the point of entering the institution. Peace, Kellaher and Willcocks (1982) have identified that very important fact of institutional life. They also point out that people who become patients have, up to that point, in one way or another managed their own activities of daily living. Often with a little of the right help they can do it again. When an older person becomes a patient, it doesn't have to mean 'closing the door on life', as Miss Newton puts it, and in her own actions demonstrated.

Part of the unpopularity of the ordinary nursing home care is due to the fact that it is 'too much of a bad thing' for many patients. Large expenditures of money are made to nurses and aides to go through nursing home populations every day to do everything for patients in block fashion: waking up, washing, toileting, bringing trays, feeding, making beds, bathing, etc., etc. Because this must be done for a very few, it has gradually come to be done for almost all. This homogenization has cost patient independence as well as money.

The Scandinavian countries have insisted upon enabling the individual to manage independently every possible part of daily life: getting up in the morning, washing, dressing, making a cup of tea or coffee, and even going out to shop. This has meant a continual search for the necessary design and supply of aids and gadgets. It has also fashioned the way that nurses, physiotherapists, physicians and home-helps care for the patient: they, too, are fundamentally enablers.

The unpopularity is in part due to the fact that nursing homes are cut off from the mainstream of health care and this often means that there is an absence of the aura of rehabilitation and hope for sufferers.

Everywhere is heard the call for medicine, nursing and the allied health professions to address the problems of the chronic illnesses as they have so resolutely attacked acute conditions. This would mean a serious investment of medical education, medical practice and medical research into the successful management of the health problems of older people. But it is not necessary to start from scratch. In Britain serious and sophisticated work in geriatrics has been developed within the framework of the National Health Service. They have found that the illnesses of older people are made manageable by a team approach which recognizes the social and emotional as well as the physical aspects of the problems. They recognize the necessity for participation by physiotherapists and occupational therapists, health visitors, social workers and, yes, home-helps, along with the traditional physician and nurse team. The World Assembly on Aging recognized the need for all of the caring professions, broadly defined, to be well educated about aging, not only because so many patients are older people, but because the treatment of problems and health promotion among younger people need to be managed with a view to what lies ahead.

In the customary academic terms, all of the above would be translated into 'a need for aging policy'. These words fail to pinpoint the direction and goals which must be identified by the decision-makers who will determine what role government will take for long-term care. It must be understood that the large amounts of money currently being spent for long-term care are to a great extent spent for the wrong things, and there are countries where resources are deployed in ways which bring about a much better life for infirm elderly people. In other words, there are ways to solve the problem of long-term care at a rate of expenditure not too different from the present rate when there is the will to find and develop these ways.

For starters, there appear to be some imperatives. The fact must be faced that a means test requiring of an infirm elderly person an admission that he is poor is truly adding insult to injury. The damage which results from cutting long-term care off from the health care system has already been mentioned. The cost of the health care people require needs to be covered by insurance regardless of the nature of their illness. To continue to exclude this very small population from insurance coverage for the kind of care they require, is truly inexcusable in countries which are putting up to 10 per cent of their gross national product into the health system.

The attitude of avoidance of governmental responsibility for long-term care is created or sustained by a number of misconceptions which need correcting:

1. The number of persons involved is not the large 'over 65' population — it is only a relatively small part of those over 80.
2. The nursing home route for providing care is an expensive route and a poor route from the patients' standpoint; certainly, it is not the only way: there are better, probably less costly alternatives.
3. We are not called upon to *begin* a new type of expenditure: we are already spending vast amounts of money for long-term care which often brings very poor results.

When these misunderstandings are cleared out of the way and the problem is faced squarely, it is more likely that long-term care will be seen as a national responsibility.

Looking at other countries' experience has shown that the governmental role needed is not simply to write cheques. That is only part of the job of the trust officer. That job requires wise investments and an overall perspective of the needs which must be met and the best ways to meet them. Governments which have faced the problem squarely with the help of private initiatives and co-operation between different parts of the public sector — health and social services and housing — have found new solutions which they themselves and others feel are more satisfactory than expensive hospital-like institutions. Once rid of the misconceptions about long-term care and with a clear view of the solutions possible, it is reasonable to expect governments to take responsibility and move ahead because they will see that it is in their own self-interest to do so.

Will the rights of citizens in long-term care be protected? Will very elderly people be restored to full citizenship? Our exploration of the subject, especially listening to the words of elderly citizens themselves, suggests that the answer to human rights protection lies squarely in the answer to the question posed about consultation and participation: Will the disabled and infirm elderly be given a voice in determining the provisions for their own future?

The evidence is truly shocking about the conditions of human rights of patients in the institutional settings of mental hospitals, nursing homes and old age homes. Instances of intentional cruelty are probably not very common, but the affronts to dignity and privacy, the denial of choice and the creation of dependent individuals seem almost universal. The concept of the infirm elderly patient according to Norman's description of '"old dears", "OAPs" and "geriatrics"' actually prevents the one thing which might start up a change in the situation: their own participation in what their conditions of care are to be. Even very infirm patients can inform us what is right and wrong about their care if they have an opportunity to talk and we take the opportunity to listen.

One country, Denmark, has shown that there are solutions for the problem of the care of very elderly people:

Today the pleasant fact is that the quality of the care of the elderly is at a very high level, which is not least due to the involvement of the elderly themselves. (EGV Dane Care, p. 1)

How long will it be before other nations can make that statement?

The interest in problems of the care of very elderly people by the Society for Law and Medicine in the United States is a very hopeful development for human rights of elderly patients. Their efforts should be welcomed, encouraged and supported by public and private groups. The same is true regarding the concern over life in institutions for the care of older people on the part of the Senioren Schutz Bund in West Germany. They, and groups like them, are to be welcomed and supported. The findings of departments and commissions set up by governments to examine conditions must be taken into account very seriously: The Equal Opportunities Commission in Britain, with their examination of problems arising in family care of elderly dependents, is a case in point.

Probably the most valuable resource for protection of human rights is lost when we fail to consult and listen to the very elderly who are recipients of care in and out of institutions. The damage to individuals which results from the violations of dignity and other basic rights is something no government can wish to continue.

What will happen with respect to human rights is dependent, however, on the answer to the first of the questions raised. It is a further reason for governments to assume far greater responsibility in the area than they have done so far, to make sure that the voice of elderly patients is a part of the decision-making about their care.

At the beginning of the study we noted the failure on the part of all of us to be ready to welcome as guests the large numbers of very elderly people who are arriving in every country of the world. Most industrialized countries are by no means ready to welcome as guests the very elderly who have already begun to arrive. If nations are to be ready by the time the generation now middle-aged is elderly, most governments will have to concern themselves with a search for better solutions.

Some better solutions are already in place in some other countries, as we have seen. Alternatives to institutional care for disabled elderly people of those kinds have been recommended to the US by Dr Robert Butler. In his 1978 article on the economics of aging, Butler wrote that we might prevent institutionalization through 'an emphasis on in-home services, on congregate housing and on programs to strengthen support networks' (p. 68).

Our comparison of national differences in responding to long-term care needs has shown that a few nations have moved very much toward the development of the approaches Butler recommended, and other nations have made great strides in some of them. The US appears far behind in most of them and remains committed to the institutional response of nursing homes. These institutions are on the increase, in most of the other countries as well as in the US.

The Sandoz Institute experts (Selby and Schechter, 1982) stressed that institutional care must be viewed only as an alternative to other approaches which are much more desirable because they provide opportunities for disabled elderly people to live relatively independent and satisfying lives. The World Assembly on Aging, like the Sandoz Institute group, recommended just what Butler had called for.

The shape of much more adequate accommodations for infirm elderly people can be seen when we look around at other countries. The very elderly guests are arriving every day and will continue arriving every tomorrow. Eventually it will be the turn of all of us who live to a ripe old age. There are ways to prepare the welcome if there is the will to prepare. Looking at the achievements of countries around us may help bring about the needed determination as well as some workable patterns with which to begin.

References

Butler, Robert, (1978) 'The economics of aging: We are asking the wrong questions.' In *The Economics of Aging*, a National Journal Issues Book. The Government Research Corporation, Washington, DC
EGV Dane Care, (1982) Ensomme Gamles Vaern, Hellerup, Denmark
Selby, P. and Schechter, M. (1982) *Aging 2000 — A Challenge for Society*. (Herein referred to as 'the Sandoz Institute Study'). MTP, Lancaster, England (Published for the Sandoz Institute for health and socio-economic studies.)
World Assembly on Aging, (1982) *Plan of Action*. From meeting of the United Nations World Assembly on Aging in Vienna, Austria, August, 1982 (Referred to herein as WAA)

LIST OF HELPFUL ADDRESSES

Federal Republic of Germany

Arbeiterwohlfahrt Bundesverband (Federal Association of
Workers' Welfare Organizations)
Oppelner Strasse 130
5300 Bonn 1

Deutscher Caritas Verband (German Caritas Association)
Karlstrasse 40
7800 Freiburg

Deutscher Verein für öffentliche und private Fürsorge (German
Association for Public and Private Welfare Policy)
Am Stockborn 1-3
6000 Frankfurt 50

Deutsches Zentrum für Altersfragen (German Center for
Gerontology)
Manfred-von-Richthofen Strasse 2
1000 Berlin 42

Diakonisches Werk der Evangelischen Kirche in Deutschland
(Social Division of the Evangelical Church of Germany)
Staffenbergstrasse 76
7000 Stuttgart 1

Kuratorium Deutsche Altershilfe (German Foundation for the
Care of the Aged)
An der Paulaskirche 3
5000 Köln 1

Senioren-Schutz-Bundes: Graue Panther (Organization for Older
People's Rights: German Gray Panthers)
Donbergerstrasse 92
5660 Wuppertal 1

Great Britain

Abbeyfield Society
35a High Street
Potters Bar
Herts. EN6 5DL

Age Concern England
60 Pitcairn Road
Mitcham
Surrey CR4 3LL

Age Concern Greater London
54 Knatchbull Road
London SE5

Anchor Housing Association
13 Magdalen Street
Oxford OX1 3BP

British Association for Services to the Elderly
3 Keele Farmhouse, Keele
Newcastle-under-Lyme,
Staffs. ST5 5AR

Centre for Policy on Ageing (location of an excellent library for
gerontology)
Nuffield Lodge Studio, Regents Park
London NW1 4RS

The Continuing Care Project
20, Westfield Road
Birmingham B15

Counsel and Care for the Elderly
131 Middlesex Street
London E17 JF

Officer for Services to the Elderly
Department of Health and Social Security
Elephant and Castle
London SE1

Help the Aged
Education Department
32 Dover Street
London W1A 2AP

King Edward's Hospital Fund for London
The King's Fund Centre (location of an excellent library for
health topics)
126 Albert Street
London NW1 7NF

Methodist Homes for the Aged
11 Tufton Street
London SW1P 3QD

National Association of Community Health Councils
362 Euston Road
London NW1 3BL

National Association of Widows
Stafford and District Voluntary Service Centre
Chell Road
Stafford ST1 62QA

National Council for Carers and Their Elderly Dependents
29 Chilworth Mews
London W2 3RG

National Council of Voluntary Organisations (publishers of a
directory)
26 Bedford Square
London WC1B 3HU

National Federation of Old Age Pensioners Associations
91 Preston New Road
Blackburn
Lancs.

Over Forty Association for Women Workers
Mary George House
120 Cromwell Road
London SW7

Pensioners Link/Task Force
17 Balfe Street
London N1 9EB

Policy Studies Institute
1/2 Castle Lane
London SW1E 6DR

Pre-Retirement Association
19 Undine Street
London SW17 8PP

Royal College of Nursing: The Geriatric Nursing Society
20 Cavendish Square
London

The Volunteer Centre
29 Lower King's Road
Berkhamsted
Herts. HP4 2AB

Other European and International Organizations

Centre de Liason, d'Etude, d'Information et de Recherche sur Les
Problèmes des Personnes Agées (Reports to the Commission of
the European Communities)
42, rue Mirabeau
75016 Paris
France

Centre for Social, Developmental and Humanitarian Affairs
Department of International Economic and Social Affairs
United Nations Secretariat
Vienna International Centre — PO Box 500
A1400 Vienna
Austria

EGV Dane Care
Danish Association for Care of the Elderly
Tingskiftevej 2
DK 2900 Hellerup
Denmark

European Community Directorate General
Employment and Social Affairs
Rue de la Loi
B 1049 Brussels
Belgium

The International Federation on Ageing, Headquarters
60 Pitcairn Road
Mitcham
Surrey
England

The Netherlands Federation for Care for the Elderly
The Hague
Netherlands

Norsk Gerontologisk Institutt (Norwegian Center for
Gerontology)
Oscargate 36
Oslo 2
Norway

Institute for Gerontology
Brunnsgatan 30
8-552 55 Jonkoping
Sweden

World Health Organization, Regional Office for Europe
Scherfigsvej 8
DK 2100 Copenhagen
Denmark

The United States

The Administration on Aging
Department of Health and Human Services
Washington
DC 20201

Alzheimer's Disease and Related Disorders Association, Inc.
360 N. Michigan Avenue
Chicago
IL 60601

American Association of Homes for the Aging
1050 17th Street NW
Suite 770
Washington
DC 20036

*American Association of Retired Persons/National Retired
Teachers Association
1909 K Street NW
Washington
DC 20049

American Civil Liberties Union Women's Rights Project
1001 East Main Street
Suite 710
Richmond
VA 23219

American Geriatrics Society
10 Columbus Circle
New York
NY 10019

American Foundation for the Blind
Unit on Aging
15 West 16th Street
New York
NY 10011

The American Society for Law and Medicine
765 Commonwealth Avenue
Boston
MA 02215

Caregivers Assistance and Resources for the Elderly Relatives
Center for the Study of Aging
State University of New York
Buffalo
NY 14214

Center for Women's Policy Studies
Older Women's Program
2000 P Street NW
Suite 508
Washington
DC 20036

Commission on Legal Problems of the Elderly
American Bar Association
1800 M St. NW
Washington
DC 20036

Children of Aging Parents
2761 Trenton Road
Levittown
PA 19056

Congressional Caucus on Women's Issues
204 Fourth St. SE
Washington
DC 20003

Gerontological Society of America
1 Dupont Circle NW
Washington
DC 20036

*Gray Panthers
3700 Chestnut Street
Philadelphia
PA 19104

International Federation of Ageing
Editorial Office
1909 K Street NW
Washington
DC 20049

National Association of Jewish Homes for the Aged
2525 Centerville Road
Dallas
TX 75228

National Caucus and Center on Black Aged
1424 K Street NW
Suite 500
Washington
DC 20005

National Commission on Working Women
Center for Women and Work
1211 Connecticut Avenue NW
Washington
DC 20036

*National Council of Senior Citizens
925 15th Street NW
Washington
DC 10005

National Council on the Aging
600 Maryland Avenue SW
Washington
DC 20024

National Health Law Program
1424 16th Street NW
Washington
DC 20036

National Home Caring Council
67 Irving Place
New York
NY 10003

National Institute on Aging
National Institutes of Health
Bethesda, MD 20014

National Interfaith Coalition on Aging
289 South Hull Street
Athens
GA 30601

National Jewish Welfare Board, Senior Advisory Services
401 South Broad Street
Philadelphia
PA 19147

National Policy Center on Women and Aging
University of Maryland
College Park
MD 20742

National Voluntary Organizations for Independent Living for the
Aging
600 Maryland Avenue SW
Washington
DC 20024

*Older Women's League
1325 Street NW
Washington
DC 20005

In the US Congress:
    The Select Committee on Aging
    House of Representatives
    Washington
    DC 20515

    The Special Committee on Aging
    US Senate
    Washington
    DC 20510

University of Michigan, Institute of Gerontology
520 East Liberty Street
Ann Arbor
Michigan 48109

---

*One of the national membership organizations for older persons.

INDEX